Irish Church Records

Irish Church Records

Their history, availability and use in family and local history research

Edited by

James G. Ryan

First Published 1992 by
Flyleaf Press
4 Spencer Villas
Glenageary
Co. Dublin
Ireland

© 1992 Flyleaf Press and the contributors

British Library Cataloguing in Publication Data

Irish Church Records: Their History, Availability
and Use in Family and Local History
I. Ryan, James G.
929
ISBN 0 9508466 4 3

Cover Design by Cathy Henderson

Printed by Colour Books, Dublin, Ireland.

CONTENTS

ACKNOWLEDGEMENTS

Thanks are due to a large number of individuals and institutions for permission to use illustrations or to provide materials for photography. Specifically, thanks are due to: Ms. Mary Shackleton, Curator of the Friends Historical Library and the Historical Committee of the Friends Historical Committee; Fr. Brian O'Ceallaigh of the South Parish, Cork City; Kevin Whelan and Cork University Press; The Wesleyan Methodist Historical Society; The Presbyterian Church, Lower Abbey Street, Dublin; The Irish Jewish Museum, Dublin; The Representative Church Body Library, Dublin; The Irish Baptist Historical Society Journal; The British Library; The National Library of Ireland and the Director of the National Archives of Ireland.

In the chapter on the Catholic records, thanks are due to Mr. David Sheehy of the Dublin Diocesan Archives for advice and assistance; to Kevin Whelan, Prof. Patrick Corish, Eileen O'Byrne and Ruth O'Halloran for commenting on the manuscript; and to the various individuals whose personal correspondence is listed in the bibliography to this chapter.

CONTRIBUTORS

Vivien Costello (nee Le Clerc) is a founder and Committee Member of the Irish Section of the Huguenot Society of Great Britain and Ireland, and has conducted research on Irish sources of Huguenot history.

Dr H.D. Gribbon is President of the Irish Baptist Historical Society, and an Honorary Research fellow in the Dept of Economic & Social History of Queen's University, Belfast.

Richard J. Harrison B.A. (TCD), M.Litt. is a historian and writer with a specific interest in the history of Irish Quaker Communities.

Marion Kelly B.Sc. (Econ) has been Honorary Archivist of the Wesley Historical Society (Irish Branch) since 1967.

Dr Christine Kinealy is a historian and writer on Irish family and social history.

Raymond Refausse is the Librarian and Archivist at the Representative Church Body Library, Dublin.

Dr James G. Ryan (Editor) is a writer and publisher on Irish family history.

Raphael V. Siev is the Honorary Curator of The Irish Jewish Museum, Dublin.

INTRODUCTION

James G. Ryan

The records of the Irish Churches are among the earliest, and are undoubtedly the most comprehensive, sources of personal information available to researchers of Irish family and social history. Despite their importance, there is little published information on the way in which these records have been compiled, or on the factors which caused such variation in the availability of records, and in the format and detail of what is recorded. This book attempts to fill this gap. It presents chapters on the records of all of the major, and several of the minor, denominations which have existed in Ireland during the last three centuries.

The earliest estimation of the religion affiliations of the people of Ireland is probably Petty's "Political Anatomy of Ireland", which was published in 1691 but most probably referred to figures compiled at Christmas of 1672. In this census Petty estimates the total population of Ireland at 1.1 million (or 200,000 families). This was made up of 800,000 Irish, 200,000 English and 100,000 Scots. Even at this early date the relationship between nationality and religion is unequivocal. Petty states that "The Scots are Presbyterian and the Irish Papist, but the English are above 100,000 legal Protestants or conformists and the rest Presbyterian, independent Anabaptists and Quakers".

In 1736 the Hearth Money collectors estimated the number of taxable families in Ireland at 105,501 Protestant and 281,401 Catholic. This figure does not take into account an estimated 2000 houses not liable for the tax due to their low value.

TABLE 1.1

The membership of the various Irish churches in each of the Provinces according to the 1861 Census.

Catholic	C.of I.	Presb.	Meth.	Indep.	Bapt.	Quaker	Other	Jew
		Leinster (Pop. 1,457,635)						
1,252,553	180,587	12,355	6,290	1,025	455	1,425	1,616	338
		Ulster (Pop. 1.914,236)						
966,613	391,315	503,835	32,030	2,749	3,438	1,369	12,331	52
		Munster (Pop. 1,513,558)						
1,420,076	80,860	4,013	4,436	498	225	884	628	2
		Connaught (Pop. 913,135)						
866,023	40,595,	3,088	2,643	260	119	17	120	1
4,505,265	693,357	523,291	45,399	4,532	4,237	3,695	14,695	393

The large variation in distribution of different religions between the four provinces (and counties) of Ireland is evident from Tables 1.1 and 1.2. Table 1.1 shows the specific distribution of the major denominations in each of the provinces of Ireland, while Table 1.2 shows the proportional distribution in each county. These are based on the 1861 census. Catholics are the most numerous almost everywhere, forming over 95% of the population of Connaught, but only 50% of the population of Ulster. Presbyterians, on the other hand are very much centred in Ulster with over 96% of their number in this province. Certain counties are predominantly Presbyterian, for instance Down (44%) and Antrim (47%). In general Connaught is the least diverse in terms of the religion of its population, having only 0.8% of its population which are neither Catholic nor Church of Ireland. Leinster and Ulster contain the greatest diversity of religions.

This distribution of religions is generally explicable by the events of Irish history. The native Irish people are almost entirely Catholic and the distribution of Catholics in Ireland is therefore indicative of the history of the Gaelic Irish. Their numbers are highest in Connaught, which has been subjected to the least influx of other nationalities, and lowest in Ulster, which has been the site of a major plantation by settlers from England, and particularly, Scotland. Because these latter Scottish settlers were predominantly Presbyterian, this church is strongest in Ulster. The Church of Ireland is also very strong in Ulster, but also relatively so in Leinster, and particularly so in Dublin which was the seat of British power in Ireland from the time of the

TABLE 1.2

The percentage of members of each of the major religions in each county in the Census of 1861

County	Catholic	Protestant	Presbyterian	Methodist
Province of Connaught (Pop. 913,135)				
Galway	96.5	3.0	0.2	0.2
Leitrim	89.8	9.1	0.3	0.8
Mayo	96.8	2.6	0.4	0.2
Roscommon	96.1	3.6	0.2	0.1
Sligo	90.1	8.4	0.7	0.6
Province of Ulster (Pop. 1,914,236)				
Antrim	27.5	20.2	47.6	2.4
Armagh	48.8	30.9	16.2	3.2
Cavan	80.5	14.9	3.5	0.9
Derry	45.3	16.9	35.1	0.6
Donegal	75.1	12.6	11.0	1.0
Down	32.3	20.5	44.5	1.4
Fermanagh	56.5	38.4	1.8	3.3
Tyrone	56.5	21.9	19.5	1.6
Monaghan	73.4	14.0	12.0	0.3
Province of Leinster (Pop. 1,457,635)				
Carlow	88.4	10.9	0.2	0.3
Dublin	75.5	20.9	1.8	0.7
Kildare	87.0	11.5	1.0	0.4
Kilkenny	94.9	4.8	0.2	0.1
Laois	88.3	10.7	0.3	0.5
Longford	90.4	8.6	0.8	0.1
Louth	91.5	6.9	1.3	0.3
Meath	93.6	5.9	0.4	0.1
Offaly	88.8	10.1	0.4	0.4
Westmeath	92.1	7.0	0.4	0.2
Wexford	90.4	8.9	0.2	0.3
Wicklow	81.0	17.7	0.3	0.8
Province of Munster (Pop.1,513,558)				
Clare	97.8	2.0	0.1	0.1
Cork	90.7	8.0	0.3	0.5
Kerry	96.7	3.1	0.1	0.1
Limerick	94.7	4.5	0.3	0.3
Tipperary	94.3	5.1	0.2	0.2
Waterford	95.1	3.9	0.4	0.2

reformation to 1921. The smaller "seceder" churches such as the Methodist and Baptist church are also strongest in Ulster and Dublin.

The category "Other" in Table 1.1, which is based on the 1861 Census, seems large at 14,695, but many of these are people who expressed their religion in terms which were not absolutely clear to the census enumerators, even though a reasonable guess can be made as to their intentions. For instance, a significant proportion were members of different sects of the Presbyterian church. The terms "Seceder, Seceding Presbyterian, United Presbyterian, Reformed Presbyterian" are among those which were used by the respondents to describe their religion. These are classified as "other" in the census. Other minor religions which are classified under this heading are Unitarian, Christian, Lutheran, Trenchite, Moravian, Congregationalist and even Sceptic and Infidel !

The histories of the Irish churches, and in particular the major churches, are inextricably bound up with the history of the nation. This is because religion has had, since the 16th century, a political as well as a spiritual dimension in Ireland. The chapters on the Church of Ireland and the Catholic Church in particular indicate the relevance of national political events to the minutiae of record-keeping. In the Catholic church of the early 18th century, the keeping of records was, for many priests, a criminal activity and records for this period are therefore rare. On the other hand, in the Church of Ireland, there was a legal incentive to registration since church records were also the State records and could be used as proof of ancestry in succession disputes etc.

Such factors are of obvious significance in determining whether records were kept by these churches. Another major factor which affected the keeping of records by each church was their internal organisation. The policies of each church regarding the form and scope of record-keeping have differed significantly among the different denominations. As important as the policy of the church was the degree to which policy was observed by individual clergymen. In the Catholic church, for instance, it would seem that many priests did not observe the rules set down by their bishops for the keeping of records. These factors have been dealt with in the respective chapters.

Each of the chapters deals with the history of the respective church, and also defines the policies of each church on record-keeping. The practices of each church in regard to recording of the various sacramental and administrative occasions are also described. In each case the availability of the records, in original or copy form, is indicated. In several chapters listings of records in specific archives are included.

Church records are a unique source of information. In their pages are the births, marriages and deaths of millions of Irish people. For a large proportion of these individuals, particularly before the mid-19th century, the church record is the only remaining evidence of their existence. The existence of the records is, ultimately due to the diligence of the many clergymen and lay-clerks who generated and maintained the records. To these people we must dedicate this book.

IRISH QUAKER RECORDS

Richard S. Harrison

This account falls into three parts; Sections 2.1-2.4 provide a brief outline of Irish Quaker History, 2.5 & 2.6 provide an outline of Quaker administrative arrangements and of the documents which resulted; and 2.7-2.14 provide an account of Quaker records and how best to use them for genealogical purposes.

2.1 Quaker Origins

The Religious Society of Friends, also known as "Quakers" or "Friends" originated in the north-west of England during the mid-seventeenth century, where it was part of a wide movement of radical dissent and spiritual enquiry. Its chief spokesman, George Fox, was born in 1624, the son of a weaver. Having endured much religious doubt and being possessed of a highly sensitive character, he sought a sense of 'true religion'. Failing to locate effective human help in his search and when 'all his hope in men was gone' he felt 'there was one, namely Jesus Christ, who could speak to his condition' (1).

The Religious Society which George Fox promoted was seen as a fundamental recovery of the Christian vision. Rejecting particular sacraments in favour of a sacramental and holistic view of life, the early Quakers believed that people could have direct access to the inspiration of the Holy Spirit, mediated through the metaphor of the 'Inward Light'. This could guide them individually and corporately and obviated the necessity for any clergy or paid ecclesiastical officials. Their silent Meetings for Worship were occasions in which any man or woman might participate and share whether vocally or in simple quiet

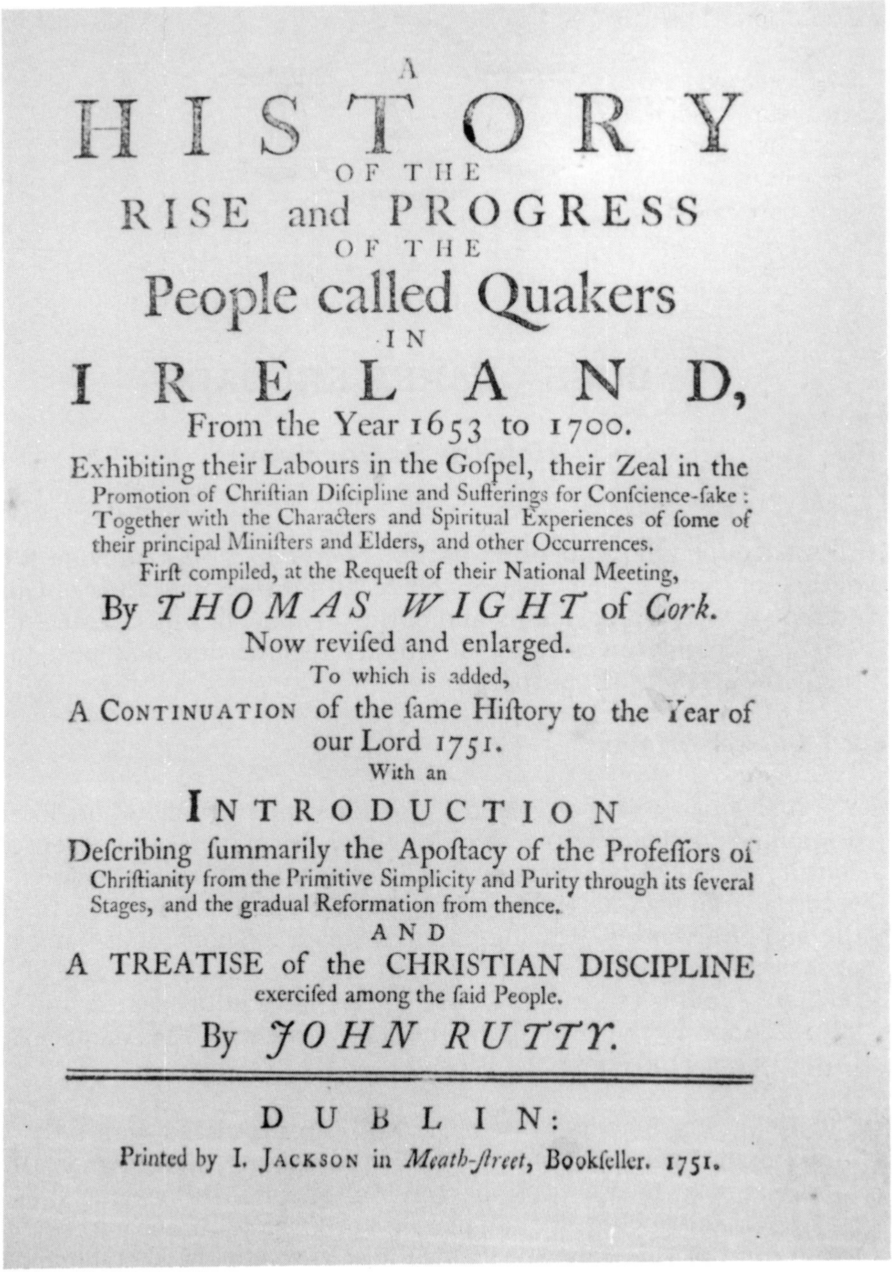

A

H I S T O R Y

OF THE

RISE and PROGRESS

OF THE

People called Quakers

·IN

I R E L A N D,

From the Year 1653 to 1700.

Exhibiting their Labours in the Gospel, their Zeal in the Promotion of Christian Discipline and Sufferings for Conscience-sake: Together with the Characters and Spiritual Experiences of some of their principal Ministers and Elders, and other Occurrences.

First compiled, at the Request of their National Meeting,

By *THOMAS WIGHT* of *Cork.*

Now revised and enlarged.

To which is added,

A CONTINUATION of the same History to the Year of our Lord 1751.

With an

INTRODUCTION

Describing summarily the Apostacy of the Professors of Christianity from the Primitive Simplicity and Purity through its several Stages, and the gradual Reformation from thence.

AND

A TREATISE of the CHRISTIAN DISCIPLINE exercised among the said People.

By *JOHN RUTTY.*

D U B L I N:

Printed by I. JACKSON in *Meath-street*, Bookseller. 1751.

Fig. 2.1 *The Title Page of Wight & Rutty's classic work on the early History of the Quakers in Ireland.*

adoration.

George Fox's insight was not merely an expression of a traditional Protestant individualism. The Quaker claims implied corporate activity and discipline among believers. The Christianity promoted by the Quakers constituted a movement rather than a credal system. Obedience to the immediate teaching of Jesus Christ implied certain ethical imperatives which for George Fox included (a) egalitarian treatment of all men and women (b) a single absolute standard of truth telling (c) the setting aside of other customs of worship with their associated ecclesiastical forms, ministers, priests and prayer-books, and the avoidance of vain and superfluous fashion. Traditional Protestants put their emphasis on the authority of the written words of scripture, while the Roman Catholic looked for the authoritative teaching and interpretation which a church anchored in history and tradition could claim. But the Quakers looked towards immediate inspiration to illuminate and confirm in their own experience the written words of scripture.

2.2 Irish Quaker Origins

In Ireland the Quaker movement emerged firstly in the formidable person of William Edmundson, who was born in 1627 in Westmoreland, England and set up business in Dublin in 1652. This was shortly after his first exposure to 'Quakerism'. Spiritual considerations as much as those of commerce encouraged him to move North to Lurgan, Co. Armagh where Ireland's first established meeting was held in 1654 *(2)*. Quakerism entered Munster in 1655 when Elizabeth Fletcher and Elizabeth Smith began preaching at Youghal, Co. Cork.

The advance of the Quaker message in Ireland was not at first as rapid as in England. However, in 1656 it had already begun to penetrate the Cromwellian army, which was then active in Ireland. It received a positive reception from the Baptist radicals who formed the army's rank and file. The names of captains and colonels occur frequently as supporters or hosts of the itinerant preachers of the infant Society. William Edmundson himself had a commission in the Cromwellian army in England. Other 'Cromwellian' surnames included Pike, Clibborn, Goodbody, Haughton, and Wright. Quakers, with their implied pacifist viewpoint, gradually withdrew from the army. A Major Barcroft is stated to have refused to accept military payment in the form of land at Athlone, for the reason that it had been gained by the sword.

A minority of those who became Quakers had been in Ireland prior to the Cromwellian invasion. The Quaker historian Isabel Grubb *(3)* notes that of the first 129 Quakers in Dublin, 24 had come from Cumberland, 33 from Yorkshire and 12 from Gloucester with other significant proportions from Lancashire, Cheshire and Westmoreland. The same pattern is reflected at a national level. Some of the first Irish Quakers were 'planters', i.e. they came to occupy land received in lieu of loans given to service army needs.

Quakers became the object of persecution by the authorities due to their refusal to take judicial oaths (on the grounds that they endeavoured to live lives of truth), their refusal to support paid clergy, and their denial of false social conventions *(4)*. However, in spite of these ongoing and extraordinary persecutions the Quaker community in Ireland prospered. A figure in the region of 5-9,000 adherents in 1690 is assumed by some authorities. The early Quakers appear to have come from a section of the English population that was well acquainted with the assumptions of capitalism and often had a knowledge of trade and of manufacturing. The Friend's helped each other and through the processes of mutual review ensured by their disciplinary structures, encouraged each other in honesty and the production of goods at a just price. They were also careful not to exploit their tenants or employees and avoided monopolies.

The dawn of a limited degree of official tolerance of Quakers was signalled in the 'Toleration Act' of 1719 which allowed the Friends the legal privilege of meeting for worship subject to their meeting houses being registered. It also permitted the use of affirmation in place of the oath in certain defined non-criminal instances and thus removed a prime difficulty in the way of Quaker traders. To one degree or another however they and Catholics and dissenters shared various legal disabilities. These were associated with the evolving 'Penal Laws' implicit in the Acts of 1704 *(See p. 110)*. Some disabilities were consequent on the establishment in law of the Episcopalian Church. Between the years 1655-1750 alone, Irish Quakers suffered distraints of £100,000 and perhaps 1,000 of them were put into prison *(4)*.

2.3 Quaker History after 1750

In 1750 there were reportedly 101 Irish 'Meetings for Worship', some of which may well have been small and held in private houses. This figure represented a wider diffusion of the Quaker population but conceals numerical decline. The Religious Society of Friends by then had become an inward-looking, 'peculiar' people marked off from the world by distinctions of speech, dress and behaviour. The Society had formalities of membership, 'birth-right' membership and processes of disownment and disunity for infringements of disciplinary arrangements. The practice of disownment for those who gave recognition to the Church of Ireland clergy, by marriage outside of the Society, was a significant factor in an ongoing decline of membership. In Dublin alone, a total of 173 disownments for this reason took place between 1761-1800. Another occasional cause of disownment was for insolvency and failure to repay creditors, seen as an infringement of 'the Golden Rule'.

The Religious Society of Friends in Ireland may be assumed to have been at a peak of financial success and social confidence in the 1840's. In spite of a large numerical decline from the earliest period, its members occupied a unique position in Irish business life and philanthropic schemes. Many of its members were noteworthy in the initiation and promotion of several industrial, business and infrastructural schemes. Notable among these are the St. George Steam Packet Company (c. 1822), the Dublin & Kingstown Railway Line (promoted in 1831) and Jacob's Biscuit Factory (1851). A number of their business schemes were notable for including medical care and improved housing for employees. Bessbrook in Co. Armagh, promoted by John Grubb Richardson (1815-90) was set up as a purpose built community for the employees of the Richardson linen factory. It was deliberately built without public-houses which were perceived as being a potent cause of social, family and personal destruction.

In 1845 the Society had 3,066 members. During the potato famine of 1845-8, the Quaker Central Relief Committee promoted the setting up of emergency soup-kitchens for the starving. These avoided all sectarian ties. Funds gathered by the international Quaker community were impartially administered through Catholic and Protestant clergy or through any person who would have sufficient expertise to do the work in places where Friends were not resident or available.

From the 1860's on the Society embarked on a course of internal reform *(5)*. A dynamism became apparent which resulted in a new leniency on marriage and other discipline questions. The Church of Ireland, which had so often been responsible for the persecution and harrassment of Quakers, had ironically become an attraction for some of them. This was partially due to the so-called 'Evangelical Revival'.

Friends were able to receive the 'evangelical revival' in terms of their own ideas about the proper place of the scripture in their Religious

Society. At a period when their numbers in Munster and in the midland areas of Leinster were in constant decline a new influx of membership was to occur in what had been the numerically weaker 'Ulster Quarterly Meeting'. This resulted very much from the setting up of 'General Meetings' which were first held in Grange and Richill in 1875. These were mission type meetings held on Quaker assumptions and occasionally using hymns. Of the membership of the Society in 1876 (2,933 members) 33.3% were in Ulster, 44.6% in Leinster and 22.4% in Munster. By 1920 the total membership had declined to 2,308 of which 49.6% were in Ulster, 38.1% in Leinster and 12.3% in Munster. Such statistics include both adults and children as 'birth-right' members, all being in the past presumed to be 'active' in the affairs of the Society. Adherents not in membership have since the latter part of the nineteenth century been separately listed in the annual statistical abstracts. They are known as 'Attenders'. The numerical decline of the Society in Ireland after 1920 was at a considerably lower rate than that of the population in general. In recent years, particularly in Munster, it has shown signs of increase mainly through accession to membership from people with no 'Quaker' ancestry, National membership is now centred on 25 local 'preparative' meetings and stands in 1991 at 1,666 members.

2.4 Notable Irish Quakers

A number of Quakers are remembered for their contributions to Irish life. The community might be assumed to have had an impact out of all proportion to its numerical size, although such an influence is not quantifiable. Among individuals remembered for their specific contributions should be mentioned the botanist William Henry Harvey (1811-66) of Limerick. Maria Haslam (nee Fisher) (1829-1922) originally from Youghal was a pioneering feminist. Mary Leadbeater (nee Shackleton) (1758-1826) was a philanthropist, a correspondent of George Crabbe, a friend of Maria Edgeworth and an author and poet in her own right. She was responsible for a diary, later published as 'The Leadbetter Papers'. This significant, humane account minutely details eighteenth century and early nineteenth century daily life in the Quaker village of Ballitore, Co. Kildare *(9).* Jonathan Pim (1806-85) a prominent Dublin businessman, took a keen interest in his fellow citizens. He was one of those active in the Quaker Central Relief Committee during the 'Great Famine' of 1845-8 and was responsible for the substantial report afterwards issued concerning its proceedings. Although Friends generally avoided all party political entanglements, his interest in social improvement led him into politics as a Liberal M.P. elected as such in 1868. He was the first Irish Quaker M.P.

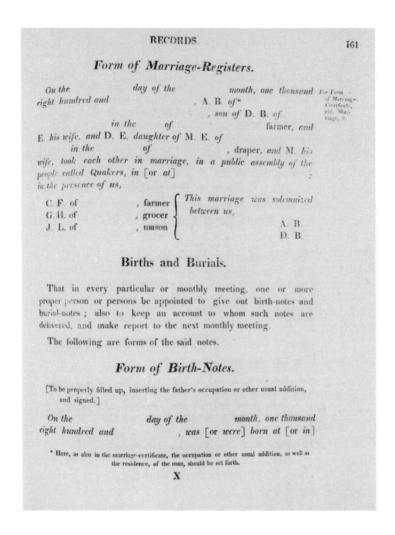

Form of Marriage-Registers.

On the   day of the   month, one thousand *For Form*
eight hundred and   , A. B. of*   *of Marriage-Certificate,*
                                , son of D. B. of   *vid. Marriage, 9.*
      in the   of   farmer, and
E. his wife, and D. E. daughter of M. E. of
      in the   of   , draper, and M. his
wife, took each other in marriage, in a public assembly of the
people called Quakers, in [or at]   ;
in the presence of us,

C. F. of   , farmer ⎧ This marriage was solemnized
G. H. of   , grocer ⎨ between us,
J. L. of   , mason   ⎩
                                          A. B.
                                          D. B.

Births and Burials.

That in every particular or monthly meeting, one or more
proper person or persons be appointed to give out birth-notes and
burial-notes ; also to keep an account to whom such notes are
delivered, and make report to the next monthly meeting.

The following are forms of the said notes.

Form of Birth-Notes.

[To be properly filled up, inserting the father's occupation or other usual addition,
and signed.]

On the   day of the   month, one thousand
eight hundred and   , was [or were] born at [or in]

* Here, as also in the marriage-certificate, the occupation or other usual addition, as well as
the residence, of the man, should be set forth.

X

Fig. 2.2   Extract from "Advice & Rules agreed to by the Yearly Meeting of
Friends of Ireland, 1811". John Jones, Dublin.

2.5 Church Discipline

Quaker records derive from the operations of the Quaker church
'discipline' which was developed   earlier in Ireland than among the

English Friends. Although 'church discipline' has undergone many changes, it is in essence the same as that put into place by William Edmundson. This 'discipline', coinciding with a visit by George Fox in 1669, resulted in the setting up of Men's and Women's Disciplinary Meetings, which are the basis for all church administration, and the source of most of the Quaker records.

The meeting for worship was the smallest local focus for transacting church affairs. Meetings for 'discipline' grew out of these. A number of such disciplinary meetings together would constitute an area known as the 'Monthly' or occasionally, as in Dublin, the 'Two weeks' Meeting. Monthly Meetings again formed units known at first as 'Six Week Meetings'. and later after a period of overlap, were to develop into the Province (or Quarterly) Meetings of Leinster, Munster and Ulster. The final unit of discipline was known as the National or 'Half-Yearly Meeting' which met for the first time in 1669. Whilst the National Meeting had a moral, spiritual and executive significance, this derived from the local units, which enjoyed a wide autonomy. At the latter end of the eighteenth century, the National Meeting became known as 'Dublin Yearly Meeting'.

Women and men transacted their own affairs in their own Disciplinary Meetings. Many Meeting Houses had a partition which would be lowered to separate the men and women from each other when they were dealing with their own administrative areas. When necessary the Clerks at each side would send in to each other notes on matters of procedures. Women's Meetings did not have the same executive authority as those of the men. Their province was chiefly in the care of the needs of their own sex. The Women's National Meeting was initiated in 1678. Men's and Women's Meetings were eventually to be amalgamated at every level. Joint Meetings were held by the National Meeting from 1885 on and have been held continually ever since 1903. There were, in addition, separate and complementary meetings for men and women 'Elders'.

2.6 Administration

One aspect of the Disciplinary Meetings was that of Administration. The Men's and Women's Monthly Meetings dealt with such practical matters as assistance to widows and orphans, the supervision of education and apprenticeships, the recording of births, marriages and deaths and the supervision of marriage procedures. They also dealt with the collection of subscriptions, the visiting of persecuted brethren in prison, the collection of information about distraints for tithes, collectively known as 'Sufferings', *(see page 34 for discussion of Tithes)* which Quakers resolutely refused to pay. They also regulated emigration and internal migrations between Monthly Meetings. Great emphasis was put on encouraging regular attendance by all members at Meetings for Worship. In the encouragement of attendance, as well as other supervisory tasks, the 'overseers' were active. Faced with a crisis in leadership and with numerical decline in membership, the administrative meetings were in 1762 thrown open to all members 'in unity'.

The separate Men's and Women's disciplinary meetings were made up of Friends with tried and tested qualities of leadership and spirituality. They were not originally open equally to all the adherents. Younger people with the required maturity would occasionally be invited to join them. They would be expected already to have lives consistent in word and deed, and to conform to the conventions of clothes and speech by which the Society was outwardly distinguished.

These special meetings operated to encourage spiritual progress and oversee the general welfare of the members. When good advice and counsel failed to win back the refractory, such individuals were faced with the penalties of disownment. Chief causes for this included the more obvious moral lapses, failure to fulfill financial obligations, or recognition of a paid clergy. Any Quaker who failed to pay debts was obliged to make over every part of his possessions to his creditors and if the due processes of law led to his imprisonment he was obliged to submit and not to conceal himself. The Quaker was expected to pay back every penny owed and not to force accommodations on his creditors. If he was willing to fulfill all the conditions, the Men's Meeting might look more favourably on him and keep his case under review, until they saw how he lived up to their expectations. Recognition of the ' Church by law established', ie the Church of Ireland, was another reason for disownment. Such recognition could take financial (ie payment of tithes), or other forms (e.g. marriage by a C of I minister).

The meetings for 'transacting the affairs of the church' were held, as they still are, in a spirit of worship designed to ascertain the will of God for the group involved in the exercise. They were held in a democratic manner but with a theocratic assumption. Being held on a basis of consensus no vote was ever taken. They enabled the young Society to hold together in the face of forces and individuals who might have destroyed it. Such meetings supplied an environment in which administrative expertise could be learned and practically applied in a

42   ANNUAL MONITOR.

ROBERT GARBUTT, *Bilsdale*, 48   3mo.   2 1849
Yorkshire.

WILLIAM GILLETT, *Brailes*, 81   9mo. 10 1849
Warwickshire.

BARBARA GOOCH, *Norwich.* 86   6mo.   6 1849

HANNAH GOODBODY,   3   9mo. 25 1848
Hillsboro', Ireland. Daughter of Thomas P. Goodbody.

THOMAS GOOSE,   89 8mo. 16 1849
Hempnall, near Tasburgh, Norfolk.

MARY GOPSILL, *Chelmsford.* 55 11mo. 14 1848

RACHEL GOUNDRY, *New-* 55 2mo. 14 1849
castle-on-Tyne. Widow of George Goundry.

SARAH GREEN, *Shillingford.* 78 12mo. 1 1848

ELIZABETH GREEN, *Shilling-* 40 9mo. 9 1849
ford, Oxon. Daughter of Hannah Green.

LUCY GREENWOOD,   37 3mo. 24 1849
Chelmsford. Daughter of E. Greenwood.

HELENA GREER, *Cork.*   38 6mo. 9 1849
Wife of Alfred Greer.

DANIEL GRIMES, *Ampthill,* 79 3mo. 13 1849
near Hitchin.

HANNAH GRIMSHAW,   80 8mo. 16 1849
Pontefract. Widow of Jonathan Grimshaw.

REBECCA GRUBB, *Clonmel.* 66 6mo. 10 1849

Fig. 2.3   *Sample page from the Annual Monitor, a register of deaths reported from each Monthly Meeting in Dublin and London Yearly Meetings.*

congenial atmosphere. Decisions arrived at in these meetings are recorded in the form of an agreed minute representing the 'sense of the meeting' and prepared by the Clerk and read out sometimes by his or her assistant. All functions were voluntarily assumed.

The Irish disciplinary structures remained independent of those of English Quakers but a special relation was assumed between the two National Meetings. These structures were reflected also in America and in each place where the Religious Society of Friends was established. All maintained, at Monthly, Provincial and National levels, an ongoing correspondence and intervisitation with each other as part of their individual administrations.

2.7 Organisation of Quaker Records

Central to any account of Irish or other Quakers is a consideration of their records, which represent the corporate genius of their Society. Not alone can the development of the Society be traced through them but numerous points of genealogical interest can be located in a consistent, internally cross-validating form. Business, or disciplinary, meetings at every level kept records of their proceedings, partly for the benefit of the members and partly as visible evidence of their proceedings at a time when the authorities and the populace at large continued to be suspicious of Quakers.

Friends records are complete and interlocking, which means that as long as a Friend was counted as a member, his or her movements can be fairly accurately plotted. Detailed family information can, in many instances, be put together about the lives of Quaker ancestors. Not all attained to the same heights of piety or the more measurable business success for which some were remarkable. Neither were all Friends equally active in the administrative affairs of the Society, but their names will inevitably occur somewhere in the records.

Quaker records are extensive, well indexed and centrally maintained in two locations in Ireland (see Section 2.8). Birth certificates, marriage certificates, burial certificates and all types of registration material exist for each Monthly Meeting of the Friends. As the result of a decision of the Yearly Meeting in the 1860's, and reflecting a similar decision in London Yearly Meetings, abstracts were made of the local monthly meeting registers of births, marriages and deaths. These abstracts are located in the Dublin Friend's Historical Library (DFHL) *(Appendix 2.2)* are retrospective to the 1670's and in some cases include earlier material probably extracted from 'family lists'. Information on births, marriages and deaths is therefore most accessible from these collections of abstracts. National Abstract Registers have been retained in Dublin since 1859. Registrations after 1859 are accessible under certain conditions on application to the Recording Clerk of the Dublin Yearly Meeting, when the same information is not recoverable from other register books in the care of the DFHL. For all practical purposes the genealogical researcher is unlikely to need to consult minute books when there are quicker and more efficient methods to access information.

An important convention in Quaker records is that the months are referred to in a simple numerical form as 'First-month' 'Second month' etc. and the days of the week as 'First-day' (Sunday), "Second-day' (Monday) etc. Before 1752, when the Julian calendar was still in use, this meant that the First-month was March and so on. When the 'new style' calender was instituted in 1752 First-month was applied to the month called by non-Quakers January and so on in numerical sequence.

2.8 Quaker Archives

Most of the Quaker records are located in the Dublin Friends Historical Library (DFHL) *(Appendix 2.2)*. Ulster Province Meeting Records and those of the Monthly Meetings in Ulster are retained by the Society's Ulster Archives Committee at Lisburn *(Appendix 2.2)*. The National Abstract Registers, including those of Ulster, are held in DFHL.

The Dublin Friends Historical Library was set up by the Dublin Yearly Meeting in 1908. The registers, minute books and archival material belonging to each Monthly Meeting were deposited with it at the time under the care of the Recording Clerk. Private papers, manuscripts, family correspondence, photographs and ephemera of all kinds have been added to the Library which has become a rich historical resource. It is of national, as well as local and Quaker, significance and bears on many aspects of Irish business and social life. Genealogical research and enquiries can be undertaken by the library for a scale of charges which can be obtained on enquiry. If it is intended to produce any printed or published item based on the collection, it is only courtesy that the correct permissions should be obtained or acknowledgements made. The DFHL is run on a voluntary basis and contributions are always appreciated so that the service can be maintained.

The Ulster Province and its subsidiary Monthly Meeting Records, held at Lisburn, were originally referenced in a different way from those of the rest of the country, but a comprehensive system of reference, devised by Professor Theodore Moody (T.C.D.) (1907-84) was put into operation for all the Irish Quaker archives in 1984. Microfilms of the Ulster Province Archives, made by the Public Record Office of Northern Ireland, were given to the DFHL and to the Lisburn Archives in 1989 where the originals continue to be held. For any researcher working in Dublin there is probably little reason to consult the records in Lisburn unless there is preference to handle original manuscript items. A preliminary letter to their keeper would elucidate if there was any specific extra material available relative to a particular genealogical enquiry.

The material at these two locations includes manuscript and printed items. Manuscript records are composed of archival and non-archival material. The archival material deals with the discipline and administration of the Society at all levels of the Preparative, Monthly, Quarterly and Yearly Meetings. The Minute Books date back in the case of the National Meeting to 1671. Province Minute Books go back for Leinster to 1670 for Munster to 1694 and for Ulster to 1674. The earliest Monthly Meeting Records are for Cork from 1675. There are very few missing years in the surviving corpus of material. It became more common during the nineteenth century for Minute Books to index subjects and names. These indexes are not always systematic and should not be relied on as a substitute for looking through the books themselves, if that is unavoidable. The archives also include correspondence, committee minutes and records of internal appointments and arrangements. The non-archival material covers private letters, diaries, journals, ephemera and other supplementary material. Among important collections of letters held in the D.F.H.L. are the Grubb Collection, Jacob family letters, the Lecky family letters, the Fennell Collection and the Leadbeater-Shackleton letters.

The Printed items include the series of the Journal of the Friends Historical Society (6). This has occasionally carried articles on Irish Quaker families and until recent years items of Irish relevance frequently occurred in the feature 'Notes and Queries'. Another vital tool of family research is the Annual Monitor (7). This venture was started in 1813 and listed deaths from every Monthly Meeting in both London and Dublin Yearly Meetings. It became the practice in it to make more extensive notes of some of the Friends listed, at first with great attention to their dying words and moments, and later to the consideration of their lives as they had been perceived. Joseph J. Green in 1894 prepared an 'Epitome' of the Annual Monitor and this covered the years 1813-92 (8). The Annual Monitor continued to be published until 1918.

Finally, a number of published histories exist for major Quaker families.   The quality of these can vary widely but they all supplement each other and may help to illuminate the usually terse 'minutes', certificates and other manuscript material. Such histories have usually been privately published. A short list of such published histories is provided with the references to this chapter.

	Carlow	Cork	Dublin	Edenderry	Grange	Limerick	Lisburn	Lurgan	Moate	M'mellick	Richhill	Tipperary	Waterford	Wexford	Wicklow	Youghall
Davis	123	123	23	23		123		1		123		123	12	123	2	
Dawson	2	23	123	.3	123	2	123	123		2	2					
Day		3														
Deale					2											
Deane	2		123					23					2		2	
Dearman		2														
Deaves	23	123	123								23			23	123	
Deeble		123	23													
Deery				3												
Deeves	See	Deaves									23					
Delahunty													2			
Delany	1 2		2	3							123				1	
Delap			123		2											
Delapp																
Dellany															23	
Dennis		123	2						?	2			2	123		2
Dent			23													
Denton			3													
Derkindren		123														
Desmanios						3										
Deverell				1												
Deverson			3													
Devitt	2		123								23		2			
Devonsher	2	123														
Dewras			2													
Deyell												1				
Dickinson	1 2		123	123				2		2	123	2	12			
Dickson			2		3										23	
Dillany														123		
Dillon																
Dinham			2													
Dirkindren	See	Derkindren														
Dixon		23	23			123	3	23			2				123	
Dobbs		23				2					2					123

Fig. 2.4   *A sample page from the Jones Index, which shows the occurrence of Birth (1), Marriage(2) or Death (3) records of each family from each of the Monthly Meetings. Note that the index does not show the number of records for each family within each Meeting.*

Three important collections of material at these archives facilitate the preliminary identification of Quaker ancestors. The first of these is the printed "Guide to Irish Quaker Records" *(9)* by Olive C. Goodbody (1898-1987), a long serving Curator of the DFHL. This contains an extensive list of the occurrence of every Quaker surname in the minute books.

A second resource is a manuscript item in the DFHL known as the 'Jones Index' This lists every family name occurring in the 'Abstract Registers' and, shows in which Monthly Meeting a birth, death or marriage was registered.

A third manuscript source is the collection of 232 accurate pedigrees bequeathed by Thomas Henry Webb to the DFHL in 1927. The pedigrees cover the major Irish Quaker families but by no means exhaust the total number of family names.

Simple lists of members, and of adherents, also exist. Some of these early lists were known as 'Family Lists' and occasionally supplementary information can be gleaned from them about the national or other origins of the Friends in question. Such 'Family Lists' were sometimes on a Monthly Meeting basis and sometimes are available for a Quarterly Meeting.

2.9 Quaker Names

Generally, a researcher will have some basis for assuming that his or her ancestors were Quakers. In an Irish context the evidence of a typical 'Quaker' surname *(Appendix 2.1)* is usually sufficient to give good grounds for such a conclusion. Of course, many surnames never became prominent enough to make them typically 'Quaker', but some names are very specifically and exclusively associated with the Quakers.

Particular family names can indicate the regional origins of some Quakers. Bewley, Goodbody, Perry, Pim, Robinson might be seen as names typical of Mountmellick and the midland counties of Leinster. In Cork, Abell, Beale, Deaves, Harvey, Pike and Wright were common. Sparrow, Woodcock, Poole and Goff were to be found in Wexford. In Limerick were to be found Alexander, Bennis, and Unthank. Typical Ulster families were, Bell, Christy, Greer, Hobson, Hogg, Nicholson, Pearson, Richardson.

So called 'native' Irish names, that is names derived from the Irish

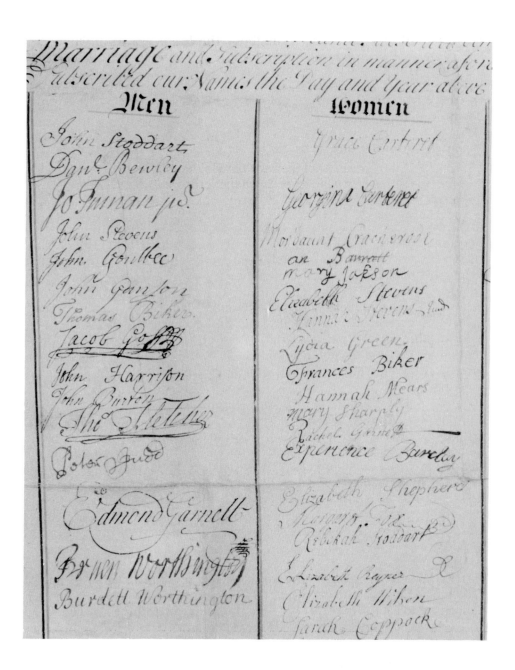

Fig. 2.5   *A detail from the Marriage document of Thomas Strettel and Elizabeth Willcocks, showing the signatures of some of those who attended.*

speaking culture, do occur throughout the history of Irish Quakers. They indicate a degree of assimilation to the wider culture of the country, chiefly as a result of a mixture with other Protestants more open to such assimilation. Lists of pupils at the 'ecumenically' mixed and Quaker-run Ballitore School in the County of Kildare indicates this. Such assimilation was necessarily wider than the evidence of paternal surnames only. Among Irish Quaker dynasties with 'native' Irish names should be mentioned Carroll, Dowd, Doyle, MacQuillan, O'Brien, O'Callaghan. Other Quaker names deriving from Scotland and therefore from a wider 'Gaelic' or 'Lowland' culture to which Ireland was linked, occur chiefly in Ulster. Some typical Ulster Quaker names might be Barclay, Bell, Christy, Greer and Douglas.

2.10 Births

Quaker children were not baptised, but births were recorded by the Monthly Meetings and these are indexed in the National Abstract Registers *(see section 2.7 & Fig. 2.2)*.

2.11 Marriages

A Quaker marriage has always been seen as a profoundly spiritual matter and not as a mere secular arrangement. The procedure was elaborate, although it was much simplified during the nineteenth century. It involved an application from the parties involved to the Women's and Men's Meeting. In the case of a marriage between members belonging to different Monthly Meetings, a clearance would also be required from the home meetings of the parties involved. The application presented had to contain a statement that the intending parties were free from all other marraige alliances and that they had proper consent from their parents and guardians. The marriage had to be in conformity with Quaker testimonies and based on a Meeting for Worship. In the course of this the man and then the woman made a simple promise after which the immediate relatives, and often all those present, subscribed their names to a marriage document. Quaker families often carefully look after such documents, some of which are hundreds of years old with exquisite penmanship and illuminations *(see Fig. 2.5)*. The Monthly Meeting would record that the marriage had taken place. A simple certificate would also be made and copies pasted in a Monthly Meeting book. The format of the entries would show the names and place of residence of the parents and of the spouses, as well as the date of marriage.

Marriages tended to be on a regional and national basis and until the

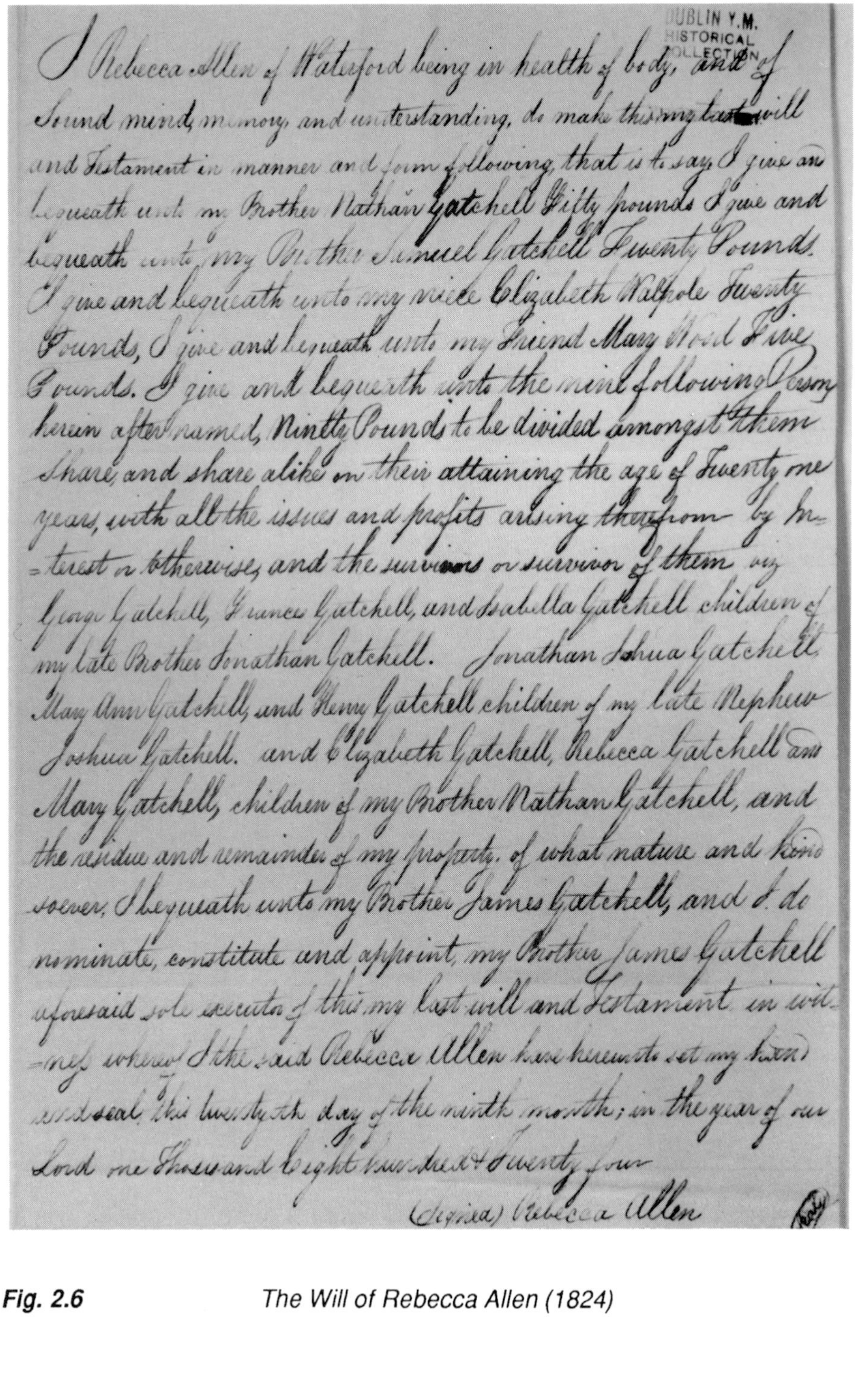

I Rebecca Allen of Waterford being in health of body, and of Sound mind, memory and understanding, do make this my last will and Testament in manner and form following, that is to say I give and bequeath unto my Brother Nathan Gatchell Fifty pounds I give and bequeath unto my Brother Samuel Gatchell Twenty Pounds. I give and bequeath unto my niece Elizabeth Walpole Twenty Pounds, I give and bequeath unto my Friend Mary Wood Five Pounds. I give and bequeath unto the nine following Persons herein after named, Ninety Pounds to be divided amongst them Share and share alike on their attaining the age of Twenty one years, with all the issues and profits arising therefrom by Interest or otherwise, and the survivors or survivor of them viz George Gatchell, Frances Gatchell, and Isabella Gatchell children of my late Brother Jonathan Gatchell. Jonathan Joshua Gatchell Mary Ann Gatchell, and Henry Gatchell children of my late Nephew Joshua Gatchell. and Elizabeth Gatchell, Rebecca Gatchell and Mary Gatchell, children of my Brother Nathan Gatchell, and the residue and remainder of my property. of what nature and kind soever, I bequeath unto my Brother James Gatchell, and I do nominate, constitute and appoint, my Brother James Gatchell aforesaid sole executor of this my last will and Testament in witness whereof I the said Rebecca Allen have hereunto set my hand and seal this twentyeth day of the ninth month; in the year of our Lord one Thousand Eight hundred & Twenty four
(Signed) Rebecca Allen

Fig. 2.6   *The Will of Rebecca Allen (1824)*

late nineteenth century any intermarriage with English or other Quakers was exceedingly rare. This contributed to the prominence of certain surnames in Irish geographical areas. Friends did of course move around. Dublin would have been a large centre where Friends from country areas would be working and likely to contract marriages with partners drawn from a wider area. The families with higher capital and more powerful business interests might naturally be most interested in cementing marriage alliances with families with similar resources and business interests. This would result in partners being drawn from a more distant area of the country.

Marriages taking place 'not according to rule' were a prime cause of disownment, or banishment, from the Society. Until 1866 it was forbidden by Quaker rules for first-cousins to contract a marriage. In such cases the parties frequently risked the discipline to be married by a clergyman of another denomination, usually of the Church of Ireland, thus doubly ensuring disownment. Even then the children of such a union might be entered by the parents as 'birthright' members of the Society.

The frequency of marriage within the Society led to the extension of a practice commonly found in Ireland, namely the giving of the maternal surname as a first-name to the child. The frequent recurrence of the same first-names and surnames contributed to the practice in documents of noting the father's first-name as an addition, as for example, Joshua Pim Joshua, Some families perpetuated a well-liked surname in this way. 'Barcroft' for example has traditionally been used as a first-name among the Haughtons of Cork.

2.12 Deaths & Wills

Deaths or burials were recorded in the Monthly Meeting Minutes, and are abstracted in the National Abstract Registers, and/or in the Annual Monitor. The format of the death or burial record is usually to show the date of death, the age of the individual, his or her parents or relict and, particularly at later periods, the address where the deceased had dwelt.

Quakers were encouraged by the Meetings to make wills so as to save trouble and confusion for the surviving families. A number of 'will books' and of wills themselves exist which list the property of Friends (see Fig. 2.6). One important collection of abstracts was edited by Beryl Eustace and Olive C. Goodbody (10) (see Fig. 2.7). Olive Goodbody's Guide (9) has another and supplementary list of abstracts of fifty such wills extracted from will books and other material.

2.13 Movement or Migration Records

Family researchers are often interested in emigration material. Minute books can be useful for the identification of certificates of emigration. Most Monthly Meetings have books of 'Removals' which should more compactly record emigration and internal migrations. The DFHL has many of the original certificates also, for which there will be separate listings. Minute Books should note that a certificate issued has been received at the place to which it was directed. In some cases certificates of removal survive which will be accessible from indexes in the DFHL. A very useful printed source on emigrations is Immigration of Irish Quakers into Pennsylvania, 1682-1750 *(11)* and Australia *(12)*

2.14 Sufferings

The lists of 'Sufferings', that is of imprisonments and persecutions and of distraints for tithes, were carefully kept by Monthly Meetings and submitted and recorded at Provincial and National levels. These were to be presented to the Government as a means of inducing a change of policy. Two manuscript books of 'Sufferings' exist for the National Meeting , dated 1653-93 and 1693-1705. They often record the names of Friends whose surnames no longer survive or whose families dropped out of the Society early on. Other provincial and monthly meeting books of 'sufferings' survive, many continuing to list distraints, such as those for 'Ministers Money' right down to the abolition of the State Church in 1871. The DFHL has many individual dockets of distraints for different periods and which are all well indexed. From a genealogical perspective the earlier manuscript books are likely to prove most helpful. The entries appear according to Province and Monthly Meeting. Many were extracted and printed in two compilations, one by Thomas Holmes & Samuel Fuller *(4)* and a second by William Stockdale *(13)*. These are noted in the bibliography following this account. A typical entry from 'Stockdale' for the year 1677 in Cavan is 'Richard Faile had taken from him for tithe by Owen Brady, tithemonger for Priest Barcroft, 35 loads of turf, and by John MacNulty, Patrick and Edmund MacCabe two car-loads of hay, 15 stooks of barley, 29 stooks of oats and 16 stooks of wheat, all worth £2.18 shillings.'

179 SHEPERD, GABRIEL, Dublin, clothier.

To my grandson John Chaytor my large Bible. To my grandson Samuel Whinery my Irish oak table. To my granddaughter Rachel Whinery my large looking glass with dressing box. To my granddaughter Mary Whinery my small looking glass. My daughter Sarah Whinery. My friend William Lapham. To my daughter Rachel Garnett, executrix, the remainder.

Dated 25 Dec. 1745.

Witnesses: William Lapham, Michael Dods, Arth. Shepheard.

D. 5. 152

180 SLEIGH, JOSEPH, Dublin, tanner.

My mother Alice Sleigh, widow, of Dublin. My five children: Rebekah, Joseph, Bathia, Esther, Francis (all under 21 years and unmarried). My friends to take my five children, viz. my mother to take my son Francis, Thomas Trafford of Wicklow to take my daughter Bathia, Anthony Sharp, Dublin, to take my daughter Rebekah, Roger Roberts to take my daughter Esther, Deborah Sandham, Youghal, to take my son Joseph. If my mother should die my friend Robert Turner to bring up my son Francis, and in case Robert Turner shall remove himself and family to Pensilvania in America I desire my executors may send him over thither. £5 to my friend Deborah Sandham.

My friends Anthony Sharp and Roger Roberts executors. My friends Robert Turner, James Turner and Thomas Atherton, Dublin, and William Edmondson, senior, Rosanaillis, Queen's Co., Thomas Carleton, Ballinaclash, Co. Wicklow and Thomas Trafford, Wicklow, overseers.

Dated 28 Dec. 1682. Proved in Prerogative Court 13 Oct. 1683.

Witnesses: James Fade, junior, the marks of Nicholas Wheland and John Haslack.

INVENTORY dated 16 Jan. 1683, appraised by John Haslacke and Christopher Hamerton. Valuations of leathers, furniture and household goods.

Memoranda: Payments made to Rebekah Sleigh now wife of Samuel Trafford; made 1692 to Esther Sleigh now wife of Abraham Merrick near Chester, and 1692 to Joseph Sleigh of Cork, and to Bathia Sleigh.

D. 4. 1

Fig. 2.7 *Sample Will Abstract from Olive Goodbody's "Quaker Records, Dublin : Abstracts of Wills (15).*

REFERENCES

1. *Braithwaite, William C.,* **The Beginnings of Quakerism** (2nd edition prepared by Henry J. Cadbury) (Cambridge, 1861).

2. *Edmundson, William.* **A Journal of the Life, Travels and Sufferings of** .. (3rd ed., Dublin 1820).

3. *Harrison, Richard S.,* **Cork City Quakers, a brief History** (forthcoming)

4. *Fuller, Samuel and Holmes. Thomas,* **A compendious view of some extraordinary Sufferings of the People called Quaker both in Person and Substance in the Kingdom of Ireland from Year 1655 to the End of George 1st Reign** (Dublin, 1731).

5. *Braithwaite, William C.,* **The Second Period of Quakerism,** (2nd edition prepared by Henry J. Cadbury) (Cambridge, 1961).

6. **Journal of the Friends Historical Society,** 1903 and in progress

7. **The Annual Monitor and Memorandum Book (1813-42) nos. 1-30, continued as The Annual Monitor for .. or Obituaries of the Members of the Society of Friends in Great Britain and Ireland (1843-1908)** n.s., [Original numbering resumed in 1909, began in error with 96 instead of 97 and corrected by the omission of no. 100].

8. *Green, Joseph J.,* (ed) **The Annual Monitor and Memorandum Book, Quaker Records, being an Index to the Annual Monitor 1813-92** (London, 1894)

9. *Goodbody, Olive C.,* **Guide to Irish Quaker Records 1654-1860** (Dublin, 1967)

10. *Eustace, P. Beryl, and Goodbody, Olive C.,* **Quaker Records Dublin - Abstracts of Wills** (Dublin, 1957).

11. *Myers, Albert Cook,* **Immigration of the Irish Quakers into Pennsylvania 1682-1750** (Swarthmore; Penn., 1902).

12. *Oats, Marjorie and William,* **A Biographical Index of Quakers in Australia before 1862.** (Hobart, 1982).

13. *Stockdale, William,* **The Great Cry of Oppression** (Dublin, 1683)

OTHER USEFUL REFERENCES

Advices and Rules agreed to by the Yearly Meeting of Friends in Ireland (2nd ed., Dublin 1841) [This volume could provide some useful explanations of Quaker administrative procedures]

Chapman, George R., **The History of Ballyhagan and Richhill Meetings 1654-1979,** (Dungannon, 1979).

Wight, Thomas and Rutty, John, **A History of the Rise and Progress of the People called Quakers in Ireland 1653-1700.** (Dublin, 1751).

Leadbeater, Mary, **Leadbeater Papers.** 2 vols. (London, 1862) [The first volume contains a useful list of the pupils at Ballitore School].

SELECT LIST OF FAMILY HISTORIES

Barrington, Amy, **The Barringtons, a Family History,** (Dublin, 1914).

Beale, Edgar, **The Earth between them,** (Sidney, 1975) [Chiefly about the Beale family of Mountmellick].

Bewley, E.I., **The Bewleys of Cumberland and their Irish and other Descendants,** (Dublin, 1920).

*Grubb, Geoffrey Watkins,***The Grubbs of Tipperary** (Cork, 1972)

Impey, E.J. A., **A Roberts Family,** (1939)

Penrose, Charles Cooper, (Compiler), **The Penrose Family of Helston, Cornwall and Wheldrake, Yorkshire and Co. Wicklow, Ireland** (New York, 1975).

Richardson, Jane M., **Six Generations of Friends in Ireland 1655-1890** (London, 1895) [Information about the Goffs of Wexford, & the Wilsons of 'Kings County']

Shackleton, Bernice Close, **The Shackletons** (Kansas, 1972)

Smith, Charlotte Fell, **James Nicholson Richardson of Bessbrook** (London, 1925).

Stewart, Margaret, **The Goodbodys of Clara,** (Dublin, 1965).

APPENDIX 2.1

LIST OF CHIEF IRISH QUAKER SURNAMES

Abbott
Abell
Adair
Alexander
Allen
Baker
Banfield
Banks
Barclay
Barcroft
Barnes
Barrington
Beale
Bell
Bennis
Bewley
Birkett
Boake
Boardman
Boles/Bowles
Brocklesby
Browett
Butler
Calvert
Carleton
Carroll
Chandlee
Chapman
Chaytor
Cherry
Christy
Church
Clark
Clibborn
Cole
Cooper
Cotter
Courtenay
Creeth
Davis

Dawson
Deaves
Devonshire
Dickinson
Dillon
Dobbs
Douglas
Doyle
Druitt
Duckett
Dudley
Edmondson
Edmundson
Elley
Eustace
Evans
Eves
Fairbrother
Fayle
Fennell
Fisher
Fitzpatrick
Fitt
Forbes
Fuller
Gamble
Garratt
Garnett
Gatchell
Glynn
Goff/Goffe
Going
Goodbody
Gough (see Goffe)
Green
Greer
Gribble
Grubb
Hall
Halliday

Handy
Hancock
Hanks
Harris
Harvey
Hatton
Haughton
Haydock
Heritage
Hewson
Hill
Hillary
Hogg
Hoope
Hoowe
Hudson
Hughes
Humphries
Hutchinson
Inman
Jackson
Jaffray
Jellicoe
Jenkinson
Jessop
King
Knott
Lamb
Leadbeater
Lecky
Lucas
Lynas
Macquillan
Malcolmson
Malone
Manders
Manliffe
Manly
Mark
Martin

Mason
Medcalf
Meyers
Miller/Milner
Moore
Morris
Morrison
Moss
Mullin
Murphy
Murray
Neale
Nevins
Newbold
Newenham
Newsom
Nicholson
Noble
O'Brien
O'Callaghan
Pattison
Pearce
Pearson
Peet
Penrose
Perry
Petticrew
Phelps
Phillips

Pike
Pillar
Pim
Poole
Rhodes
Richardson
Ridgway
Roberts
Robinson
Rooke
Russell
Sandwith
Scott
Shackleton
Sikes
Simmons
Sinton
Smith
Smithson
Sparrow
Stephens
Stott
Strangman
Strettell
Taylor
Thacker
Thomas
Thompson
Todhunter

Tolerton
Trapnell
Turner
Turtle
Unthank
Uprichard
Wakefield
Walker
Walpole
Walsh
Wardell
Waring
Watson
Webb
Wheddon
White
Whitfield
Whitten
Wigham
Wight
Wilcocks
Wilkinson
Williams
Wilson
Wright
Woodcock
Woods
Wyly

APPENDIX 2.2

QUAKER ARCHIVES

Dublin Friends Historical Library
(Curator, Mary Shackleton),
Religious Society of Friends in Ireland,
Swanbrook House,
Morehampton Road, Dublin 4,
Telephone: (01) 68 71 57.
Opening Hours; Thursday 11.00 a.m. - 1.00 p.m.

Religious Society of Friends,
Ulster Quarterly Meeting,
Archives Committee,
Meeting House,
23 Railway Street,
Lisburn,
Co. Antrim,
Northern Ireland QT 28 (Keeper, G. Leslie Stephenson).

Friends Historical Library,
Friends House,
Euston Road,
London N.W. 1 2BJ,
England (Librarian, Malcolm Thomas)
Telephone: 03 071 387 3601

3

THE RECORDS OF
THE CHURCH OF IRELAND

Dr. Raymond Refausse

The records of the Church of Ireland (the Anglican or Protestant Episcopal Church in Ireland) are unique among those of the Christian churches in Ireland for they are not alone the chronicles of a religious denomination, but are also the transactions of a part of the machinery of government. From the 16th to the 19th century the Church of Ireland was the state church established by law and so, although it was always a minority church, it exercised a degree of influence and wielded an authority disproportionate to its numerical strength. Its parishes were units of local government, its courts were the centres of matrimonial and testamentary jurisdiction, its prelates and clergy were often important officers of state, and, perhaps most importantly, its parish churches were for periods the scenes of the only acts of worship which were permitted under the law.

The laws which created the framework of the Established Church were never uniformly applied but were nonetheless of sufficient significance to have created, by the middle of the 18th century, the fabric of the protestant ascendancy. Membership of the Established Church was the key, not alone to ecclesiastical advancement, but to the attainment of public office and the ownership of land. Thus to the ranks of the Church of Ireland were attracted not only those who were convinced by its theology but many who out of political, social or economic expendiency found it prudent to become, at least nominally, members of the Established Church *(1)*.

This unusually wide range of people is catalogued and characterized in various fashions in the parish records. They appear particularly in the registers of baptisms, marriages and burials but are also to be found to a significant extent in the records of the vestries and in the parish deeds.

The registers are the best known and most important class of parish record and their importance is reflected in the fact that their care and custody has periodically occupied government since the early 17th century and are today to a significant degree governed by statute law.

There are three distinct categories of parish registers:

- Registers containing records of baptisms and burials up to and including 1870, and records of marriages up to and including 31 March 1845. These are public records in Northern Ireland and National Archives in the Republic of Ireland : that is, they are the property of the state.

- Registers containing records of marriages from April 1845. These were created under the terms of an act of 1844 which provided for the civil registration of protestant marriages.

- Registers containing details of baptisms and burials from 1871. These are the direct responsibility of the Church of Ireland.

The registers in the first of these categories are of course the most significant since they predate the introduction of civil registration of births, marriages and deaths in 1864. To this category I shall return shortly but first something should be said of the other categories.

The 1844 <u>Act for Marriages in Ireland: and for Registering such Marriages</u> (2) introduced civil registration of protestant marriages. From April 1845 parishes were supplied with proforma marriage registers by the Registrar General in Dublin and the clergy were required by law to record in a prescribed fashion the marriages which they performed. These registers were to be kept in duplicate and , on completion, one copy was returned to the local registrar and the other remained in the parish. There was, however, no prohibition on parishes maintaining their own separate ecclesiastical registers of marriage. Indeed for a short period some continued to do so but these are of no informational significance since the detail required for the civil register was more comprehensive than that which had theretofore been collected by the Church.

Conſtitutions and Canons Eccleſiaſtical.

with another, or be his own Judge; but ſhall truly pay the ſame as hath been accuſtomed to their Parſons, Vicars and Curates, without any Reſtraint or Diminution. And for ſuch lack and default as they can juſtly find in their Parſons, Vicars and Curates, they ſhall ſeek for Reformation to their Ordinaries, and other Superiors, who upon complaint and due Reproof thereof, ſhall reform the ſame accordingly.

XLVI. *A Regiſtry to be kept of Chriſtenings, Weddings, and Burials.*

IN every Pariſh Church and Chapel, within this Realm, ſhall be provided one Parchment Book, at the charge of the Pariſh, wherein ſhall be written the Day and Year of every Chriſtening, Wedding, and Burial, which ſhall be in the Pariſh, from the time that this Canon ſhall be eſtabliſhed. And for the ſafe keeping of the ſaid Book, the Church-wardens, at the charge of the Pariſh, ſhall provide one ſure Coffer, with three Locks and Keys, whereof the one to remain with the Miniſter, and the other two with the Church-wardens ſeverally: So that neither the Miniſter without the Church-wardens, nor the Church-wardens without the Miniſter, ſhall at any time take that Book out of the ſaid Coffer. And henceforth upon every Sabbath-day, immediately after Morning and Evening Prayer, the Miniſter and Church-wardens, ſhall take the ſaid Parchment Book out of the ſaid Coffer: And the Miniſter in the preſence of the ſaid Church-wardens ſhall write and record, in the ſaid Book, the Names of all Perſons chriſtened, together with the Names and Surnames of their Parents; and alſo the Names of all Perſons married and buried in that Pariſh the Week before, by the Miniſter or his Curate, and the Day and the Year of every ſuch Chriſtening, Marriage and Burial And that done, they ſhall lay up the Book in the Coffer, as before. And the Miniſter and Church-wardens, unto every Page

of that Book, (when it ſhall be filled with ſuch Inſcriptions) ſhall ſubſcribe their Names. And the Church-wardens ſhall once every Year, within one Month after the 25th Day of *March*, tranſmit unto the Biſhop of the Dioceſs, or his Chancellor, a true Copy of the Names of all Perſons chriſtened, married, or buried in their Pariſh in the Year before (ended the ſaid 25th Day of *March*,) and the certain Days and Months, in which every ſuch Chriſtening, Marriage and Burial was had, to be ſubſcribed with the Hands of the ſaid Miniſter and Church-wardens, to the end the ſame may faithfully be preſerved in the Regiſtry of the ſaid Biſhop: Which Certificate ſhall be received without Fee. And if the Miniſter or Church-wardens ſhall be negligent in the performance of any thing herein contained, it ſhall be lawful for the Biſhop, or his Chancellor, to convent them, and proceed againſt every of them as contemners of this our Conſtitution.

XLVII. *None to marry within the Degrees prohibited.*

NO Perſon ſhall marry within the Degrees prohibited by the Laws of God, and expreſſed in a Table ſet forth by Authority in *England*, in the Year of our Lord God, 1563. And all Marriages ſo made and contracted, ſhall be adjudged inceſtuous and unlawful, and conſequently ſhall be diſſolved, as void from the beginning. And the Parties ſo married, ſhall be by courſe of Law ſeparated. And the aforeſaid Table ſhall be in every Church publickly ſet up, and fixed at the charge of the Pariſh.

XLVIII. *None to marry under twenty-one Years, without their Parents conſent.*

NO Children under the Age of twenty one Years compleat, ſhall contract themſelves to marry without the conſent of their Parents, or of their Guardians and Governors, if their Parents be deceaſed.

(c)   XLIX.

Fig.3.1   The 46th Canon from the Constitutions and Canons Ecclesiastical of the Irish Church ... of 1634, setting out the instructions for the keeping of a registry of Christenings, Weddings, and Burials.

The process of keeping the registers in duplicate was supplemented by a requirement that the clergy should make quarterly returns of the marriages in their parishes. These returns now form the corpus of the information which is maintained in the General Register Office in Dublin (and, from 1922, in the General Register Office of Northern Ireland in Belfast). Thus for information on Church of Ireland marriages from 1845 the principal sources are the General Register Offices. The duplicate registers which are retained in the custody of the church may of course be searched but in normal circumstances they will not contain any information which is not available from the General Register Offices. There have, however, been instances, although few, in which the General Register Offices have not held a record of a post-1845 marriage: in such circumstances, of course, recourse to the register in church custody is an appropriate course of action.

The civil registration of protestant marriages foreshadowed by some twenty years the introduction of civil registration of all births, marriages and deaths in 1864. From that date Church of Ireland registers of baptisms and burials ceased to be records of the first instance since for most practical purposes the information on births and deaths (and marriages) can be more easily obtained from the General Register Offices. However, it is worth pointing out that the information maintained by the church in its post-1864 registers of baptisms and burials is not, as in the case of marriages, exactly the same as that required by the State for the registration of births and deaths. Most obviously, the Church's registers record the dates and places of baptisms and burials. These do not appear in the civil records of births and deaths. Unlike their Roman Catholic counterparts, the Church of Ireland registers of baptisms rarely contain information on god-parents or sponsors.

The parish registers which are of greatest importance and which have justifiably commanded most attention are those which are public records and national archives and which cover the years before the introduction of civil registration. In the following discussion the term parish register is taken to mean only registers of baptism and burials up to and including 31 December 1870, and registers of marriage up to and including 31 March 1845.

An early attempt, in 1617, had been made to require clergy to keep registers and to make regular returns to a 'Public Register' in Dublin. Although there is evidence to suggest that this system functioned to some extent from 1617 to 1620, by that latter date it seems to have fallen into disuse and no records emanating from this initiative are

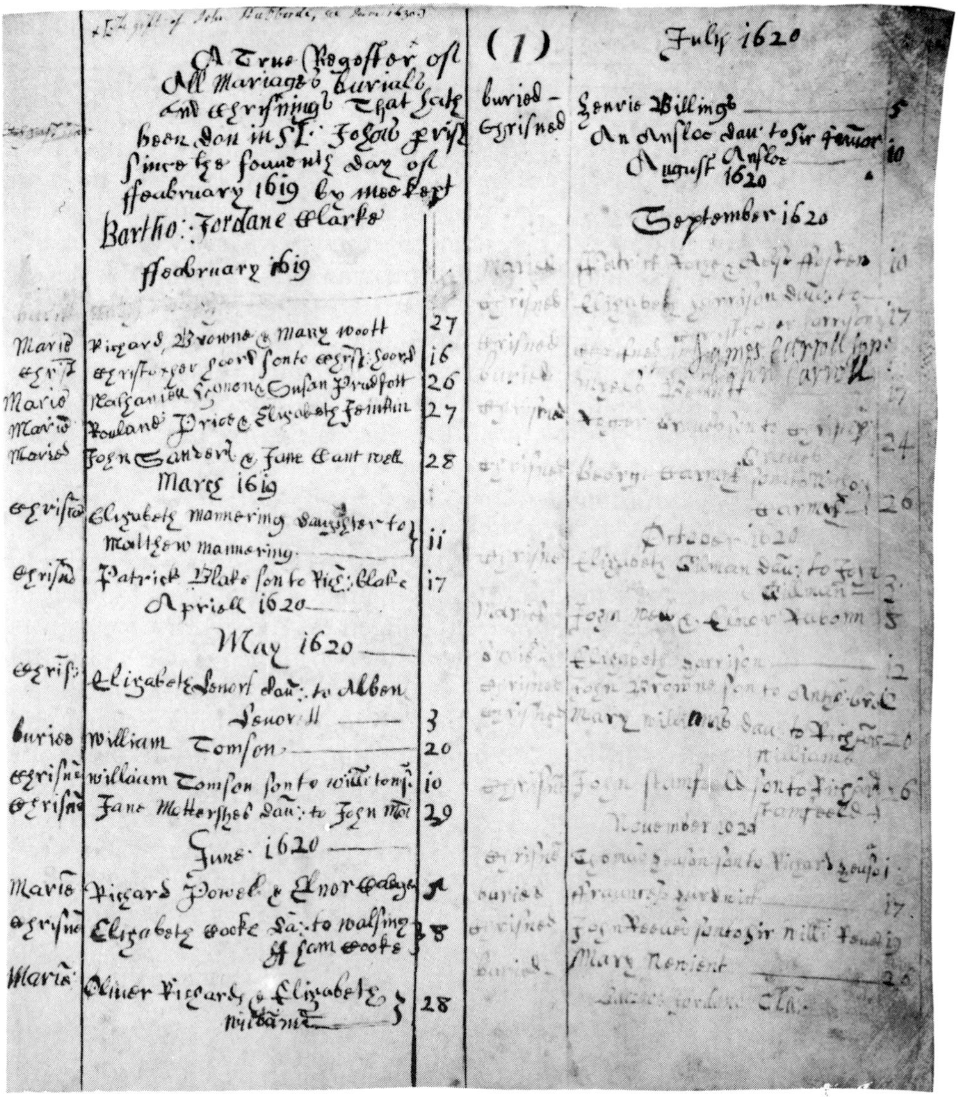

Fig.3.2   A page from the Register of St. John the Evangelist, Dublin of
1619. This is the earliest surviving Church of Ireland register.

known to survive *(3)*.

It was not therefore until after the promulgation of the 1634 Canons of the Irish Church (Fig. 3.1) that there was a sustained requirement of the clergy to keep parish registers. The 46th Canon required "A Registry to be kept of Christenings, Weddings, and Burials" in each parish and further required that "one sure Coffer" should be provided for its safe custody. On each Sunday the minister was to enter in the register, in the presence of the church-wardens, all the details of baptisms, marriages and burials which had taken place during the previous week. At the bottom of each completed page the minister and churchwardens were to sign their names, confirming the veracity of the entries, and once a year (within a week of 25 March) they were to submit to the bishops a copy of all the entries for the preceding year. This regulation was in essence a copy of the 70th Canon of the English Church which was promulgated in 1538.

By the standards of the day this was a clear and relatively comprehensive initiative covering the keeping, storing and copying of parish registers. Its effects, however, judged on the evidence which is available today, were not immediate. Only two parishes, St. John the Evangelist (1619) *(Fig. 3.2)* and St. Bride (1633), both in Dublin, are known to have had registers predating the Canon *(3)*. In the remaining years of the decade following the promulgation of the Canon, only four parishes are known to have had registers - St. Michan (1636), St. Audeon (1636), St. Catherine (1639), all in Dublin, and Blaris (1639) in Co. Antrim *(4)*. It is of course probable that other parishes were keeping registers in the 17th century - the limited operation of the 1617 measure suggests as much - but it is not possible to quantify or detail this assertion since no significant inventories of parish records were compiled until the late 19th century by which time some early records had certainly been lost.

The Canons of the Church continued to be the only significant regulation governing the keeping of parish registers until the mid 19th century. There had been an attempt to introduce a form of civil marriage during the Commonwealth *(5)* and the Irish Record Commissioners had made recommendations for the safer custody of registers in the early 19th century *(6)*. However, nothing had come of these initatives and it was not until the introduction of civil registration of marriages in 1845 that canon law was significantly supplemented by statute law.

The information which is available in the early registers is sparse. The

1634 Canons required only that there should be recorded " the Names of all Persons christened, together with the Names and Surnames of their Parents; and also the Names of all Persons married and buried and the Day and the Year of every such Christening, Marriage and Burial....": this information, as in all Church of Ireland parish registers, is written in English. Occasionally these rather terse entries were augmented with some detail on places of residence but for the 17th and 18th centuries such additions were not commonplace. Furthermore, dates of birth or death are rarely provided in these registers and so these details must be inferred from the dates of baptism and burial. In most circumstances burial seems to have taken place within two or three days of death but the interval between birth and baptism was longer. Clearly baptism immediately after birth was not the norm for the 15th Canon of 1634 required clergy "not to defer Christening if the Child be in danger." However in an age when infant mortality in Ireland was conspicuously higher than today it seems likely that most parents would have sought to have their children baptised within a matter of weeks rather than months. The registers of baptisms for this period are the most useful as they alone provide information on two generations.

The rather sparse information in these registers may owe something to the fact that these were records of local events and thus more detailed information about the persons involved and their families would be well known locally. Baptisms, marriages and burials were, almost exclusively, conducted in the parish church. Some baptisms, particularly of those who were near the top of the social ladder, or of children who were near death, were conducted privately. However, essentially baptism was, as the Book of Common Prayer set out, "The Ministration of Public Baptism of Infants, to be used in the Church". The clergy were instructed to warn people "that without .... great cause and necessity, they procure not their children to be baptised at home in their houses." When baptisms were conducted privately the details were entered in the parish register and annotated to indicate that the ceremony had been private. There is no reason to suppose that there has been any significant under-recording of such events.

Burial was usually also a local occasion and took place in the churchyard adjoining the parish church. It was not until the second half of the 19th century that churchyards in urban locations were filled up and burial had to take place in an independent or local authority cemetery at a distance from the parish church. In most of these instances the burial register was closed when the churchyard was full and subsequent burials were recorded in the registers of the

BAPTISMS solemnized in the Parish of *Aughavale*
in the County of *Mayo* in the year 18**65**

When Baptized.	When Born.	Child's Christian Name.	Parent's Name. Christian.	Surname.	Abode.	Quality, Trade, or Profession.	By whom the Ceremony was performed.
1865 Feb 22 1865 No. 61	Feb 20 1865	Eliza	Robert & Eliza	McNabb	Ardigomon	Farmer	Allan James Nesbitt Curate
1865 March 29th 1865 No. 62	March 16 1865	Sarah	George & Ann	Shaw	Westport	Labourer	Allan James Nesbitt Curate
1865 April 23 No. 63	March 31 1865	Louisa Mary	John Edmund & Isabella	Whaite	Westport	adjutant of South Mayo Militia	Allan James Nesbitt Curate
1865 May 11 No. 64	1865 March 25	Ellen Elizabeth	John or Lydia true	Wolfenden	Westport	Corn - merchant	[illegible] Curate
1865 May 19 No. 65	1865 May 16	Susan	John & Ann	Gibbons	Westport	Labourer	Allan James Nesbitt Curate
1865 July 2 No. 66	March 19 1865	Thomas William	Thomas & Mary Ann	Deniston	Westport	Land agent	D.B.M.A.
1865 Sep 17 1865 No. 67	Sep 10 1865	Sarah Jane	William & Jane	Ormsbey	Carraubauon	Farmer	William McCausLand Ch
1865 Oct 4 1865 No. 68	Sep 13 1865	Charles Frederick Zacharias	William & Amelia	Gray	Westport	Coast guard	Allan James Nesbitt Curate

Fig.3.3 *A page from the 1865 Baptismal Register of Aughaval, Co. Mayo. This register is of the form introduced in 1820 which includes date of birth, parent's abode and father's occupation.*

appropriate cemetery. Marriages also invariably took place in the parish church and usually in the church of the bride.

In the early years of the 19th century *pro forma* registers were introduced. The first of these seems to have been supplied by William Watson of Capel Street, Dublin in about 1807. These registers not only provided for the recording of more information than theretofore, but they also included a specimen page which clearly illustrated how the clergy were to keep the registers. The entries of baptisms now included the date of birth as well as the date of baptism *(Fig. 3.3)* while the burial records added an address (although usually only the name of the parish), the age of the deceased and where appropriate some indication of a family relationship (e.g. the names of parents or a wife, sometimes with an address). The marriage entries, however, were the most detailed. As well as the names of the parties and the date of the ceremony the new marriage register now included the addresses of the parties (again usually only the name of the parish) and the names and addresses of the witnesses. Such witnesses were frequently other menbers of the family. In addition, provision was now made for the parties to sign the register or, where the parties were illiterate, to make their mark.

These *pro forma* registers were further improved in the 1820's with the appearance of a register which increased the information which was to be recorded at baptisms. In addition to the dates of birth and baptism and the child's and the parents' names, now was added the parents' address and the "Quality, Trade or Profession" of the father *(see Fig. 3.3)*. This style of register (although increasingly divided into separate registers for baptisms, marriages and burials) has continued to be the norm for baptisms and burials until the present day. The new form of register was evidently judged to be highly appropriate, because from 1834 it was printed on the authority of the Ecclesiastical Commissioners for Ireland, the body responsible for the administration of the temporalities of the Church of Ireland (ie the revenues of the Church arising from secular sources such as rents etc) (7).

The adoption of pro-forma registers by the parish clergy in the 19th century seems to have been both widespread and swift. There was no compulsion to do so since the Canons remained the only binding regulations governing how registers should be kept but the convenience of ready-made registers, especially when they carried the imprimatur of the Ecclesiastical Commissioners, was evidently compelling.

The Canons of the Church did not set out specific reasons for the keeping of parish registers and their very silence on this subject suggests that even in the early 17th century the *raison d'etre* for such elementary record keeping was obvious. By recording baptisms, marriages and burials, the Church was presumably keeping a record of its members in the same way that any organisation would do today. However, by the 19th century these records had assumed an historical significance which owed little to their Christian origins. The Irish Record Commissioners noted in 1812 "... the great utility which might be derived from the registers in guarding the evidence of title and pedigrees ..."(8) while in more direct language the Daily Express in 1876 reported that in cases where parish registers were not scrupulously kept "it is impossible to estimate the amount of injury which may have been caused to persons whose right to property may be dependent upon proof of title contained in these records" (9). Thus the registers evolved both as religious and legal records which determined membership of a Christian community and also established family relationships which could be invoked in law to prove rights of inheritance.

As the Daily Express pointed out, the significance of parish registers depended to a large extent on how scrupulously they were kept and how safely they were stored. It is difficult to judge how faithfully the registers were kept: whether the details of each ceremony were accurately copied into the register, whether all ceremonies were recorded, what percentage of the residents in any parish actually came before the clergy to have their children baptised or their unions sanctified. The Canons had required that the minister, in the presence of the churchwardens, should make weekly entries of baptisms, marriages and burials. However, it seems that this duty was often delegated to parish clerks and it is not clear whether their work was supervised or checked. During the 18th century the entries in the parish of St. Audoen, Dublin were made almost exclusively by the parish clerk and, although each page is signed by the rector and the church-wardens, the relatively modest number of entries suggests significant under-recording. Furthermore it is clear that by the 19th century the discipline of recording entries each week was not uniformly observed. In some registers there are pages of entries which have clearly been copied at the same time and it would be prudent to be cautious about the accuracy of such repetitious exercises. Indeed there are occasions (for example, in the 19th century register of Rathdrum, Co. Wicklow) on which some details have been completely omitted from the registers. This suggests that the clergy's notes were not always scrupulously kept. In the mid-19th century the growing appreciation of the importance of parish registers as potential evidence of title prompted a debate about the conditions under which they were stored. In 1812 the Irish Record Commissioners had recommended that the parish registers should be stored in a central repository *(10)* and their desire for improved conditions of storage was not misplaced. The earliest registers of St. Werburgh, Dublin had perished in a fire in the church in 1754 *(11)* while in 1802 the rector of Marmullane, Cork noted that the pages of his register prior to October 1801 had been removed by an unknown person. The 1634 Canon had, of course, required that the registers were to be kept in a "sure Coffer" but the fact that the Marmullane register had been stored in an unlocked box suggests that this injunction was not uniformly observed *(12)*.

In 1869 the Church of Ireland was disestablished, that is it ceased to be the Established, or State, Church. It was concern over the status of the parish registers following disestablishment that eventually prompted action by the government on the custody of registers. Prior to 1869 the Church of Ireland had been part of the state establishment and as such the presumption appears to have been that its records were covered by the Public Records Act of 1867 and thus were the

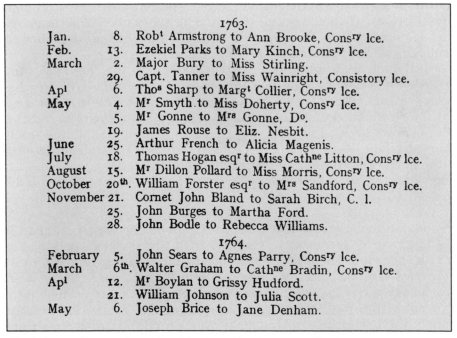

1763.

Jan.	8.	Robt Armstrong to Ann Brooke, Cons^{ry} lce.
Feb.	13.	Ezekiel Parks to Mary Kinch, Cons^{ry} lce.
March	2.	Major Bury to Miss Stirling.
	29.	Capt. Tanner to Miss Wainright, Consistory lce.
Ap^l	6.	Thos Sharp to Marg^t Collier, Cons^{ry} lce.
May	4.	Mr Smyth to Miss Doherty, Cons^{ry} lce.
	5.	Mr Gonne to Mrs Gonne, D^o.
	19.	James Rouse to Eliz. Nesbit.
June	25.	Arthur French to Alicia Magenis.
July	18.	Thomas Hogan esq^r to Miss Cath^{ne} Litton, Cons^{ry} lce.
August	15.	Mr Dillon Pollard to Miss Morris, Cons^{ry} lce.
October	20th.	William Forster esq^r to Mrs Sandford, Cons^{ry} lce.
November	21.	Cornet John Bland to Sarah Birch, C. 1.
	25.	John Burges to Martha Ford.
	28.	John Bodle to Rebecca Williams.

1764.

February	5.	John Sears to Agnes Parry, Cons^{ry} lce.
March	6th.	Walter Graham to Cath^{ne} Bradin, Cons^{ry} lce.
Ap^l	12.	Mr Boylan to Grissy Hudford.
	21.	William Johnson to Julia Scott.
May	6.	Joseph Brice to Jane Denham.

Fig.3.4   *Extract from the "Marriage Entries in the Registers of the Parishes of St. Marie.....(1627-1800)", published by the Parish Register Society of Dublin, 1915.*

property of the state. Following disestablishment the Church became a private organisation and thus legislation was introduced in 1875 and 1876 to ensure that the registers remained in public ownership. It had been intended by the 1875 Act that all parish records would be transferred to the Public Record Office in Dublin but this legislation was amended in the following year. Under the terms of the 1876 Act only registers of baptisms and burials up to and including 31 December 1870, and registers of marriages up to and including 31 March 1845, were to be deemed public records and provision was made for their retention in parish custody providing the Master of the Rolls was satisfied with the conditions in which they were stored *(13)*. A large proportion of the registers were, however, transferred to the Public Record Office.

The single most significant consequence of this legislation is the one fact which apparently everyone knows about Church or Ireland parish registers: that they were burnt in the fire in the Public Record Office of Ireland in 1922. In fact the registers of 1006 parishes had been transferred to the Public Record Office by 1922. Of these registers, only four were saved *(14)* although the registers of 637 parishes survived in local custody. In addition all but three of the parochial returns, the annual abstracts of baptisms, marriages and burials which were required under the 1634 Canons, were destroyed *(15)*.

These losses were mitigated to some extent by the fact that some parishes had copied their registers and for others the registers had been printed. Investigations by the Public Record Office in the wake of the fire established that 124 parishes held copies in whole or in part of the registers which they had transmitted to Dublin, while the Public Record Office itself held copies from a further 23 parishes *(16)*. Subsequent investigations suggest that more material has survived in copy form than had been originally estimated but it is not yet possible to detail this impression.

In addition the registers of a number of parishes had been printed. In the forefront of this activity was the Parish Register Society of Dublin which, between 1905 and 1915, produced volumes relating to 16 churches *(Fig. 3.4)*. All of these, except Templemore (Derry) were Dublin city parishes *(17)*. Similar transcription work was printed in the Journal of the Irish Memorials Association and some 19th century parish histories include substantial extracts from the parish registers.

The original registers which have survived date predominantly from the 18th and 19th century, with an emphasis on the latter. Only four parishes have original registers pre-dating 1650. These are St. John

(Dublin) 1619 *(see Fig. 3.2)*, Blaris (Lisburn, Co. Antrim) 1637, Templemore (Londonderry) 1642, Holy Trinity (Cork) 1643. A further 45 parishes have registers which begin between 1650 and 1700. In contrast a little over 200 parishes have original registers which begin in the 18th century while some 340 parishes have registers which begin in the first half of the 19th.

Many of these registers have remained in the custody of the parishes while others have been deposited in the Public Record Office of Northern Ireland, the National Archives of Ireland (formerly the Public Record Office of Ireland) or the Representive Church Body Library in Dublin. The National Archives hold the registers for 10 parishes in the Republic of Ireland while the Public Record Office of Northern Ireland in Belfast have registers from some 30 parishes in Northern Ireland. Both repositories have been active also in microfilming. In Belfast there are microfilms of all those parish registers which are public records, from the six counties of Northern Ireland and similar films for the parishes in the other three counties which make up the historic province of Ulster (ie Cavan, Monaghan and Donegal). In Dublin, the National Archives has filmed registers in the dioceses of Cashel, Cork, Limerick, Tuam, Meath and Kildare, Glendalough and Ferns.

The Representative Church Body Library in Dublin, which is the Library of the Church of Ireland, has been providing accomodation for church records since 1939. Since 1981, with the appointment of an archivist, and the provision of modern purpose built storage accommodation, the accession of parish registers has increased. The Library now holds registers for over 250 parishes in the Republic of Ireland, of which 100 pre-date civil registration. In addition, the Library has transcripts of, or extracts from, the registers of a further 17 parishes, the original registers of which were destroyed in 1922. It is located at Braemor Park, Rathgar, Dublin 14.

There are a number of modern published guides of Irish parish registers *(18)* which provide a useful introduction to the subject. The information from these guides on the survival and custody of Church of Ireland registers can easily be updated by application to the Representive Church Body Library. At present there is an increasing tendency to deposit original registers in the Public Record Office of Northern Ireland and the Representive Church Body Library. Details of the registers in the latter are published bi-ennially in the <u>Irish Genealogist</u> while an up to date handlist is available from the Library. The holdings of the former are detailed periodically in the <u>Reports of the Deputy Keeper of the Records.</u> Those registers which remain in the

New St Michans Parish January the 28: 1722

An assessment made pursuant to an Act of Vestery bearing date Thursday the 20 day of December 1722 for the Sume of 68.0.11½, Grounded upon a Report of the Committee appoynted the 29 of November Last to Inspect & Examin the Severall and Respetive debts due from this Parish for Sallerys, and Severall other Debts and Publick uses, as by the said Act of vestery may more ptiularly appeare, Which said Sume is acordingly applotted upon the Severall and Respective Inhabitants of the said Parish, and to be Collected by Mr Joseph Hollingsworth, mr Constant, mr Rowland Parker, and mr Thomas Rice, Sides men, and overseers of the said Parish who are appoynted Collectors thereof, according to the Respetive names, & Sumes hereunto annexed, as follows

Mr Jos. Hollingsworth, & Mr Constant Collects for the East part of the said Parish.

The First Ward	£	s	d	Arrears	Bridgman Constable	£	s	d
The Inns					Mich. Doyle	0	0	8
John Mullenex	0	2	2	3. d	Mr Carroll	0	0	6
mr Horish Tennt	0	0	10	0.3	Widdow Hoskinson	0	1	0
Widdow Brady	0	1	2		Ensigne Palfrey	0	1	0
Lady Dunn	0	4	0		From The Inns to Charles Street			
mrs Skeahy	0	2	6		William Leynard	0	1	2
mr O'Brian	0	2	6		Councill. Saunders	0	2	4
mr John Moore	0	3	4		William Delany	0	1	8
Widdow Alderson	0	2	6					
mr Dillon	0	5	0		Charles Street			
mr Tobin	0	5	0		West Side S. End			
John Waite Esqr	0	2	4		William Cook	0	3	8
Widdow Cannon	0	1	6		Widdow Mcnamarah	0	1	8
mrs Eastwood	0	5	10		Robert Johnston	0	3	0
mr Emerson	0	3	0		Pat Cannon	0	1	8
Widdow Dowlen	0	2	8		Richard Thorowgood	0	2	0
					mr Garrt Byrne	0	1	8
Lucey Lane					mrs Forrest	0	2	0
Mrs Crimsby	0	1	8		mr John Drewry	0	2	0
Peter Orrill	0	1	2		Nich Tully	0	2	0
mr Byrne	0	1	2		Willm Callahan	0	2	0
mr Connor	0	1	2		mr Dueney	0	3	4
Wid Dunn	0	1	0	1.0	Doctr Hoyle	0	2	6
James Malone Waast	0	0	0		mr Robert King	0	2	6
John Behan	0	0	8		mrs Tho Mcsoolery	0	2	6
Peter Walsh	0	0	8					
	2	11	10			2	0	10

Fig.3.5 *A page from the Cess Applottment Book of St. Michan Dublin, for January 28th 1722, showing the persons liable to pay parish cess (a form of tax) on some of the streets in the parish.*

custody of the parishes are the responsibility of the local clergy, the names and addresses of whom, together with the parishes for which they are responsible, are printed annually in the Church of Ireland Directory.

The Constitution of the Church of Ireland explicitly recognizes a right of public access to parish registers. Clergy are required ".. at all reasonable times, on demand to allow search in such registers..." and to provide certified copies of entries. Certified copies of entries can also be provided by the repositories which hold original registers and only certified copies made from the original entries are acceptable under law as valid proof of a baptism, marriage or burial. It is not the policy of the Church of Ireland or the major repositories to permit the photocopying of parish registers. A fee is levied for the issue of certified copies and also for the search if it is made in registers which are still in the custody of the local clergy. Clergy may undertake a search on behalf of a researcher but they are not obliged to do so. The responsibility for a search is essentially that of the researcher or his agent.

The parishes of the Established Church of Ireland were both religious and civil units with the civil functions being those of an embryonic local government. These activities are detailed in the records of the vestry. The Select Vestry was in effect a committee of rate paying Protestants which levied small local taxes for the maintenance of the Church and its officers. Of greater importance was the General Vestry which, after the abolition of the penal laws, was composed of all ratepayers irrespective of their religion. The General Vestry levied a local tax, or cess, which paid for local services such as the repair of roads, the cleaning of streets, and the provision of fire brigades and parish constables (19). The records of the applotment, or assessment, of the parish cess, which survive either as individual volumes or among the vestry minutes, provide lists of ratepayers, often arranged street by street, which can be a useful supplement to the parish registers. The parish of St. Michan, Dublin has a particularly fine set of cess applotment books dating from 1711 to 1835 (Fig. 3.5).

In addition the vestry records can contain valuable detail on the administration of the parish and on the personalities involved. The parish of St. John the Evangelist, Dublin has a remarkable collection of records which detail those who served in the parish watch (an embryonic police force) from the 1720's until the 1780's; the records of St. Mark's Dublin list the parish poor in the late 18th century (20); while the pew register of St. Werburgh's is a catalogue of the prominent figures in the Dublin public life in the first half of the 18th century.

Inevitably such records are richest for the large cities and particularly for Dublin where there was a sufficiently large Protestant populace to exercise effective control, and a large enough body of ratepayers to require a variety of services and to be able to financially support such provision. Some rural parishes did operate a vestry system as complete and sophisticated as in the cities - Derriaghy in Co. Antrim is a good example of this - but in general the amount of useful information to be gleaned from the extant records of rural parishes before the mid 19th century is limited. However for any parish for which the registers have not survived, the vestry records are worth investigating as a substitute source of genealogical information.

Some vestry records were destroyed in the fire in the Public Record Office in Dublin in 1922 as they were bound in the same volume as parish registers. Others have certainly been lost through misfortune or more often through neglect - they have never been viewed as important in the same legal sense as registers and thus there have never been any regulations governing their care and custody. There is no comprehensive inventory of vestry records but information on those which survive and on their custody can usually be provided by the Representative Church Body Library. The vestry records of a few parishes have been published either as complete volumes as in the case of Derriaghy, *(21)* or as extracts in parish histories or in the editions of periodicals such as the Irish Builder.

Finally some mention should be made of parish deeds and particularly of those for the years predating the establishment of the Registry of Deeds, which contains records of registered deeds of transfer of ownership or interest in property from 1708.

Five Dublin parishes are known to have had significant collections of medieval and early modern deeds. Of these only the collection of the parish of St. John survives. Those for St. Nicholas Within, St. Catherine and St. James, and St. Werburgh were destroyed in the fire in the Public Record Office in Dublin in 1922. However, for all of these, except St. Nicholas, the information from the deeds has survived to some extent.

The collection of the parish of St. John the Evangelist is obviously the most important because of its physical survival. It is also the most significant as it is the largest of these collections, with 203 deeds covering the period c. 1233-1704. These deeds are now in the Library of Trinity College, Dublin *(22)*. The deeds of St. Werburgh were 160 in number and covered the period 1317-1662 while for St. Catherine and St James there were 37 deeds covering the period 1296 - 1743. The deeds of these four parishes were calendared in the <u>Proceedings of the Royal Irish Academy</u> in 1916 and 1919 *(23)* while there is a complete transcript of those for St. Catherine and St. James in the Representative Church Body Library *(24)*. The original deeds were written in Latin but the printed calendars are in English while the transcript of the deeds of St. Catherine's parish is in both Latin and English.

All these collections contain significant information on family relationships, occupations and places of residence as well as details of the transfer and ownership of land and property. The deeds are particularly useful for the period before the earliest surviving Church of Ireland parish register in 1619.

The parish records of the Church of Ireland are a unique and invaluable source for genealogists and local historians - but they are not easy to use. They demand preparation to discover where they are and how much of them survives, patience to gain familiarity with many different styles of handwriting, and above all industriousness to work through quantities of unindexed manuscript material. For researchers with these qualities the use of parish records can be very rewarding.

REFERENCES

1. For a short introduction to the history of the Church of Ireland see *K.Milne*, **The Church of Ireland: A History** (Dublin 2nd Ed. 1981). For an overview of Church of Ireland records see *R. Refausse " The Archives of the Church of Ireland: an Introduction"* in **Irish Archives Bulletin** Vol 11, 1981.

2. **7 & 8 Victoria c 81.**

3. *J. Mills* (Ed.) **The Registers of St John the Evangelist, Dublin. 1619 - 1699.** (Dublin 1906).

4. Ibid.

5. *J. Mills* (Ed.) **The Register of the Liberties of Cashel 1654 - 1657.** (Dublin 1907).

6. **Irish Record Commission. Second Annual Report, March 1812.**

7. See **Church Temporalities (Ireland) Act 1833**, (3 & 4 William IV C. 37).

8. **Irish Record Commission** (see 6).

9. Cited in *G. O'Duill* *"Church Records after Disestablishment"* in **Irish Archives Bulletin,** Vol 5, 1975.

10. **Irish Record Commission** (see 6).

11. *S.C. Hughes* **The Church of St Werburgh Dublin,** (Dublin 1889).

12. **Parish Records of Marmullane (Cork).** Representative Church Body Library, Dublin P. 197.

13. For an extensive discussion of this debate see *G. O'Duill* (9 above).

14. These registers are listed in the **55th Report of the Deputy Keeper of the Public Records in Ireland (1928),** App IV.

15. Ibid.

16. These copies are listed in the **56th Report of the Deputy Keeper of the Public Records in Ireland (1931),** Appendices VII & VIII.

17. The publications of the Parish Register Society were as follows;
    J. Mills (Ed.) **The Registers of St John the Evangelist, Dublin 1619 -1699** (Dublin 1906);
    J.H. Bernard (Ed.) **The Registers of.St Patrick, Dublin 1677 - 1800** (Dublin 1907);
    H.J.Lawlor (Ed.) **The Registers of Provost Winter (Trinity College Dublin) 1650 - 1660** (Dublin 1907);
    J. Mills **The Registers of the Liberties of Cashel 1654 - 1657** (Dublin 1907);
    H.S.Guinness (Ed.) **The Register of the Union of Monkstown (Co. Dublin) 1669 - 1786** (Dublin 1908);
    H. Wood (Ed.) **The Registers of St Catherine, Dublin 1636 - 1715** (Dublin 1908);
    H.F. Berry (Ed.) **The Registers of St. Michan, Dublin 1636 - 1700** (Dublin 1909);

R. *Hayes* (Ed.) **The Register of Derry Cathedral. Parish of Templemore 1642 - 1703** (Dublin 1910);
J. *Mills* (Ed.) **The Registers of St Peter and St. Kevin, Dublin 1663 -1761** (Dublin 1911);
J. *Mills* (Ed.) **The Registers of St Nicholas Without, Dublin 1694 -1739** (Dublin 1912);
D.A. *Chart.* (Ed.) **Marriage Entries from the Registers of St. Andrew, St. Anne, St Audoen, & St. Bride (Dublin) 1632 - 1800.** (Dublin 1913);
A.E.*Langman* (Ed.) **Marriage Entries in the Registers of ...S. Marie, St Luke, St Catherine & St Werburgh 1627 - 1800** (Dublin 1915).

18.	J. G. *Ryan* **Irish Records - Sources for Family & Local History** (Salt Lake City 1988); and **A Guide to Tracing your Dublin Ancestors** (Dublin 1988);
B.*Mitchell* **A Guide to Irish Parish Registers** (Baltimore 1988)

19.	For a further discussion of the role of the vestry see
D.H. *Akenson* **The Church of Ireland; Ecclesiastical Reform and Revolution 1800 - 1885** (Yale 1971) pp 52-55.

20.	See R. *Lavelle* & P. *Huggard* "*The Parish Poor of St. Marks*" in D. *Dickson* (Ed.) **The Gorgeous Mask** (Dublin 1987)

21.	W.N.C.*Barr* & W.C. *Kerr* (Eds) **The Oldest Register of the Parish of Derryiaghy 1696 - 1772.** (Derryiaghy 1981).

22.	These deeds are in the Library of Trinity College Dublin MS 1477.

23.	J.L.*Robinson* "*On the ancient Deeds of the Parish of St. John, Dublin*" in **Proc. R.I.A. Vol. XXXIII**, Section C, No. 7, July 1916;
H.F. *Twiss* "*Some ancient deeds of the parishes of St Catherine & St James, Dublin* and *"Some ancient Deeds of the Parish of St. Werburgh, Dublin"*, in **Proc. R.I.A. Vol XXXV**, Section C, Nos 7 & 8.

24.	Representative Church Body Library MS 15/3/1

APPENDIX 3.1

The following list details those registers of baptisms, marriages and burials which had been deposited in the Representative Church Body Library by 1 June 1992. These Registers are available to readers in the Library which is located at Braemor Park, Rathgar, Dublin 14. An asterisk beside the name of a parish indicates that the records are, in whole or in part, copies of or extracts from original registers which were destroyed in the fire in the Publin Record Office of Ireland in 1922. The list also contains records from some non-parochial ministries such as military chapels of ease : these have been included because these ministries produced registers of baptisms, marriages or burials.

COUNTY CARLOW

Parish	Baptisms	Marriages	Burials
Bilboa		1846-1956	
Carlow	1695-1885	1695-1915	1698-1894
Clonagoose		1846-1954	
Clonmelsh		1846-1934	
Dunleckney	1791-1837	1791-1957	1791-1837
Kellistown		1854-1917	
Kiltennel	1837-1875	1837-1950	1837-1957
Lorum		1845-1954	
Nurney		1845-1954	
Old Leighlin*	1781-1813	1790-1855	1781-1813
Tullow	1696-1844	1700-1843	1700-1844
Wells	1870-1957	1803-1915	1802

COUNTY CAVAN

Parish	Baptisms	Marriages	Burials
Kingscourt		1845-1949	
Moybologue		1878-1956	
Swanlibar	1798-1863	1798-1952	1798-1883
Templeport	1837	1845-1954	1878-1906

COUNTY CLARE

Parish	Baptisms	Marriages	Burials
Clare Abbey		1845-1901	
Clondegad		1845-1885	1882-1915

Clonlea	1879-1947	1845-1946	1877-1951
Kildysert	1881-1920	1847-1918	1882-1915
Kilfarboy		1845-1957	
Kilfenora		1853-1918	
Kilfieragh		1845-1954	
Kilfinaghty		1862-1939	
Killard		1848-1933	
Kilmanaheen	1886-1972	1845-1920	
Kilmurry	1889-1918	1845-1905	1892-1954
Kilnaboy	1799-1931	1802-1961	1821-1831
Kilnasoolagh	1731-1829	1746-1954	1739-1829
Kilrush	1741-1840	1766-1841	1743-1841
Kilseily	1881-1915	1848-1905	1877-1951
Quin	1907-1954	1845-1915	1906-1927

COUNTY CORK

Parish	Baptisms	Marriages	Burials
Abbeymahon*	1782-1852	1738-1852	1732-1852
Ballymodan	1695-1878	1695-1958	1695-1878
Blackrock	1828-1897	1828-1981	1830-1946
Brinny*	1797-1884	1797-1844	1797-1844
Canaway		1845-1872	
Carrigaline	1724-1756	1726-1792	
Carrigtwohill		1848-1955	
Catherlog		1870-1955	
Clondrohid		1848-1884	
Douglas	1789-1818	1792-1893	1790
Dungourney	1850-1954		
Frankfield		1847-1955	
Inchigeelagh	1900	1845-1865	
Inishannon	1693-1844	1693-1911	1693-1844
Kilbrittain*	1832-1876	1830-1868	
Killeagh*	1782-1863	1778-1840	1787-1868
Kilroan	1885-1920	1846-1920	
Knockvilly*	1837-1883	1844-1848	1837-1883
Leighmoney	1869-1943		
Marmullane	1801-1873	1802-1954	1803-1873
Midleton*	1699-1881	1728-1823	1696-1877
Rathclaren*	1780-1875	1780-1849	1792-1875
Rathcooney	1750-1897	1749-1954	1750-1853
Templemichael	1845-1853		
Templenacarriga			1883-1932

COUNTY DONEGAL

Parish	Baptisms	Marriages	Burials
Aughanunshin		1845-1971	
Conwal	1876-1951	1845-1988	1878-1906
Gartan	1881-1959	1845-1946	
Leck	1878-1975	1846-1959	1878-1900

CITY AND COUNTY OF DUBLIN

Parish	Baptisms	Marriages	Burials
Arbour Hill Barracks	1848-1922		1847-1884
Baggotrath	1865-1923	1882-1923	
Balgriffin	1820-1945	1846-1956	1821-1945
Beggars' Bush Barracks	1868-1921		
Castleknock	1709-1959	1710-1956	1710-1963
Christ Church Cathedral	1740-1838	1717-1826	1710-1848
Clonsilla	1830-1901	1831-1956	1831-1902
Cloughran*	1782-1852	1738-1852	1732-1852
Cloughran	1870-1891	1858-1875	1872-1938
Donnybrook	1712-1957	1712-1956	1712-1873
Dun Laoghaire- Christ Church	1852-1899	1875-1956	
Dun Laoghaire- Mariners	1843-1970	1875-1972	
Female Penitentiary	1898-1907		
Finglas			1877-1956
Free Church	1902-1987		
Irishtown	1812-1973	1824-1956	1807-1866
Kilmainham	1857-1982	1861-1981	
Kilternan	1817-1895	1817-1954	1817-1936
Malahide	1822-1964	1825-1956	1822-1876
Missions to Seamen	1961-1981		
Molyneux Chapel	1871-1926		
Mulhuddert		1871-1944	
Newcastle Lyons	1768-1847	1772-1946	1776-1847
North Dublin Union	1906-1918		

Parish	Baptisms	Marriages	Burials
Pigeon House Fort	1872-1901		
Portmarnock*	1820-1876	1825-1951	1820-1875
Portobello Barracks	1859-1869		
Richmond Barracks	1857-1922		
St. Aidan	1910-1961		
St. Ann	1873-1938	1845-1978	1780-1816
St. Audeon	1672-1916	1673-1947	1673-1885
St. Augustine	1911-1965		
St. Bride		1845-1887	
St. Catherine	1699-1966	1679-1966	1679-1898
St. George	1794-1875	1794-1956	1824-1908
St. James	1730-1963	1742-1963	1742-1989
St. John	1619-1878	1619-1878	1619-1850
St. Kevin	1883-1980	1884-1977	
St. Luke	1713-1974	1716-1973	1716-1974
St. Mark	1730-1971	1730-1971	1733-1923
St. Mary	1697-1972	1697-1880	1700-1858
St. Mathias	1867-1955	1873-1955	
St. Michael*	1674-1686	1663-1765	1678-1750
St. Michan*	1701-1787	1796-1809	1727-1745
St. Nicholas Within	1671-1866	1671-1865	1671-1863
St. Nicholas Without	1694-1861	1699-1861	1694-1875
St. Paul	1698-1987	1699-1982	1702-1892
St. Peter	1669-1974	1670-1975	1670-1883
St. Stephen	1837-1912	1862-1956	
St. Thomas	1750-1970	1750-1980	1762-1882
St. Victor	1897-1954	1916-1956	
St. Werburgh	1704-1913	1704-1956	1704-1843
Sandymount	1850-1861		
Santry	1754-1875	1754-1831	1753-1875
South Dublin Union	1864-1898		
Trinity	1871-1918	1874-1915	

COUNTY FERMANAGH

Parish	Baptisms	Marriages	Burials
Enniskillen*	1667-1789	1668-1794	1667-1781

COUNTY GALWAY

Parish	Baptisms	Marriages	Burials
Ballinakill	1775-1914	1792-1928	1803-1951
Castlekirke	1879-1925		1879-1963
Dunmore	1884-1914	1846-1903	1887-1938
Headford	1888-1941	1845-1920	1885-1975
Kilconla		1846-1906	
Killeraght		1846-1936	
Killererin*	1811-1828	1818-1828	1818
Kilmoylan	1866		
Moylough	1826-1922	1823-1844	1843-1940
Renvyle	1884-1918	1869-1910	1871-1932
Ross		1856-1950	
Sellerna	1897-1913	1856-1950	1898-1919

COUNTY KERRY

Parish	Baptisms	Marriages	Burials
Cahir	1878-1947	1847-1876	
Kenmare	1818-1873	1819-1950	1818-1849
Kilcrohane		1846-1930	
Kilgarvan	1811-1850	1812-1947	1819-1960
Kilmore	1826-1960	1850-1925	
Templenoe		1849-1920	

COUNTY KILDARE

Parish	Baptisms	Marriages	Burials
Ballinafagh	1876-1954	1851-1957	1877-1964
Celbridge	1777-1977	1777-1975	1787-1882
Clane		1850-1956	1906-1947
Clonaslee	1814-1989	1814-1981	1816-1985
Donadea	1890-1968	1846-1939	1892-1920
Fontstown	1814-1840	1811-1856	1811-1869
Lea	1830-1852	1841	1842-1886
Newbridge Garrison	1867-1922		
Straffan	1838-1881	1838-1950	1841-1940

COUNTY KILKENNY

Parish	Baptisms	Marriages	Burials
Ballaghtobin		1882-1936	

Parish	Baptisms	Marriages	Burials
Burnchurch	1881-1942	1845-1929	1882-1980
Callan	1892-1966	1846-1954	1894-1982
Castlecomer	1799-1839	1799-1845	1799-1901
Colliery	1838-1858	1839-1844	
Ennisnag		1851-1954	
Gowran	1885-1977	1845-1956	
Graiguena-managh	1804-1805	1846-1933	
Grange Sylvae		1850-1921	
Innistiogue	1797-1878	1797-1953	1798-1886
Kells		1845-1924	
Kilmocahill		1848-1864	
Kilmoganny	1819-1845	1826-1873	1828-1845
Knocktoper	1884-1959	1849-1940	1887-1983
Mothel	1810-1843	1811-1950	1817-1842
Powerstown		1854	
Rathcool	1836-1844	1842	
Rower	1888-1943	1849-1937	1883-1985
Shankill		1845-1950	
Tascoffin		1853-1880	
Thomastown	1895-1965	1845-1949	1870-1987
Ullard		1857	

COUNTY LAOIS

Parish	Baptisms	Marriages	Burials
Durrow*	1731-1841	1731-1836	1731-1836

COUNTY LIMERICK

Parish	Baptisms	Marriages	Burials
Ballinlanders		1852-1877	

COUNTY LONGFORD

Parish	Baptisms	Marriages	Burials
Forgney	1808-1918	1804-1952	1804-1914
Shrule	1854-1863		

COUNTY LOUTH

Parish	Baptisms	Marriages	Burials
Dunleer*	1787-1792	1738-1796	1729-1795

COUNTY MAYO

Parish	Baptisms	Marriages	Burials
Aasleagh		1859-1956	
Achill	1854-1896	1855-1936	
Aughaval	1801-1887	1802-1854	1820-1903
Ayle	1825-1892	1828-1904	1828-1893
Ballinchalla	1831-1835	1832-1917	1831-1836
Ballinrobe	1796-1912	1809-1862	1809-1974
Ballycroy		1855-1898	1883-1962
Ballyovie	1879-1951	1854-1954	1880-1966
Bulnahinch		1854-1873	
Castlemore	1890-1911	1847-1908	
Cong	1746-1863	1745-1956	1745-1863
Crossboyne	1877-1924	1854-1937	1879-1973
Dugort		1845-1888	
Kilcolman	1877-1932	1846-1949	1878-1969
Kilcommon	1921-1926	1845-1937	1920-1959
Kilmaine	1744-1927	1744-1891	1744-1958
Kilmeena	1887-1904	1845-1917	
Knappagh		1855-1952	
Louisburgh		1846-1952	
Mayo		1849-1862	

COUNTY MEATH

Parish	Baptisms	Marriages	Burials
Clonard		1846-1850	
Colpe	1810-1822	1845-1937	
Delvin	1817-1947	1817-1942	1817-1989
Drogheda -			
St. Mary	1763-1839	1763-1956	1763-1838
Drumconrath	1799-1826	1820-1956	1821-1826
Duleek	1880-1965	1845-1973	1881-1973
Julianstown	1778-1811	1791-1887	1778-1974
Kilbride - Castlecor		1845-1955	
Killeagh	1886-1948	1846-1929	1900-1985
Kilmainhamwood	1881-1892	1856-1876	
Nobber		1850-1945	
Parish	Baptisms	Marriages	Burials
Oldcastle	1814-1884	1814-1954	1814-1890
Painstown	1833-1917	1835-1919	1834-1908
Painstown-			
St. Anne		1859-1919	1864-1913

Parish	Baptisms	Marriages	Burials
Syddan	1720-1825	1721-1949	1725-1824

COUNTY MONAGHAN

Parish	Baptisms	Marriages	Burials
Clontibret*	1864-1865		1864-1865

COUNTY OFFALY

Parish	Baptisms	Marriages	Burials
Ballyboy	1709-1847	1709-1819	1709-1868
Castlejordan	1702-1964	1707-1941	1704-1863
Clonmacnoise		1845-1893	
Drumraney		1847-1860	
Lemanaghan	1885-1975	1845-1951	1884-1988
Liss		1963-1983	

COUNTY ROSCOMMON

Parish	Baptisms	Marriages	Burials
Athlone - St. Peter	1873-1941	1845-1941	
Kiltoom	1797-1943	1802-1910	1801-1840

COUNTY SLIGO

Parish	Baptisms	Marriages	Burials
Ballisodare		1845-1954	
Emlafad	1762-1882	1762-1875	1762-1941

COUNTY TIPPERARY

Parish	Baptisms	Marriages	Burials
Ardfinnan	1877-1937		
Clonmel	1791-1807		
Terryglass	1809-1862	1809-1916	1809-1882
Tubrid	1892-1905		

COUNTY WESTMEATH

Parish	Baptisms	Marriages	Burials
Almorita		1846-1937	
Ardnurcher	1873-1982	1848-1974	
Athlone - St. Mary	1768-1903	1767-1890	1747-1892

Ballyloughloe	1877-1955	1845-1945	1877-1970
Ballymore		1850-1923	
Benown		1847-1934	
Castlepollard		1845-1953	
Churchtown		1846-1876	
Collinstown	1838-1963	1838-1963	1837-1960
Drumcree*	1816-1983	1848-1977	
Enniscoffey	1881-1953	1845-1925	1891-1976
Foyran	1890-1960	1878-1939	
Kilbeggan	1881-1959	1845-1940	1882-1988
Kilbixy		1848-1947	
Kilcleagh	1873-1985	1845-1990	1876-1989
Kilkenny West	1783-1956	1783-1913	1784-1862
Killucan	1696-1863	1787-1857	1700-1888
Kinnegad	1892-1917	1845-1894	1895-1956
Leney	1840-1843	1845-1945	1840-1841
Mayne	1808-1983	1809-1980	1808-1991
Moydrum		1885-1954	
Moyliscar		1845-1956	
Mullingar		1845-1956	
Portnashangan		1846-1979	1880-1977
Rathconnell			1881-1895
Stonehall	1878-1941		
Willbrook	1756-1783	1775	

COUNTY WEXFORD

Parish	Baptisms	Marriages	Burials
Inch		1845-1920	

COUNTY WICKLOW

Parish	Baptisms	Marriages	Burials
Donard		1848-1955	1888-1965
Donoughmore	1720-1888	1720-1856	1720-1929
Dunlavin	1697-1934	1697-1956	1697-1934
Glenealy	1808-1880	1808-1864	1817-1871
Rathdrum	1706-1845	1706-1870	1706-1916

PRESBYTERIAN CHURCH RECORDS

Christine Kinealy

Presbyterian church registers are an invaluable source for the genealogy and history of the Presbyterian people of Ireland. These registers, however, also present the same problems as those of other Irish churches. Namely, they are not standardised in format or layout, there are frequent gaps in the recording of information, the nature of the recorded information differs from year to year and area to area, and the quality of handwriting changes from minister to minister. In addition, the degree of care which was given to compiling and preserving these books varies greatly. Most significantly for the family researcher, however is the fact that Presbyterian records generally do not begin until the nineteenth century.

4.1. History

The lack of early registers for the Presbyterian Church is partly explained by the external factors affecting its history. Irish Presbyterianism originated from Scottish Presbyterianism which, in turn, had its roots in the Protestant Reformation of the sixteenth century. This movement, which was started by Martin Luther and developed by John Calvin, was brought to Scotland by John Knox in 1559 and quickly became firmly established. Subsequently, religious persecution resulted in some Presbyterians emigrating as a means of escape. The Irish Presbyterian church was established at the beginning of the seventeenth century largely by Scottish Presbyterian tenantry who chose to settle on the newly planted counties of Ulster. These counties had been set aside for settlement by British planters as part of the Plantation of Ulster in 1608-1610. The growth of the early

Presbyterian Church in Ireland was fostered by Scottish "planter" landlords such as Sir Arthur Chichester and Sir Robert Adair. The links between the Irish and Scottish Presbyterian Churches have remained strong; for many years, for example, Irish Ministers were sent to Scotland to be educated for the ministry.

The history of the early Presbyterian Church in Ireland is a history of external suppression and internal ideological conflict. From the sixteenth century the Church of Ireland (also known as the Episcopalian, Anglican or Established Church) was the state church in Ireland (see p. 41 for further details). The fact that the Presbyterian Church did not conform to Church of Ireland doctrinal practices meant that, like the Catholic Church, it was subject to intermittent periods of repression from the state. Throughout the seventeenth and early eighteenth centuries a series of laws were introduced which endeavoured to restrict Presbyterian worship not only in Ireland but also in Britain.

At the end of the sixteenth century, legislation was introduced in Ireland which obliged all Presbyterian ministers to swear an oath to the Book of Common Prayer of the Church of Ireland. Ministers who refused to do so, as frequently happened, could be deposed from their ministry. These laws also prohibited Presbyterian ministers from marrying or burying members of their own congregations unless these ceremonies were performed according to the rites of the Church of Ireland. This meant that marriages that were not celebrated in this way could be deemed invalid, the children illegitimate, and that the parents could even be tried in the local Diocesan Court for immoral behaviour. Although this action was rarely taken, such restrictions meant that ceremonies were sometimes carried out secretly according to the rites of the Presbyterian Church or, if property was involved, were performed in a nearby state church. Inevitably these restrictions meant that the recording of these ceremonies was less complete than it otherwise would have been and it explains why Presbyterian registers (like those of other dissenting groups) begin later and are generally less complete than those of the Church of Ireland parishes in the same areas.

As had been the experience of the Catholic Church, by the end of the eighteenth century a softening in the Government's attitude towards the Presbyterian Church was apparent. In 1782, marriages solemnised by Presbyterian ministers were legalised, although it was not until 1845 that marriage between a Presbyterian and a member of the Church of Ireland was recognised as valid. In 1869, following the Church

Mr. Thomas Wardrop's

Name	Address	No. of Pew
Mr. Thos. Wardrop	Orbiston House, Rathgar	75 & 76
Mrs. Wardrop	do. do.	4
Miss Wardrop	do. do.	4
Miss Agnew	do. do.	4
Mr. Wm. Renwick	Watling Street	67
Mrs. Stevenson	21. Garville Avenue	1
Mr. W. C. Stevenson	do. do.	do.
Mrs. Cochrane	do. do.	do.
Mrs. Tweeny	Widow's House, Whitefriar St.	
Mr. Wm. Wardrop		76
Mrs. Wardrop		do.
Miss Jeffcoat		do.
Mr. Jas. Johnston	42. Kingsland Park	9
Mr. John Arthurs	12. Pleasant Street	25
Mr. John Fisher	do. do.	15
Mr. John Veitch	do. do.	69
Mrs. R. Anderson	78. Newington Terr. Rathmines	32
Mrs. McDonald	do. do.	do.
Mr. Saml. Styles	15. New Bride Street	52
Mr. John C. Wilson	80. Kenilworth Square	30

Fig 4.1 A sample page from the "List of Adherents and Members of the United Presbyterian Church, Lower Abbey Street, Dublin" showing the members in Mr. Thomas Wardrop's District in the 1880's.

Disestablishment Act, the Church of Ireland was no longer the official Church of the state and no denomination was to be shown preferential treatment.

In many ways, the treatment of the Presbyterian church was similar to that of other non-conformist dissenter groups. This is ironic in view of the fact that some of the Presbyterians had left Scotland in order to avoid religious persecution. These restrictions, in turn, contributed to the decision of many Ulster Presbyterians to flee Ireland. These Ulster Scots, or Scots Irish, went in particular to North America where their influence in the movement for American Independence was significant. In Ireland during the 18th century a movement for independence developed and reached a climax with the rebellion of 1798. This movement was also significantly influenced and led by Presbyterians who found common cause with their Catholic countrymen in a desire to throw off British control of Ireland, including its repression of their respective religions.

At the same time that Presbyterians were being repressed by the state, divisions were also taking place within the church itself. Although many of these disputes had their roots in the Scottish Presbyterian Church, they quickly transferred to Ireland where they found ready supporters and opponents. Between 1719-26 the Presbyterian church suffered from an internal disagreement which resulted in the formation of a breakaway group known as "Non-Subscribers". They were so called because they refused to subscribe to the Westminister Confession of Faith which was generally accepted as the most complete statement of Presbyterian doctrinal standards.

An even larger division ocurred in the 1740's when a group of Scottish Presbyterians, known as Seceders, who also had differences with the main Presbyterian Church, started to establish congregations in Ireland. They opened their first church near Templepatrick, Co. Down in 1744 and other churches quickly followed this. The Seceders also established their own ecclesiastical council - the Secession Synod - which remained separate from the main Ulster Presbyterian Synod until 1840.

The Seceders, in turn, divided into Burghers and Anti-Burghers. Again this division had its origins in Scotland and, in this case, had little relevance within Ireland. This split arose over the question of whether Scottish Presbyterians should take the Burgess Oath which would allow them to sit on town councils. Around the same time another group was established known as Reformed Presbyterians or

Covenanters. These were people who upheld the Covenant of 1643 to establish and defend Presbyterianism. The Covenanters were adherents of a pure and strict interpretation of the Presbyterian faith. As a result of these doctrinal splits, some areas found themselves with more than one Presbyterian church within the same locality and, to avoid confusion, the churches were referred to as the "First" and "Second" church.

However, in spite of early persecution and many internal doctrinal differences, the Irish Presbyterian Church flourished. By 1660 there were an estimated 100,000 Presbyterians in Ulster, and by 1708 there were 130 Presbyterian congregations throughout Ireland.

To facilitate this rapid growth, the Synod of Ulster was established at the end of the seventeenth century. In the South of Ireland, a Synod of Munster was also formed and the Southern Association, which was a loose grouping of Non-Subscribing Presbyterians. Despite the various divisions, the Synod of Ulster remained the main governing assembly of the Presbyterian church until 1840 when it joined with the Secession Synod to form the General Assembly of the Presbyterian Church in Ireland. The structure of the Synod and, later, the General Assembly reflected the self-governing and democratic principles of Presbyterianism rather than the more rigid, hierarchical structures of other churches. The Synod represented all its ministers equally and also a portion of its laity. It had the ultimate authority for ensuring that ministers performed their duties, but it was rarely a problem in a system where the congregation chose their own ministers.

By the middle of the nineteenth century the General Assembly was responsible for approximately 433 congregations representing about 650,000 people or almost 8% of the Irish population. A second Evangelical Revival ocurred in 1859, the 'Year of Grace' when a wave of religious fervour spread across North America and the United Kingdom. By 1901, almost 10% of the Irish population was Presbyterian.

4.2 Church Organisation and Practice

The ecclesiastical and administrative structure of the Presbyterian church differed from that of other, older denominations. From the beginning it was less hierarchical than other churches: each congregation chose its own ministers and paid his stipend; the ministers were ordained by Presbyters, that is ministers who were already ordained; and each minister was answerable to the Synod or

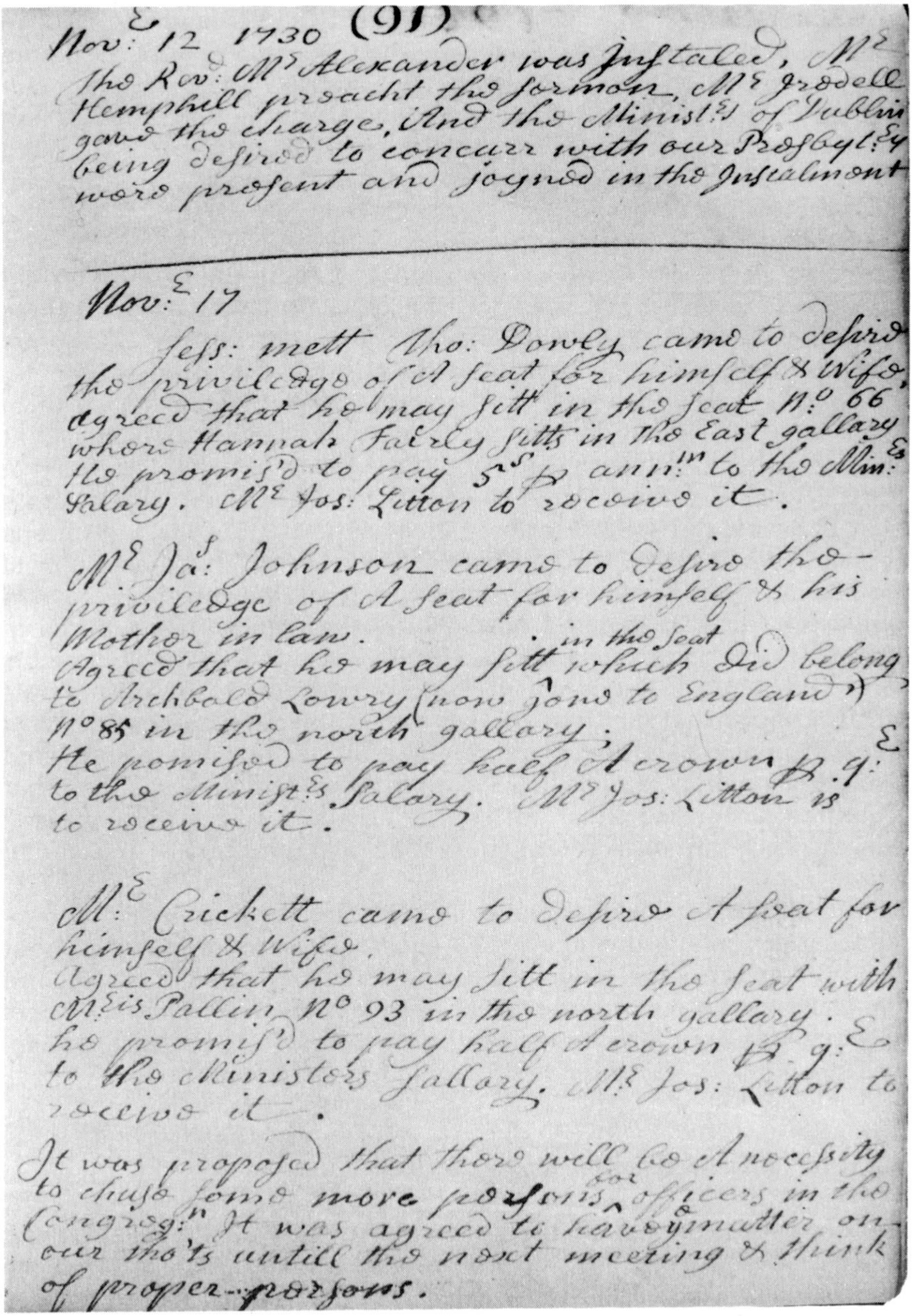

Nov: 12 1730 (91)
the Rev. Mr. Alexander was instaled, Mr.
Hemphill preacht the sermon, Mr. Iredell
gave the charge, And the Ministrs of Dublin
being desired to concurr with our Presbytery
were present and joyned in the Instalment

Nov: 17

Sess: mett tho: Dowly came to desire
the priviledge of A seat for himself & Wife,
agreed that he may sitt in the seat No 66
where Hannah Fairly sitts in the East gallary
He promis'd to pay 5s p annm to the Min:
Salary. Mr Jos: Litton to receive it.

Mr Jas: Johnson came to desire the
priviledge of A seat for himself & his
Mother in law.   in the seat
Agreed that he may sitt which did belong
to Archbald Lowry (now jone to England)
No 85 in the north gallary;
He promised to pay half A crown p: q:
to the Ministrs Salary. Mr Jos: Litton is
to receive it.

Mr Crickett came to desire A seat for
himself & Wife,
Agreed that he may sitt in the seat with
Mris Pallin, No 93 in the north gallary.
he promis'd to pay half A crown p: q:
to the Minister's Salary. Mr Jos: Litton to
receive it.

It was proposed that there will be A necessity
to chuse some more persons for officers in the
Congregn. It was agreed to have ye matter on
our tho'ts untill the next meeting & think
of proper persons.

Fig. 4.2   A sample page of a Kirk Session Minutes of Plunkett Street
            Presbyterian Church, Dublin.

General Assembly, which represented all clergymen equally. Within the congregations, however, economic distinctions were visible in the ability of a wealthy family to purchase its own pew in the church; and to purchase a plot of ground within a graveyard for the use of the family and descendants.

Presbyterian ministers lived in manses, and unlike their Roman Catholic counterparts, they were free to marry if they chose. The manses were sometimes attached to small farms which the ministers worked themselves. Apart from the stipend contributed by the congregation, Presbyterian ministers intermittently received an allowance from the state known as the "Regium Donum" or King's Gift. This was given to the Synod which divided it equally amongst its minsters. During periods of repression, however, such as 1685-1691 and 1714-19 this grant was withdrawn. Following disestablishment in 1869 (see page 51) the "Regium Donum" was abolished although each minister received a capital sum in its place. The Presbyterian church always laid particular emphasis on the education of its ministry. As early as 1691 the Synod decreed that no-one should become a minister without a degree. In the seventeenth and eighteenth centuries most ministers attended either Glasgow or Edinburgh University for their degree. Following the establishment of the Belfast Academical Institute in 1814, the majority of prospective ministers were trained on home ground.

Each local kirk (or church) consisted of the minister and a popularly elected group of Elders who were laymen. It was the function of the Elders to help the minister in matters of church administration and each was given responsibility for a district within the congregation. Within these communities, the Elders were undoubtedly powerful: they advised on who could be admitted as communicants and who could be baptised into the congregation. Cases of immoral behaviour were also brought before them during the Kirk Sessions, a form of ecclesiastical court.

Because the growth of the Presbyterian Church occurred spontaneously, the development of Presbyterian congregations did not correspond geographically with the established civil parish structure. Congregations were usually formed on an 'ad hoc' basis, that is, in response to local demand, although the permission of the Synod (after its formation) had to be first sought. Because of the relative ease of this process, established congregations frequently divided to form new congregations, sometimes known as 'Second' or 'Third' church. The formation of new congregations reflected patterns of population distribution and growth. Many of the congregations were situated in Ulster, particularly counties Down and Antrim, which are the traditional strongholds of Presbyterianism. Although some congregations were formed outside Ulster, they tended to be quite small and at the end of the nineteenth century, 96% of all Presbyterians lived within Ulster *(Table 1.2)*.

For the reasons outlined earlier, Presbyterian registers generally start later than those of the Church of Ireland. The earliest surviving parish register in Ireland is for the parish of Antrim in County Antrim which dates back to 1674. Unfortunately, other registers for this period are rare and for the most part they do not commence until the nineteenth century. It was not until 1819 that the Synod required ministers to keep a register of baptisms and marriages. Even when this was done, the recording of this information did not become widespread until after 1830.

Prior to the nineteenth century, ministers of the Church of Ireland claimed the right to perform birth, death and marriage ceremonies for all Protestants, regardless of denomination. Because these ceremonies were not legally recognised unless a Church of Ireland rector officiated, some Presbyterians did marry within the state church. This was done occasionally to protect inheritance and property rights (see page 50 for further discussion of this). It is therefore prudent for family historians to check the registers of all nearby Church of Ireland parishes when searching for Presbyterian ancestors

At the end of the eighteenth century there was a discernible softening in the State's repressive attitude towards the Presbyterian Church in Ireland. In 1782 marriage between two Presbyterians was made legal, although marriage between a member of the Church of Ireland and a Presbyterian still remained invalid. This ambiguous situation caused dissatisfaction amongst the increasingly powerful Presbyterian community. The matter came to a head in the 1840's when a court declared such marriages to be insolvent and the children of the unions illegitimate. The resultant agitation by the Presbyterians led to a significant change in the marriage laws in Ireland. In 1844 an Act was passed which came into effect in April 1845, and legalised such unions. The law also required that all Protestant marriages were to be registered by the state even though they could be performed within a church. This Act was a precursor of the more comprehensive Act of 1864 which required that all births, deaths and marriages in Ireland were to be registered by the state. The significance of the 1844 Act - apart from its obvious value for genealogists - lies in the fact that it

●

marks the emergence of a Protestant alliance in Ireland. Presbyterians were now being treated in the same way as other Protestant groups, including the Church of Ireland. At the same time, the involvement of the state in such activities meant that for the first time these ceremonies had to be recorded, and recorded in a standardised form. The value of these records, all of which survive, for genealogists is considerable. They are available in the Registrar General's Office in Dublin, 8/11 Lombard Street, Dublin 2.

4.3 Baptismal Records

Entries in the Presbyterian registers, like those of other denominations, were not standardised and their contents vary from parish to parish. In general, baptismal entries provide the name of the child and its parents. In the nineteenth century it became increasingly common to include the mother's maiden name, the date of birth, the name of the sponsors and the address of the parents (usually a townland) (see Fig. 4.3). Presbyterian baptisms did not always closely follow the birth of a child and sometimes the records will show that 4 or 5 children within a family were baptised together. This possibly was a reflection on the energy of the minister of the congregation or perhaps more simply was due to the parent's lack of cash to pay for the ceremony. The Presbyterian baptismal records are available in the local parish, in the Presbyterian Historical Society (1), or in the Public Record Office of Northern Ireland (PRONI) (2). The records currently held by the latter are listed in Appendix 4.2, although the collection is being continually added to.

Illegitimacy in the parish registers is recorded in a variety of ways. These range from the euphemistic "natural" to the obviously judgemental "born in fornication". The condemnation apparent in the latter statement shows the concern of the Presbyterian church with its moral role. Such pronouncements in the registers are not unusual. In general, the Presbyterian church tended to be stricter about illicit sex than the other churches. In cases of illegitimacy the guilty parties (the putative father was usually named) were required to undergo an "examination" by the Elders which was recorded in the Kirk Session Book (see 4.6). A common form of punishment was that they were required to sit or stand on a "stool of repentance" in front of the local congregation and confess their sins. Because of this, it is perhaps not surprising that many women chose to baptise their illigimate children in neighbouring churches.

BIRTH AND BAPTISMAL REGISTER, for

NAME OF CHILD.	SEX.		NAME OF FATHER.	MAIDEN NAME OF MOTHER.
	Male.	Female.		
Henry Smith	Male	—	Henry Smith	Mary Affleck
Annie Thomson	—	Female	James McKechnie	Margaret Galt
Elizabeth Boyd	—	Femal	James Forbes	Wilhemina Trutter
William Turner	Male	—	Andrew Turner	Mary Agnes Davidson
Jane Stewart	—	Female	John Stewart	Margaret Scott
Francis Walter Neilson	Male	—	William Neilson	Mary Anne French
Jessie Cameron	—	Female	Donald Burns Cameron	Jessie Thomson
Samuel George Brady	Male	—	Robert Brady	Mary Stewart
Alexander Smith Morrison	Male	—	Robert Morrison	Jane McHardy
Jessie Leringe Dawson	—	Female	Henry B Dawson	Arnot L McClymont
George Robinson	Male	—	Andrew Robinson	Robina Selmond
Robert Peel Thomson	Male	—	Robert Peel Thomson	Bathia Jackson
Alicia Wishart	—		Daniel Wishart	Olivia Brown
Andrew Bisland Marshall	Male	—	Robert Marshall	Marion Bisland
Jemima Turner	—	Female	James Turner	Marion Smith
Ellen Simpson	—	Female	Alexander Stevenson	Ellen Simpson
Matthew Finlay Guthrie	Male	—	Robert Harvey	Agnes Guthrie
Hugh Edgar Mackinnon	Male	—	Hugh Mackinnon	Anna Livingstone
Rebecca Slater Gibson	—	Female	Henry Gibson	Rebecca Slater
Charlotte Edgar	—	Female	James Edgar	Elizabeth Arthur
James Edgar	Male	—	James Edgar	Elizabeth Arthur
Elizabeth Edgar	—	Female	James Edgar	Elizabeth Arthur
William Arthur Edgar	Male	—	James Edgar	Elizabeth Arthur
Agnes Kerr	—	Female	William Kerr	Katherine Swan
Jane Hosie	—	Female	John Hosie	Elizabeth Stewart
James Hosie	Male	—	John Hosie	Elizabeth Stewart
Hugh Kirkwood	Male	—	Thomas Kirkwood	Mary McGuiness
C. Kennedy Brown			Wm Brown	Sarah Kennedy
Thomas Law	Male	—	John Anderson Law	Agnes Ferguson
John Cranston	Male	—	Thomas Cranston	Eleanor Carson

Fig. 4.3 A sample page from a very detailed baptismal register - of the for the years 1885-1887

CHURCH.

Employment or Profession of Father	When Born	Where Born – Parish, Place, Town or Street	Date of Baptism	By whom Baptized
Carpenter	*1885* Augt 2	Temple Cottages	*1886* Jan 29	Rev. Wm Proctor
Cashier	*1885* Novr 28	15 Annadale Avenue	Feb 14	Rev. Wm Proctor
Brass founder	*1885* Decr 22	3. Arranmore Avenue	Feb 14	Rev. Wm Proctor
Clerk	*1885* Dec 12	2. Killarney Avenue	Feb 14	Rev. Wm Proctor
Cooper	*1886* Feby 5	31 Ethana Cottages	March 14	Rev. Wm Proctor
Accountant	Feby 1	6. Blessington Street	Mar 14	Rev Wm Proctor
Lithographer	Mar 19	30. Elizabeth St. Clonliffe	May 16	Rev. Wm Proctor
Missionary	April 14	6½ Whitefriar Street	May 16	Rev. Wm Proctor
Boot maker	Mar 17	13 Lower Abbey Street	May 16	Rev Wm Proctor
Missionary	Mar 30	31 North Strand	June 13	Rev. Wm Proctor
Architect &c.	Apl 17	3. St. Patrick's Terrace St. Lawrence Road	June 13	Rev. Wm Proctor
Dentist	June 14	199 St. Merrypark St	July 11	Rev. Wm Proctor
	June 10	34	July 11	Rev. Wm Proctor
Brass founder	Augt 2	145 Church Road	Sept 19	Rev. Wm Proctor
Lithographic Printer	July 12	28 Buckingham Buildings	Sept 19th	Rev. Wm Proctor
Printer	Sept 2	25. Spencer Street	Sept 28th	Rev. Wm Proctor
Engineer	June 19	10. Strandville Avenue	Sept 28	Rev. Wm Proctor
Agent	July 20	217 Clonliffe Road	Oct 24	Rev. Wm Proctor
Lithographic Printer	Sept 2	9 Carlingford Road	Oct 24	Rev. Wm Proctor
Agent for Dye Works	*1872* April 6	3. College Street	*1886* Oct 4th	Rev. Wm Proctor
Agent for Dye Works	*1873* Oct 8	3. College Street	Oct 4th	Rev. Wm Proctor
Agent for Dye Works	*1876* Oct 27	3. College Street	Oct 4th	Rev. Wm Proctor
Agent for Dye Works	*1885* Oct 27	3. College Street	Oct 4th	Rev. Wm Proctor
Plumber Gasfitter	June 15	8. Georges Quay	Nov 14	Rev. Wm Proctor
Grocer				
Grocer	*1886* Sept 8	40. Capel Street		
Coppersmith	*1887* Jan 4	2817		
Mate	Nov 13	2 Wms Ferm Stony 11		Rev Wm Proctor
Stereotyper	March	55 G. Temple Buildings	April 10	Rev. Wm Proctor
Founder	March 26	79. Palmerston Place	May 31	Rev. Wm Proctor

United Free Church of Scotland, commonly known as Scot's Church, Dublin

4.4 Marriage Registers

Marriage registers, especially the early ones, usually contain at least the names of the couple and the name of the father of the bride *(Fig. 4.4)*. The Presbyterian Church required that prior notice of marriages be given to the Kirk Session, so even where marriage registers do not exist, a record of the event might be found in the Session Minute Book *(see 4.6)*. Although weddings were supposed to be performed in a church, it was quite common for this ceremony to be performed at home (usually that of the bride) if a fee was paid to the minister. When searching for a Presbyterian marriage, apart from searching the registers of all local Established Churches, it is also worth checking the indexes to Marriage License Bonds (1629-1864). Although these Bonds were also under the control of the Established Church, they were used by Presbyterians who wished to be married immediately or in their own home. Most of the surviving indexes to these bonds are deposited in the National Archives in Dublin.

In 1819, the Presbyterian Synod decreed that each minister was to keep a register of all marriages celebrated by him. This register was to include the date of marriage, the name of the contracting parties, the congregation in which they resided and the names of at least two witnesses. Following the commencement of civil registration of Protestant marriages in 1844, the quantity and quality of information increased dramatically. Church of Ireland and Presbyterian ministers became state registrars of marriages and were required to record the names of the couple, their age ("full age" denotes over 21), their marital condition (batchelor, spinster etc), their rank or profession, their residence at the time of marriage, their father's name and his rank or profession, and the name of two witnesses. For genealogists, therefore, these records are obviously an extremely rich source of information. They are available at the Registrar General's Office in Dublin and are indexed by name of both bride and groom.

The 1844 Act further required that these marriages were to take place with open doors, in the presence of a registrar and, if the couple were under 21, with the prior consent of the parents. Within the Presbyterian church itself this act made it necessary for each Presbytery to appoint a minister who was to liaise with the local registrar, and to send a quarterly report on registered marriages to the General Registrar in Dublin. The thoroughness of this whole process was indicative of the fact that the Government was taking its new role in the marital affairs of the nation very seriously.

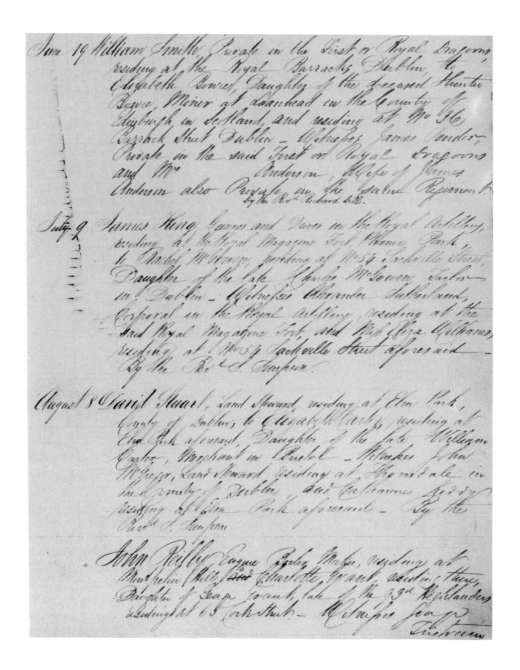

Fig. 4.4 *A sample page from the Marriage Register of the Presbyterian Congregation of Usher's Quay, Dublin.*

4.5 Burial Records

The Penal Laws prevented people who were not members of the Established Church from maintaining their own graveyard. In fact, up to the nineteenth century, dissenting ministers could not legally perform burial services unless a Church of Ireland rector was present. Because of this, it was not unusual to find Presbyterians (including their ministers) buried in Church of Ireland cemeteries. In effect therefore, the burial grounds of the Established Church became 'ecumenical' as they were used by people of all denominations. When searching for burial information concerning a Presbyterian ancestor (or any dissenting ancestor) it is therefore vital to search the registers of the local Established Churches. Even when all such restrictions were removed, Presbyterian churches rarely kept burial records and even where they do exist, they provide no more than the name and age of the deceased. Civil registration of deaths did not commence until 1864. Because of the relative absence of direct records of death, the value of gravestone inscriptions should not be underestimated *(see Appendix 4.1)*.

4.6 Other Church Records

Although early Presbyterian church registers are rare, other forms of church record have survived and can be of equal value to the family historian. The most important of these are the Session Minute Books or Kirk Session Minutes. These books are the minutes of the meetings of the congregation Elders *(Fig. 4.2)*. They often include such valuable items as the arrival of new people in the parish, comments on the baptisms and marriages of members of the congregation, and the names of people who were summoned before the Session in order to be disciplined for their misdemeanours.

Also of value, if they survive, are Certificates of Transference, and Communicant's Roll Books. The former were given to people who moved from one congregation to another, as a testimony of their good standing within the community. They are therefore particularly useful when trying to trace migrants to and from a congregation. The Communicant's Roll Books list the individuals who received communion on each Sabbath *(Fig.4.5)*. This information was subsequently collected during a visitation from the Presbytery. They also occasionally provide details of births, deaths, and marriages within the congregation. The additional records therefore, are a unique source of information which provide facinating insights into the lifestyle of Presbyterian ancestors.

5.

COMMUNICANTS' ROLL BOOK for the

No.	NAME OF COMMUNICANT.	PLACE OF RESIDENCE.	Profession, Occupation, or Designation	ADMISSION. For First Time. Month. Day
				18

No 3. Mr. Wm Wardrop's

Mr. Wm Wardrop	Hamilton, Ailesbury Road Donnybrook	Builder.	
Mrs Wardrop	do		
Miss Jeffcott	do		
X Mr. Robert Gregg	6. Eccles Street	Ironmonger	
Mrs Gregg	do		
Mr. Wm Stewart	5. Hendrick Street	Blacksmith	
Mrs Stewart	do		
Mr. Wm Todd	75. Eccles Street	Seedsman	
Mrs Todd	do		
Mr. John W. Burns	Prospect Villa Glasnevin	Warehousman	
Mrs Burns	do		
Mr. A. A. Black	5. Connaught Street Phibsboro'	Carpet Salesman	
Mrs Black	do		
Mr. Alex. Burnett	77 Prussia Street		
Mrs Burnett	do		
Mr. Alex. Cranston	do	Printer	
Mr. J. Kincaid	16. Stoney Batter		
Mrs Kincaid	do		
Mr. John Dawson	8. Dalymount Cottages Phibsboro'	Draper	
Mrs Dawson	do		
Mr. J. Ballantyne	13. Victoria Terrace Royal Canal	Litho Printer	
Mrs Ballantyne	do		
Mr. A. McAlister	70. Kirwan's Cottages Manor Street		
Mrs McAlister	do		

Fig. 4.5   *A sample page from a Communicant's Roll Book of the United Presbyterian Church, Lower Abbey Street, Dublin for 1885.*

There are also a variety of other sources which were not originated by the Presbyterian church but which nevertheless provide information on Presbyterian Church history and organisation. For the early period, the most useful of these are the intermittent religious returns commissioned by the Government in the seventeenth and eighteenth centuries. These include a "census" of 1740 which lists Protestant householders in counties Antrim, Armagh, Donegal, Londonderry and Tyrone, but little information beyond this. A "census" in 1766 required Church of Ireland ministers to compile lists of householders in their parish, showing religious denominations. Unfortunately, not all of this census survives. In 1821 the first real all-Ireland census was taken but it was not until the second census in 1831 that details concerning religious persuasion were included. Although censuses were taken every 10 years after 1821, unfortunately most of the nineteenth century ones were destroyed, only fragments of them surviving. The 1901 census therefore, is the first one to survive intact for all of Ireland. All of these censuses and 'census substitutes' are available in the National Archives in Dublin. They are not indexed except for Co. Longford for which an index has been published (3).

For the nineteenth century information from the above sources can be supplemented by various directories and almanacs. The most useful of these is Simms and McIntyre's "The Belfast Almanac" 1837 which provides names and addresses of members of the Synod of Ulster, whilst William McCombs "Presbyterian Almanac" of 1851 includes information about the various congregations. Further valuable information can be found in a number of secondary sources, the most useful being "Irish and Scotch Ancestral Research" by Margaret Dickson Falley (1962); "A History of Presbyterianism in Dublin and in the South and West of Ireland" by C. H. Irwin (1886); "The Seceders in Ireland with Annals of their Congregations" by Rev. D. Stewart (1950); "A History of Congregations of the Presbyterian Church of Ireland and Biographical notices of the eminent Presbyterian Ministers and Laymen" by Rev. W. D. Killen (1886); "The Presbyterian Orphan Society 1866-1966" by John M. Barkley (1967); "The Fasti of the Irish Presbyterian Church 1613-1840" by Rev. J. McConnell, and "The Presbyterian Church in Ireland Directory" which is published annually by the Presbyterian Historical Society and which provides the names and addresses of the current ministers of the Presbyterian Church.

4.7 *Locations of Church Records*

For the most part, Presbyterian parish registers are held locally in the custody of the Presbyterian minister. A list of these and their date of commencement is given in Appendix 4.3. As is the case with the registers of other denominations, it may not be possible to see them without first obtaining the permission of the present-day minister. A list of the addresses of all Presbyterian ministers can be found in the The Presbyterian Church in Ireland Directory. However, the Public Record Office of Northern Ireland (PRONI) probably has the biggest single collection of Presbyterian church registers. Most of these registers are available on microfilm and are from all nine counties of Ulster, where the vast majority of Presbyterians lived. A list of the registers currently held by the PRONI is given in Appendix 4.2. All of these Presbyterian records can be consulted by the Public. The Presbyterian Historical Society *(1)* also has copies of some of the oldest parish registers but they are not generally available to members of the public.

In conclusion, for the period prior to 1864, parish registers together with Kirk Session Minute Books are an important source of information. Whilst it is true that they can be erratic, frustrating, difficult and time-consuming to use, a successful search in the registers is extremely rewarding. The fact that before 1864 the information provided was rarely standardised but was rather provided at the whim of the local minister, means that many gems of personal information can be found amidst the details of births, deaths and marriages.

REFERENCES

(1)   *Presbyterian Historical Society, Church House, Fisherwick Place, Belfast BT1 6DW.*

(2)   *Public Record Office of Northern Ireland, 66 Balmoral Avenue, Belfast BT9 6NY.*

(3)   *Longford & its People, by David Leahy (Flyleaf Press, Dublin 1990).*

APPENDIX 4.1

PRESBYTERIAN GRAVESTONE INSCRIPTIONS

Because Presbyterians rarely kept burial registers, gravestone inscriptions often provide information which cannot be found elsewhere. In the late nineteenth century, The Irish Memorial Association published the useful volumes Memorials of the Dead which is a valuable record of gravestones no longer standing. Over the past few years, there has been a renewed interest in transcribing inscriptions from graveyards and churches all over Ireland. The most comprehensive collection of inscriptions has been compiled by Professor R S J Clarke and published by the Ulster Historical Foundation. The list below gives the main Presbyterian graveyards which have been transcribed by the Foundation. They cover the period up to 1900.

PRESBYTERIAN GRAVEYARDS IN CO. DOWN

Gravestone Inscriptions.

Vol. 1.	Carryduff Presbyterian Graveyard.
	Castlereagh Presbyterian Graveyard
	Gransha Presbyterian Graveyard
	Hillhall Presbyterian Graveyard
	Knockbreckan Reformed Presbyterian Graveyard
	Moneyrea Presbyterian Graveyard
Vol. 3.	Malone Presbyterian Graveyard
Vol. 4.	Drumbo Presbyterian Graveyard
Vol. 5.	Ballygowen Presbyterian Graveyard
	Comber Presbyterian Graveyard
	Raffrey Presbyterian Graveyard
	Ravara Presbyterian Graveyard
Vol. 7.	Downpatrick Non Subscribing Presbyterian Graveyard
	Downpatrick Presbyterian Graveyard
	Killyleagh Presbyterian Graveyard
Vol. 8.	Ballee Presbyterian Graveyard
Vol. 9.	Ballynahinch First Presbyterian Graveyard
	Ballynahinch Second Presbyterian Graveyard
	Clough Presbyterian Graveyard

Clough Non Subscribing Presbyterian Graveyard
Magherahamlet Presbyterian Graveyard

Vol. 10.   Mourne Presbyterian Graveyard

Vol. 12.   Ballyback Presbyterian Graveyard
Kurcubbin Presbyterian Graveyard

Vol. 14.   Ballyhemlin Presbyterian Graveyard
Cloughy Presbyterian Graveyard

Vol. 15.   Glastry Presbyterian Graveyard

Vol. 16.   Ballycopeland Presbyterian Graveyard
Millisle Presbyterian Graveyard

Vol. 17.   Ballygilbert Presbyterian Graveyard
Bangor Presbyterian Graveyard
Conlig Presbyterian Graveyard
Groomsport Presbyterian Graveyard

Vol. 18   Annahilt Presbyterian Graveyard
Carnacreevy Presbyterian Graveyard
Gilnahirk Presbyterian Graveyard
Loughaghery Presbyterian Graveyard
Maze Presbyterian Graveyard
Moira Non Subscribing Presbyterian Graveyard
Moira Presbyterian Graveyard
Carryduff Presbyterian Graveyard
Castlereagh Presbyterian Graveyard
Knockbracken Reformed Presbyterian Graveyard

Vol. 19.   Donaghcloney Presbyterian Graveyard
Dromara First Presbyterian Graveyard
Dromara Second Presbyterian Graveyard
Dromara Reformed Presbyterian Graveyard
Dromore First Presbyterian Graveyard
Dromore Second Presbyterian Graveyard
Dromore Non-Subscribing Presbyterian Graveyard
Drumlough Presbyterian Graveyard
Garvaghy Presbyterian Graveyard
Kilkinamurray Presbyterian Graveyard
Waringstown Presbyterian Graveyard
Vol 20.   Banbridge, Downshire Rd., Non-Subscribing
Pres. Graveyard
Banbridge First Presbyterian Graveyard
Banbridge, Scarva Street, Presbyterian Graveyard
Magherally Presbyterian Graveyard
Tullylish Presbyterian Graveyard

PRESBYTERIAN GRAVEYARDS IN CO. ANTRIM

Vol. 2.   Ballycarry Non-Subscribing Presbyterian
Graveyard
Raloo Non-Subscribing Presbyterian Graveyard
Raloo Presbyterian Graveyard

APPENDIX 4.2

PRESBYTERIAN REGISTERS IN THE PRONI

The Public Record Office of Northern Ireland has the largest single collection of Presbyterian Church Registers. These registers are on microfilm and the list is being continually updated. Copies of these microfilms have been presented by the Ulster Historical Foundation to the Presbyterian Historical Society. The following list of microfilms in PRONI provide the dates for which these records survive. Their PRONI call number is recorded on the list opposite eg. MIC 1P/ (stated number)

Church Name & Dates of Available Records	Order No. (MIC 1P/...)	Church Name & Dates of Available Records	Order No. (MIC 1P/...)
BELFAST		BELMONT	118
ACADEMY ST. (Ekenhead)	8 + 56	Bapt. 1862-1920	
Marr. 1866-1926.		Marr. 1862-1901	
Bapt. 1864-1929		BERRY ST.	21 + 56
AGNES ST.	47	Bapt. 1869-1984	
Bapt. 1868-18881		Marr. 1869-1974	
ALBERT ST.	16	COLLEGE SQ.	107
Marr. 1845-1933		Marr. 1845-1906	
Bapt. 1852-1921		CRESCENT	57
ALEXANDRA (See York Street)		Bapt. 1831-1974	
Bapt. 1840 1908		Marr. 1831-1908	
Marr. 1840-1928		DONEGAL PASS	116
BALLYMACARRETT (1st)	15	Bapt. 1868-1973	
Bapt. 1837-1921		Marr. 1873-1922	
Marr. 1845-1928		DUNCAIRN	41
BALLYSILLAN	22	Bapt. 1861-1985	
Bapt. 1839-1870		Marr. 1862-1904	
Marr. 1845-1902			

Church Name & Dates of Available Records	Order No. (MIC 1P/...)
EKENHEAD (Academy St.)	8
Marr. 1866-1926	
Bapt. 1864-1929	
EGLINTON	40
Marr. 1840-1844, 1853-1933	
Bapt. 1840-1937	
FISHERWICK	92
Bapt. 1810-1965	
Marr. 1845-1915	
FITZROY	14
Bapt. 1820-1923	
Marr. 1821-1845	
GT. VICTORIA ST.	74
Bapt. 1860-1876	
Marr. 1861-1867	
MCQUISTON MEMORIAL	100
Bapt. 1893-1941	
Marr. 1893-1901	
MALONE	2
Bapt. 1838-1920	
Marr. 1837-1982	
MAY ST.	9
Marr. 1835-1926	
Bapt. 1835-1931	
NEWTONBREDA	51
Bapt. 1846-1986	
Marr. 1845-1920	
ROSEMARY ST.	21
Bapt. 1853-1904	
Marr. 1741-1846	
ST. ENOCHS	21
Bapt. 1853-1904	
Marr. 1852-1907	
SINCLAIR SEAMAN'S	55
Bapt. 1854-1958	
Marr. 1855-1958	
TOWNSEND ST.	336
Bapt. 1835-1901	
Marr. 1845-1907	
WESTBOURNE	11
Bapt. 1880-1920	
Marr. 1881-1924	
YORK STREET	112
Bapt. 1840-1908	
Marr. 1840-1933	

Church Name & Dates of Available Records	Order No. (MIC 1P/...)
CO. ANTRIM	
AHOGILL (1st)	64
Bapt. 1841-1922	
Marr. 1841-1845, 1845-1920	
AHOGILL (Trinity)	136
Bapt. 1835-1901	
Marr. 1836-1920	
AHOGILL (Brookside)	95
Bapt. 1859-1962	
Marr. 1846-1911	
ANTRIM (1st) (Millrow)	3
Bapt. 1850-1951	
ANTRIM (2nd) (Hugh St.)	346
Bapt. 1850-1951	
ARMOY	290
Bapt. 1842-1906	
Marr. 1815-1920	
BALLYCARNY	330
Bapt. 1832-1969	
Marr. 1832-1945	
BALLYCASTLE	115
Bapt. 1829-1967	
Marr. 1829-1922	
BALLYCLARE	324
Bapt. 1857-1906	
Marr. 1857-1909	
BALLYEASTON (1st)	24
Marr. 1813-1821	
Bapt. 1813-1821	
BALLYEASTON (2nd)	124
Bapt.1821-1967(1862-1863 missing)	
Marr.1826-1936 (1842-1844 missing)	
Burls1842-1918 (1850-1900 missing)	
BALLYLINNEY	327
Bapt. 1851-1922	
Marr. 1845-1906	
BALLYMENA (1st)	144
Bapt. 1824-1838	
Marr. 1825-1906	
BALLYMENA (West)	105
Bapt. 1829-1945	
Marr.1830-1903 (1833-1844 missing)	

Church Name & Dates of Available Records	Order No. (MIC 1P/...)
BALLYMENA (Wellington St)	27
Bapt. 1863-1962	
Marr. 1845-1936	
BALLYMENA (High Kirk)	27
Bapt. 1866-1926	
Marr. 1845-1936	
BALLYMONEY (1st)	363
Bapt. 1866-1926	
Marr. 1845-1926	
BALLYMONEY (Trinity)	35
Marr. 1845-1921	
BALLYMONEY (St. James)	266
Bapt. 1835-1940	
Marr. 1835-1903	
BALLYNURE	103
Bapt. 1819-1917	
Marr. 1827-1901	
BALLYWAT	379
Bapt. 1867-1927	
Marr. 1845-1914	
BALLYWEANEY	82
Bapt. 1862-1967	
Marr. 1845-1900	
BALLYWILLAN	368
Bapt. 1862-1939	
Marr. 1846-1909	
BENURDEN	19
Bapt. 1864-1913	
Marr. 1864-1912	
BROUGHSHANE (1st)	76
Bapt. 1836-1894	
Marr. 1845-1870	
BROUGHSHANE (2nd)	77
Bapt. 1868-1986	
Marr. 1864-1906	
BUCKNA	322
Bapt. 1841-1893	
Marr. 1845-1907	
BUSHMILLS	113
1 death 1864	
BUSHVALE	362
Bapt. 1858-1934	
Marr. 1848-1909	

Church Name & Dates of Available Records	Order No. (MIC 1P/...)
CAIRNCASTLE	328
Bapt. 1832-1944	
Marr. 1832-1936	
CARNALBANAGH	351
Bapt. 1862-1949	
Marr. 1867-1936	
CARNMONEY	137
Bapt. 1819-1968	
Marr. 1819-1841	
CARRICKFERGUS(1st)	157
Bapt. 1823-1901	
Marr. 1845-1905	
Marr. 1840-1914	
CLOUGH	312
Bapt. 1865-1987	
Marr. 1873-1907	
CLOUGHWATER	320
Bapt. 1852-1955	
Marr. 1845-1923	
CONNOR	162
Bapt. 1819-1963	
Marr. 1845-1900	
CROAGHMORE	370
Bapt. 1852-1964	
Marr. 1866-1917	
CRUMLIN	125
Bapt. 1838-1913	
Marr. 1846-1936	
CULLYBACKEY (see Cunningham Memorial below)	
CUNNINGHAM MEMORIAL	88
Bapt. 1812-1843, 1848-1935	
Marr. 1813-1838, 1845-1919	
CUSHENDALL	352
Bapt. 1854-1947	
Marr. 1853-1935	
CUSHENDUN	352
Bapt. 1854-1947	
Marr. 1853-1935	
DERVOCK	
Bapt. 1827-1838, 1850-1970	
Marr. 1828-1841, 1845-1903	
DONEGORE (1st)	79
Bapt. 1806-1870	
Marr. 1806-1987	

Church Name & Dates of Available Records	Order No. (MIC 1P/...)	Church Name & Dates of Available Records	Order No. (MIC 1P/...)
DONEGORE (2nd) Bapt. 1845-1936 Marr. 1848-1987	153	**LARNE (1st)** Bapt. 1813-1902 Marr. 1846-1902	335
DRUMNEAGH Bapt. 1864-1906 Marr. 1845-1912	374	**LARNE (2nd, or Gardenmore)** Bapt. 1861-1906 Marr. 1846-1906	263
DUNLOY Bapt. 1841-1925 Marr. 1842-1936	117	**LISBURN (1st)** Bapt. 1824-1871 Marr. 1824-1845	159
DUNLUCE Bapt. 1865-1953 Marr. 1845-1912	367	**LISBURN (Railway Street)** Bapt. 1860-1870 Marr. 1861-1872	74
ESKYLANE Bapt. (not received) Marr. 1874-1902	311	**LISBURN (Sloan Street)** Bapt. 1861-1921 Marr. 1868-1887	356
FINVOY Bapt. 1843-1933 Marr. 1843-1907	321	**LOUGHMORNE** Bapt. 1848-1853 & 1892-1952 Marr. 1863-1930	161
GARRYDUFF Bapt. 1885-1985 Marr. 1851-1936	265	**LYLEHILL** Bapt. 1830-1966 Marr. 1889-1936	98
GLENARM Bapt. 1836-1920	350	**MAGHERAGALL** Bapt. 1878-1903 Marr. 1845-1911	81
GLENWHIRRY Bapt. 1845-1928 Marr. 1845-1927	151	**MAGHERAMOURNE** Bapt. 1880-1930 Marr. 1881-1919	349
GRANGE Bapt. 1824-1913 Marr. 1824-1926	375	**MOSSIDE** Bapt. 1842-1930 (1873 missing) Marr. 1842-1936 Burials. 1855-1877	91
ISLANDMAGEE (1st) Bapt. 1829-1935 Marr. 1829-1905	326	**MUCKAMORE** Bapt. 1861-1985 Marr. 1845-1936	277
ISLANDMAGEE (2nd) Bapt. 1854-1937 Marr. 1848-1933	337	**NEWTOWNCROMMELIN** Bapt. 1835-1954 Marr. 1836-1899	319
KELLS Bapt. 1873-1897 Marr. 1889-1921	310	**PORTGLENONE (1st)** Bapt. 1826-1920 Marr. 1845-1933	24
KILBRIDE Bapt. 1848-1923 Marr. 1849-1934	331	**PORTGLENONE (2nd)** Bapt. 1826-1910 Marr. 1822-1910	357
KILLYMURRIS Bapt. 1862-1925 Marr. 1855-1908	309	**PORTGLENONE (3rd)** Bapt. 1869-1944 Marr. 1845-1911	334

Church Name & Dates of Available Records	Order No. (MIC 1P/...)
RALOO	354
Bapt. 1842-1927	
Marr. 1841-1900	
RAMOAN	366
No pre-1900 Bapt. exist	
Marr. 1845-1910	
RANDALSTOWN (1st)	99
Marr. 1845-1922	
Bapt. 1853-1944	
RANDALSTOWN (2nd)	86
Bapt. 1881-1986	
Marr. 1845-1936	
RASHARKIN	292
Bapt. 1834-1919	
Marr. 1845-1919	
TEMPLEPATRICK	325
Bapt. 1831-1965	
Marr. 1831-1965	
TOBERDONEY	371
Bapt. (no pre-1900 Baptisms exist)	
Marr. 1864-1913	
TOBERLEIGH	
Bapt. 1829-1944	
Marr. 1845-1907	
WHITEABBEY	84
Bapt. records destroyed in fire	
WOODBURN	160
Bapt. 1863(or 5) -1952	
Marr. 1866-1932	
Bapt. 1820-1966	
Marr. 1821-1845	

CO. ARMAGH

Church Name & Dates of Available Records	Order No. (MIC 1P/...)
AHOREY	353
Bapt. 1834-50	
Marr. 1834-1933	
ARMAGH (1st)	4
Bapt. 1707-1949	
Marr. 1707-1910	
ARMAGH (2nd & 3rd)	281
Bapt. 1825-1986	
Marr. 1825-1907	
ARMAGH ROAD, (See Portadown)	
Bapt. 1825-1985	
Marr. 1869-1930	

Church Name & Dates of Available Records	Order No. (MIC 1P/...)
ARMAGHBRAGUE	297
Bapt. 1908-84	
Marr. 1840-1936	
BELLVILLE	271
Bapt. 1863-1980	
Marr. 1875-1934	
CLARE	50
Bapt. 1824-1945	
Marr. 1825-1936	
DRUMINNIS	286
Bapt. (not received)	
Marr. 1846-1936	
KEADY (1st)	71
Bapt. 1838-1938	
Marr. 1845-1920	
LOUGHGALL	287
Bapt. 1842-1965	
Marr. 1845-1925	
LURGAN (1st)	71
Bapt. 1746-1965	
Marr. 1845-1929	
LURGAN (Hill Street)	109
Bapt. 1861-1961	
Marr. 1864-1916	
MOUNTNORRIS	29
Bapt. 1810-1848	
Marr. 1804-1827	
PORTADOWN (1st)	52
Bapt. 1839-1954	
Marr. 1838-1900	
PORTADOWN (Armagh Road)	269
Bapt. 1868-1985	
Marr. 1869-1930	
REDROCK	285
Bapt. 1808-1986	
Marr. 1812-1936	
RICH HILL	372
Bapt. 1848-1960	
Marr. 1845-1936	
TANDRAGEE	258
Bapt. 1830-1913	
Marr. 1835-1916	
TARTARAGHAN	288
Bapt. 1853-1962	
Marr. 1845-1921	

Church Name & Dates of Available Records	Order No. (MIC 1P/...)
TULLYVALLEN	29
Bapt. 1834-1885	
CO. CAVAN	
BAILIEBOROUGH (1st)	145
Bapt. 1861-1983	
Marr. 1745-1955	
BAILIEBOROUGH (2nd or Trinity)	143
Bapt. 1863-1983	
Marr. 1845-1952	
BALLYCONNELL	276
Bapt. (Not received)	
Marr. 1918-30	
BALLYJAMESDUFF	268
Bapt. 1826-1980	
Marr. 1845-1955	
BELLASIS	267
Bapt. 1877-1985	
Marr. 1845-1951	
BELTURBET	272
Bapt. 1845-1957	
Marr. 1858-1924	
CARRIGALLEN	163
Bapt. 1837	
Marr. 1845-1909	
COOTEHILL (1st)	178
Bapt. 1870-1982	
COOTEHILL (2nd)	177
Bapt. 1822-1921	
Marr. 1845-1879	
CORGLASS	145
Bapt. 1861-1983	
Marr. 1845-1955	
CORLEA	158
Bapt. 1836-1982	
Marr. 1835-1844	
CORRANEARY (sic Coronary)	179
Bapt. 1825-1961	
Marr. 1863-1955	
DRUMKEERAN	166
Bapt. 1835-99	
Marr. 1835-1947	
KILLESHANDRA	164
Bapt. 1841-1896	
Marr. 1741-76	

Church Name & Dates of Available Records	Order No. (MIC 1P/...)
KILMOUNT	213
Bapt. 1866-1972	
Marr. 1862-1907	
SEAFIN	144
Marr. 1846-1956	
SMITHBOROUGH	200
Bapt. 1868-1983	
Marr. 1883-1927	
CO. DONEGAL	
BALLINDRAIT	185
Bapt. 1819-1923	
Marr. 1845- 1901	
BALLYARNET	239
Bapt. 1852-1891	
Marr. 1848-1903	
BALLYLENNON (1st & 2nd)	207
Bapt. 1829-1983	
Marr. 1831-1878	
BALLYSHANNON	5
Bapt. 1836-1962	
Marr. 1837-1952	
BUNCRANA	32
Bapt. 1836-1966	
Marr. 1845-1937	
BURT	33
Bapt. 1833-1878	
Marr. 1837-1907	
CARNDONAGH	237
Bapt. 1830-1928	
Marr. 1845-1950	
CARNONE	221
Bapt. 1834-1984	
Marr. 1846-1916	
CARRIGART	216
Bapt. 1844-1984	
Marr. 1846-1954	
CONVOY	220
Bapt. 1822-1914	
Marr. 1846-1938	
CROSSROADS	259
Bapt. 1811-1854	
Marr. 1819-1956	

Church Name & Dates of Available Records	Order No. (MIC 1P/...)	Church Name & Dates of Available Records	Order No. (MIC 1P/...)
DONEGAL (1st & 2nd)	6	MOVILLE	241
Bapt. 1824-1962		Bapt. 1833-1934	
Marr. 1824-1953		Marr. 1845-1936	
Death. 1860-1880		NEWTOWNCUNNINGHAM	188
DONAGHMORE	217	Bapt. 1830-1974	
Bapt. 1844-1961		Marr. 1830-1944	
Marr. 1819-1905		Death. 1880-1901	
DUNFANAGHY	152	PETTIGO	66
Bapt. 1830-1830		Bapt. 1844-1917	
Marr. 1830-1845		Marr. 1846-1926	
FAHAN	306	RAMELTON	142
Bapt. 1899-1986		Bapt. 1806-1904	
Marr. 1845-1955		Marr. 1807-1944	
FANNET	232	RAMELTON (2nd)	210
Bapt. 1859-1952		Bapt. 1808-1911	
Marr. 1827-1955		Marr. 1808-1910	
GORTLEE	226	RAMELTON (3rd)	209
Marr. 1872-1922		Bapt. 1839-1902	
INCH	313	Marr. 1839-1926	
Bapt. (not received)		RAPHOE (1st & 2nd)	1;183;184
Marr. 1845-1947		Bapt. 1829-1923	
KILMACRENNAN	141	Marr. 1829-1945	
Bapt. 1848-1979		RATHMULLAN	231
Marr. 1846-1920		Bapt. 1854-1984	
KNOWHEAD	238	Marr. 1845-1908	
Bapt. 1826-1948		RAY (1st)	187
Marr. 1846-1909		Bapt. 1855-1982	
LETTERKENNY (1st)	223	Marr. 1845-1928	
Bapt. 1821-1900		RAY (2nd)	186
Marr. 1864-1901		Bapt. 1882-1982	
Death. 1845-1929		Marr. 1845-1937	
LETTERKENNY (2nd)	225	ST. JOHNSTON	206
Bapt. 1821-1858		Bapt. 1838-1949	
Marr. 1821-1843		Marr. 1835-1901	
LETTERKENNY (3rd)	222	STRANORLAR	218
Bapt. 1841-1924		Bapt. 1821-1932	
Marr. 1845-1928		Marr. 1846-1914	
MALIN	236	TRENTA	224
Bapt. 1866-1983		Bapt. 1836-1886	
Marr. 1845-1948		Marr. 1838-1938	
MILFORD	244	Death. 1843-1887	
Bapt. 1839-1902			
Marr. 1845-1927		**CO. DOWN**	
MONREAGH	233	ANAGHLONE (1st & 2nd)	134
Bapt. 1845-1984		Bapt. 1868-1968	
Marr. 1894-1933		Marr. 1852-1924	

Church Name & Dates of Available Records	Order No. (MIC 1P/...)
ANAHILT	360
Bapt. 1780-1939	
Marr. 1803-1931	
BALLYBLACK	318
Bapt. 1821-1948	
Marr, 1820-1915	
Death. 1821-1852	
BALLYDOWN	169
Marr. 1845-1911	
Bapt. 1875-1985	
BALLYFRENIS	315
Bapt. 1862-1917	
Marr. 1864-1901	
BALLYNAHINCH (1st)	302
Bapt. 1841-1986	
Marr. 1870-1900	
BALLYNAHINCH (2nd & 3rd)	
Later Edengrove	110
Bapt. 1820-1966	
Marr. 1820-1931	
BALLYRONEY	168
Bapt. 1818-1845	
Marr. 1819-1845-1906	
BALLYWALTER (1st & 2nd)	104
Bapt. 1920-1923	
Marr. 1803-1949	
BANBRIDGE (Scarva Street)	178
Marr. 1782-1933	
BANBRIDGE (Presbyterian)	138
Marr. 1857-1883	
BANGOR (1st)	23
Bapt. 1852-1888, 1895-1926	
Marr. 1829-1844	
BANGOR (2nd or Trinity)	256
Bapt. 1829-1984	
Marr. 1829-1844	
BOARDMILLS (1st)	72
Bapt. 1782-1933	
Marr.1783-1814,1823-1844,1846-1929	
BOARDMILLS (2nd or Killaney)	102
Bapt. 1782-1933	
Marr. 1782-1814, 1823-1929	
BROOKVALE	132
Bapt. 1891-1968	
Marr. 1867-1936	

Church Name & Dates of Available Records	Order No. (MIC 1P/...)
CARGYCREEVY	358
Bapt. 1887-1941	
Marr. 1870-1923	
CARROWDORE	316
Bapt. 1843-1940	
Marr. 1843-1907	
CARRYDUFF	154
Bapt. 1854-1914	
Marr. 1846-1970	
CASTLEWELLAN	198
Bapt. 1845-1964	
Marr. 1845-1915	
CLONDUFF	126
Bapt. 1842-1968	
Marr. 1864-1936	
CLOUGH	308
Bapt. 1791-1953	
Marr. 1842-1890	
CLOUGHEY	314
Bapt. 1841-1946	
Marr. 1864-1936	
COMBER (1st)	58
Bapt. 1847-1870	
Marr. 1845-1870	
CONLIGH	94
Bapt. 1845-1919	
Marr. 1850-1935	
DONACLONEY	342
Bapt. 1798-1956	
Marr. 1845-1909	
DONAGHADEE (1st)	167
Bapt. 1822-1950	
Marr. 1822-1936	
DONAGHADEE (Short Street)	341
Bapt. 1849-1966	
Marr. 1850-1936	
DONAGHCLONEY (See Donacloney)	
DONAGHMORE	129
Bapt. 1804-1968	
Marr. 1845-1936	
DOWNPATRICK	156
Bapt. 1827-1977	
Marr. 1827-1845-1913	
DROMARA	89
Bapt. 1763-1806, 1810-1816	
Marr. 1800-1816, (1802 missing)	

Church Name & Dates of Available Records	Order No. (MIC 1P/...)
KILKEEL	205
Bapt. 1842-21 & 1875-1964	
Marr. 1842-1957	
KILKINAMURRY	305
Bapt. pre-1900 bapts	
Marr. 1845-1926	
KILLANEY & BOARDMILLS (2nd)	102
Bapt. 1846-1950	
Marr. 1847-1923	
KILLYLEAGH (1st)	53
Bapt. 1693-1881	
Marr. 1692-1872	
KILLYLEAGH (2nd)	261
Bapt. 1840-1968	
Marr. 1846-1906	
LEGACURRY	345
Bapt. 1866-1950	
Marr.(no pre-1900 marriages)	
LEITRIM	246
Bapt. 1839-1901	
Marr. 1836-1936	
Deaths 1837-92	
LISSARA	299
Bapt. 1809-1909	
Marr 1811-1900	
Burr. 1809-1888	
LOUGHAGHERY	119
Bapt. 1803-1939	
Marr. 1801 -1936	
Burials. 1868-1917	
LOUGHBRICKLAND	181
Bapt. 1842-1903	
Marr. 1880-89	
MAGHERAHAMLET	300
Bapt. 1831-1986	
Marr. 1831-1936	
Burials. 1909 -	
MAGHERALLY	211
Bapt. (not received)	
Marr. (not received)	
MOURNE	365
Bapt. 1839-1946	
Marr. 1845-1903	
NEWRY (Downshire Road)	106
Bapt. 1849-1965	

Church Name & Dates of Available Records	Order No. (MIC 1P/...)
NEWTOWNARDS	
(Greenwell Street)	317
Bapt. 1866-99	
Marr. 1870-1936	
NEWTOWNARDS (2nd)	333
Bapt. 1832-1940	
Marr. 1833-1842	
NEWTOWNARDS (Strean)	361
Bapt. 1888-1943	
Marr. 1867-1935	
PORTAFERRY	137
Bapt & Marr. 1699-1786	
Bapt. 1822-1864	
Marr. 1822-1845	
Burr. 1836-1867	
RAFFREY	130
Bapt. 1843-1968	
Marr. 1845-1915	
RATHFRILAND	131
Marr. 1845-1936	
ROSSTREVOR	260
Bapt. 1851-1986	
Marr. 1852-74-1910	
SAINTFIELD (1st)	298
Bapt. 1854-1986	
Marr. 1845-1905	
SAINTFIELD (2nd)	289
Bapt. 1831-93	
SCARVA	182
Bapt. 1845-1936	
Marr. 1807-1964	
SEAFORDE	355
Bapt. 1826-1925	
Marr. 1827-1936	
SPA	301
Bapt. 1880-1986	
Marr. 1875-1936	
WARINGSTOWN	270
Bapt. 1862-1985	
Marr. 1854-1926	
WARRENPOINT	307
Bapt. 1832-1986	
Marr. 1823-1907	

Church Name & Dates of Available Records	Order No. (MIC 1P/...)
CO. FERMANAGH	
AUGHENTAINE	80
Bapt. 1836 - 1888	
Marr. 1845 - 1970	
BALLYHOBRIDGE	274
Bapt. 1846 - 1905	
Marr. 1854 -1936	
CAVANALECK	80
Bapt. 1819 - 1986	
ENNISKILLEN	282
Bapt. 1819 - 1986	
Marr. 1819 - 1845	
IRVINESTOWN	66
Bapt. 1842 - 1918	
Marr. 1848 - 1934	
LISELLAW	284
Bapt. 1851 - 1984	
MAGUIRESBRIDGE	69
Marr. 1845 - 1872	
Marr Reg. 1845 - 1920	
Bapt. 1860 - 1871	
Bapt Reg. 1860 - 1885	
TEMPO	9
Bapt. 1874 - 1951	
Marr. 1845 - 1934	
CO. LONDONDERRY	
AGHADOWEY	123
Bapt. 1855 - 1870	
Marr. 1845 - 1923	
BALLYKELLY	208
Bapt. 1826 - 1983	
Marr. 1699 - 1920	
BALLYRASHANE	70
Bapt. 1863 - 1928	
Marr. 1846 - 1936	
BALTEAGH	228
Bapt. not received	
Marr. 1845 - 1920	
BANAGHER	227
Bapt. 1834 - 1984	
Marr.1845 - 1920	
BELLAGHY	377
Bapt. 1862 - 1887	
Marr 1845 - 1919	

Church Name & Dates of Available Records	Order No. (MIC 1P/...)
BOVEEDY	18
Bapt. 1841 - 1928	
Marr. 1842 - 1929	
BOVEVAGH	229
Bapt. 1818 - 1896	
Marr. 1842 - 1929	
CASTLEDAWSON	90
Bapt. 1809 - 1901	
Marr. 1805 - 1932	
CHURCHTOWN	347
Bapt. 1840 - 1970	
Marr. 1845 - 1936	
COLERAINE (1st)	54
Bapt. 1845 - 1901	
Marr. 1845- 1901	
COLERAINE (3rd - Terrace Row)	101
Bapt. 1862 - 1939	
Marr. 1835 - 1903	
COLERAINE (New Row)	31
Bapt. 1842 - 1986	
Marr. 1809 - 1928	
CUMBER UPPER	148
Bapt. 1874 -1983	
Marr. 1845 - 1936	
CUMBER LOWER	147
Bapt. 1827 - 1867	
Marr. 1843 - 1845	
CURRAN	338
Bapt. {No pre-1900 baptisms exist}	
Marr. 1845 - 1936	
DRAPERSTOWN	343
Bapt. 1876 - 1947	
Marr. 1845 - 1923	
DROMORE	373
Bapt. 1889 - 1987	
Marr. 1869 - 1987	
DUNBOE (2nd)	149
Bapt. 1864 - 1983	
Marr. 1845 - 1913	
FAUGHANVALE	190
Bapt. 1819 - 1983	
Marr. 1845 - 1968	
GARVAGH (1st)	257
Bapt. 1795 - 1816	
Marr. 1795 - 1844	

Church Name & Dates of Available Records	Order No. (MIC 1P/...)
GARVAGH (2ND)	17
Bapt. 1830 - 1921	
Marr. 1830 - 1934	
Burr. 1853 - 1896	
GORTNESSY	189
Bapt. 1839 - 1983	
Marr. 1845 - 1977	
KILREA (1st)	53
Bapt. 1825 - 1859, 1862 - 1870	
Marr. 1825 - 1830, 1845 - 1899	
KILREA (2nd)	261
Bapt. 1840 - 1885, 1903 - 1930	
Marr. 1845 - 1929	
LARGY	180
Bapt. 1845 - 1872	
Marr. 1845 - 1936	
LIMAVADY (1st)	34
Marr. 1832 - 1841	
Bapt. 1832 - 1839, 1861 - 1870	
LONDONDERRY (Carlisle Road)	67
Marr. 1839 - 1891	
Bapt. 1838 - 1921	
LONDONDERRY (Great James S)	150
Bapt. 1837 - 1984	
Marr. 1837 - 1984	
LONDONDERRY (2nd or Strand)	293
Bapt. 1845 - 1918	
Marr. 1847 - 1909	
MAGHERA	376
Bapt. 1843 - 1962	
Marr. 1843 - 1936	
MAGILLIGAN	215
Bapt. 1814 - 1857	
Marr. 1814 - 1845	
MONEYDIG	93
Bapt. 1857 - 1923	
Marr. 1852 - 1928	
MONEYMORE (1st)	339
Bapt. 1827 - 1959	
Marr. 1827 - 1936	
MONEYMORE (2nd)	340
Bapt. 1845 -1949	
Marr. 1868 - 1910	
TOBERMORE	344
Bapt. 1860 - 1905	
Marr. 1845 - 1918	

Church Name & Dates of Available Records	Order No. (MIC 1P/...)
CO. MONAGHAN	
BALLYALBANY	146
Bapt. 1802 - 1848	
Marr. 1807 - 1830	
BALLYBAY (1st)	171
Bapt. 1834 - 1982	
Marr. 1834 - 1956	
BALLYBAY (2nd)	197
Marr. 1845 - 1906	
BROOMFIELD	192
Bapt. 1841 - 1973	
Marr. 1842 - 1956	
CAHANS	172
Bapt. 1858 - 1971	
Marr. 1845 - 1894	
CARRICKMACROSS (or Corvally)	214
Bapt.1832 - 1955	
Marr. 1838 - 1955	
CASTLEBLANEY (1st)	196
Bapt. 1823 - 1934	
Marr. 1845 - 1922	
CASTLEBLANEY (2nd or Frankford)	191
Bapt. 1920 - 1981	
Marr. 1845 - 1916	
CLONES	273
Bapt. 1856 - 1984	
Marr. 1859 - 1956	
CLONTIBRET (1st)	176
Marr. 1845 - 1919	
Bapt. 125 - 1898	
CLONTIBRET (2nd)	175
Bapt. 1856 - 1905	
Marr. 1845 - 1956	
CORVALLEY (sic Corvally)	214
Bapt. 1832 - 1955	
Marr. 1838 - 1955	
CRIEVE	194
Bapt. 1819 - 1953	
Marr. 1845 - 1944	
DERRYVALLEY	173
Bapt. 1816 - 1833 (copies) + 1833 - 1928	
Marr. 1833 - 1953	

Church Name & Dates of Available Records	Order No. (MIC 1P/...)	Church Name & Dates of Available Records	Order No. (MIC 1P/...)
DRUM (1st)	201	AUGHNACLOY	38
Bapt. 1866 - 1931		Bapt. 1812 - 1827, 1830 - 1870.	
Marr. 1845 - 1936		Marr. 1812 - 1824, 1830 - 1841,	
DRUM (2nd)	202	1845 - 1870	
Bapt. 1868 - 1983		BADONEY	278
Marr. 1845 - 1904		Marr. 1845 - 1912	
DRUMKEEN	174	BALLYGAWLEY	61
Bapt.1856 - 1981		Bapt. 1842 - 1863, 1864 - 1984	
Marr. 1845- 1904		Marr. 1845 - 1862, 1864 - 1895	
GLASSLOUGH	219	BALLYMAGRANE	39
Bapt. 1836 - 1974		Bapt. 1851 - 1870	
Marr. 1845 - 1956		Marr. 1845 - 1870	
GLENNAN	155	BALLYNAHATTY (1st & 2nd)	97
Bapt. 1820 - 1981		Bapt. 1845 - 1968	
Marr. 1805 - 1820		Marr. 1843 - 1894	
LOUGHMOURNE	193	BENBURB	60
Bapt. 1846 - 1965		Marr. 1845 - 1885, 1885 - 1936	
Marr. 1851 - 1945		Bapt. 1874 - 1936	
MIDDLETOWN (see under Glasslough)		BRIGH	13
MONAGHAN (1st)	199	Marr. 1837 - 1920	
Bapt. 1821 - 1983		Bapt. 1837 - 1926	
Marr. 1821 - 1834 + 1845 - 1907		CALEDON	25
MONAGHAN (2nd)	146	Bapt. 1870	
Bapt. 1802 - 1948		Marr. 1848 - 1867	
Marr. 1807 - 1830		CARLAND	28
NEWBLISS	275	Bapt. 1759 - 1799, 1847 - 1986	
Bapt. 1856 - 1984		Marr. 1770 - 1802, 1840 - 1914	
Marr. 1845 - 1923		CARNLOUGH (no pre 1900 records)	
ROCKCORRY	195	CARNTALL (Or Clougher)	96
Bapt. 1860 - 1982		Bapt. 1819 - 1845	
Marr. 1845 - 1955		Marr.1829 -1845	
SCOTSTOWN	203	CASTLECAULFIELD	121
Bapt. 1855 - 1963		Bapt. 1855 - 1947	
Marr. 1846 - 1935		Marr.1834 - 1919	
STONEBRIDGE	165	CASTLEDERG (1st)	73
Bapt. 1846 - 1980		Bapt.1823 - 1985	
Marr. 1845 - 1956		Marr. 1845 - 1898	
		CASTLEDERG (2nd)	248
		Bapt. 1880 - 1985	
CO. TYRONE		Marr. 1861 - 1935	
ALBANY (see under Stewartstown)	13	CLADY	50
ALT	249	Bapt.	
Bapt. (no pre 1900)		Marr. 1845 - 1871	
Marr. 1845 - 1955		CLENANESS (Upper)	44
ARDSTRAW	50	Marr. 1860 - 1869	
Bapt. 1837 - 1890		Bapt. 1868 - 1870	
Marr. 1837 - 1936			

Church Name & Dates of Available Records	Order No. (MIC 1P/...)	Church Name & Dates of Available Records	Order No. (MIC 1P/...)
CLENANEES (Lower) Marr. 1849 - 1870 Bapt. 1811 - 1872 Deaths 1865 - 1870	45	FINTONA Bapt. 1836 - 1875 Marr. 1836 - 1929	283
CLOUGHERNEY Bapt. 1865 - 1984 Marr. 1845 - 1930	246	GILLYGOOLEY Bapt. 1848 - 1984 Marr. 1845 - 1934	234
COOKSTOWN (1st) Marr. 1845 - 1870 Bapt.1836 - 1950 Bapt. 1836 - 1870	43 & 139	GLENELLY Bapt. (not received) Marr. 1845 - 1915	280
CORRICK Bapt. (not received) Marr. 1851 - 1935	279	GLENHOY Bapt. 1832 - 1984 Marr. 1869 - 1907	255
CREEVAN (see under Ballymatty 2nd)		GORTIN Bapt. 1843 - 1985 Marr. 1845 - 1935	253
CROCKANTANTY Bapt. (not received) Marr. 1876 - 1924	254	KILLETER Bapt. 1839 - 1981 Marr. 1839 - 1911	252
CROSSROADS (see under Mountjoy) Bapt. 1821 - 1979 Marr. 1845 - 1924		LECKPATRICK Bapt. 1838 - 1935 Marr. 1835 - 1930	49
DOUGLAS Bapt.1840 - 1925 Marr. 1832 - 1936	50	MAGHERAMASON Bapt. 1878 - 1939 Marr. 1881 - 1927	369
DROMORE Bapt. 1863 - 1986 Marr. 1835 - 1914	247	MINTERBURN Marr. 1845 - 1870 Bapt. 1829 - 1870	26
DRUMLEGAGH Bapt. 1863 - 1986 Marr. 1845 - 1930	303	MOUNTJOY (Crossroads) Bapt. 1821 - 1979 Marr. 1845 - 1924	242
DRUMQUIN Bapt. 1845 - 1884 Marr. 1845 - 1870	65	MOY Bapt. 1852 - 1854, 1871 - 1986 Marr. 1854 - 1917	36
DUNGANNON Bapt. 1790 - 1886 Marr. 1785 - 1884	3a	NEWMILLS Bapt. 1850 - 1952 Marr. 1846 - 1928	295
EDENDERRY Bapt .1845 - 1945 Marr.1845 - 1935	108	NEWTOWNSTEWART (1st & 2nd) Marr. 1845 - 1880, 1883 - 1907 Bapt. 1848 - 1868, 1890 - 1985	59
EGLISH Bapt. 1856 - 1963 Marr. 1846 - 1936 Burls. 1858 - 1927	122	OMAGH(1st) Bapt. 1856 - 1968 Marr. 1845- 1927	128
		OMAGH (2nd) Bapt. 1821 - 1942 Marr. 1846 - 1990	235

Church Name & Dates of Available Records	Order No. (MIC 1P/...)	Church Name & Dates of Available Records	Order No. (MIC 1P/...)
POMEROY	120	SIXMILECROSS (No pre-1900 records)	
Bapt. 1841 - 1967		STEWARTSTOWN (1st)	48
Marr. 1845 - 1936		Bapt. 1814 - 1871	
SANDHOLES	42	STRABANE (1st)	10
Bapt. 1863 - 1870		Bapt 1828 - 1937	
Marr. 1845 - 1870		Marr. 1845 - 1879, 1881 - 1919	
SESKINORE	245	STRABANE (2nd)	10
Bapt. 1863 - 1937		Bapt. 1844 - 1916	
Marr. 1843 - 1928		Marr. 1864 - 1874	
SION	251	URNEY	250
Bapt. 1866 - 1936		Bapt. 1937 - 1930	
Marr. 1866 - 1884		Marr. 1866 - 1926	

APPENDIX 4.3

PRESBYTERIAN REGISTERS IN LOCAL CUSTODY

Presbyterian Registers in local custody giving the earliest date at which these registers commence. It is first advisable to confirm with the local minister that these registers have not been moved to a different location. Their addresses can be found in the Annual "Presbyterian Church in Ireland Directory".

CO. ANTRIM

Ahoghill (Brookside)	1845	Cullybackey	1812
Armoy	1815	Cushendall	1853
Ballycarry	1832	Dervock	1828
Ballycastle	1829	Dunluce	1805
Ballyeaston 1st	1821	Finvoy	1843
Ballyeaston 2nd	1826	Glenarm	1850
Ballylinney	1837	Glenwhirry	1845
Ballymena 1st	1825	Grange	1824
Ballymena 2nd	1837	Islandmagee (First)	1829
Ballymena West Church	1829	Kilroughts (First)	1836
Ballymoney (First)	1817	Kilroughts (Second)	1858
Ballymoney (St. James)	1825	Loughmorne	1848
Ballyweaney	1845	Mosside	1843
Ballywillan	1816	Newtowncrommellin	1835
Broughshane (1st)	1830	Portglenone (First)	1848
Buckna	1841	Portrush	1848
Carrickfergus (First)	1823	Raloo	1840
Connor	1819	Randalstown (1st)	1837
Crossgar	1839	Randalstown (2nd)	1838
Crumlin	1839	Rasharkin	1834
		Toberkleigh	1830

CO. ARMAGH
Aghorey	1845
Armagh (Second)	1825
Clodymore	1843
Clare	1838
Creggan	1835
Cremore	1831
Drumbanagher	1832
Drumhillory	1829
Keady (Second)	1819
Kingsmills	1842
Knappagh	1842
Lislooney	1836
Loughgall	1842
Lurgan (First)	1749
Markethill (First)	1821
Newtownhamilton (Second)	1823
Portadown (First)	1822
Poyntzpass	1840
Richhill	1845
Tandragee	1835
Tartaraghan	1845
Tassagu	1843
Tullyallen	1795
Tyrone's Ditches	1864
Vinecash	1838

CO. DOWN
Ballyblack	1845
Clough	1836
Banbridge	1851
Kingsmills (Jerrettspass)	1842
First Newtownards	1833
Second Newtownards	1834
Warrenpoint	1832

BELFAST CITY
Argyle Place	1853
Ballymocant	1837
Ballysillan	1839
Berry St.	1861
College Square North	1840
Crescent	1831
Fisherwick	1810
Fitzroy	1820
May St.	1845
Malone	1837
Rosemary St.	1723
Townsend St.	1835
St.	1854

CO. CAVAN
Bailieborough (1st) B	1852
Bailieborough (2nd) B	1865
Ballyhobridge	1840
Ballyjamesduff	1845
Cavan	1851
Corlea	1835
Cootehill	1828
Seafin	1871

CO. CORK
Bandon	1842
Cobh	1847
Cork	1832

CO. DONEGAL
Ballindrait	1819
Ballyshannon	1836
Buncrana	1830
Burt	1834
Carndonagh	1830
Convoy	1822
Crossroads	1853
Donaghmore	1844
Donegal	1825
Fannet	1859
Knowhead (Miff)	1826
Letterkenny	1841
Monreagh	1845
Moville	1834
Newtowncunningham	1830
Ramelton	1808
Raphoe	1829
Rathmullan	1854
St. Johnston	1838
Trentagh	1836

CO. DOWN

Anaghlone	1839
Annalong	1840
Ballyblack	1845
Ballygilbert	1841
Ballygrainey	1838
Ballynahinch 1st	1841
Ballynahinch 2nd	1827
Ballywalter (1st)	1808
Ballywalter (2nd)	1833
Bellasis	1845
Bessbrook	1854
Boardmills First	1824
Carrowdore	1843
Carryduff	1854
Castlereagh	1809
Clonduff	1842
Clough	1836
Cloughley	1841
Comber 1st	1845
Comber 2nd	1845
Conlig	1845
Donacloney	1798
Donaghadee 1st	1822
Donaghadee 2nd	1849
Donaghmore	1804
Downpatrick	1827
Dromoira 1st	1817
Dromore 1st	1834
Drumgooland	1833
Drumlee	1826
Drumlough	1827
Dundrod	1829
Fourtowns	1822
Gilford	1843
Greyabbey	1845
Groomsport	1841
Hillhall	1845
Hillsborough	1832
Holywood 1st	1846
Holywood 2nd	1856
Katesbridge	1866
Kilkeel	1842
Killinchy	1835

Leitrim	1837
Lissara	1809
Loughaghery	1801
Loughbrickland	1842
Magherahamlet	1831
Magherally	1837
Maze	1856
Millisle	1773
Mintersburn	1829
Moira	1845
Mourne	1840
Newmills	1838
Newry 1st	1829
Newtownards 1st	1833
Newtownards 2nd	1834
(Regent St.)	1835
Raffrey	1843
Rathfriland 2nd	1864
Rathfriland 3rd	1834
Rostrevor	1851
Ryans	1857
Saintfield 1st	1851
Saintfield 2nd	1837
Seaforde	1826
Tullylish	1813
Warringstown	1864
Warrenpoint	1832

CO. DUBLIN

Abbey St.	1779
Clontarf	1830
Ormond Quay	1787

CO. FERMANAGH

Cavanleck	1853
Enniskillen	1837
Irvinestown	1867
Lisbellaw	1848
Pettigo	1844

CO. GALWAY

Galway	1831

CO. KERRY
Tralee — 1840

CO. LAOIS (QUEENS)
Mountmellick — 1849

CO. LEITRIM
Carrigallen — 1801
Drumkeenan — 1835

CO. LIMERICK
Limerick — 1829

CO. LONDONDERRY
Aghadowey — 1855
Balteagh — 1868
Banagher — 1834
Boveedy — 1841
Castledawson — 1835
Cloughwater — 1845
Cumber (Lower) — 1837
Cumber (Upper) — 1834
Curran — 1840
Derramore — 1825
Draperstown — 1837
Drumachose — 1838
Dungiven — 1834
Garvagh 1st — 1795
Garvagh 2nd — 1830
Glendermoty — 1855
Gortnessy — 1839
Kilrea (First) — 1825
Limavady (First) — 1832
Limavady (Second) — 1845
Londonderry (First) — 1815
Londonderry, St. James St. — 1837
Londonderry, Carlisle Rd — 1838
Londonderry, Strand — 1847
Maghera — 1843
Magilligan — 1814
Moneymore — 1820
Myroe — 1850
Portstewart — 1829
Saltersland — 1845

CO. LONGFORD
Corboy — 1839
Longford — 1834
Tully — 1844

CO. LOUTH
Corvally — 1840
Dundalk — 1819

CO. MAYO
Ballina (Dromore) — 1846
Killala — 1849

CO. MEATH
Ervey — 1862

CO. MONAGHAN
Ballyalbany — 1802
Ballybay — 1833
Ballyhobridge — 1846
Broomfield — 1841
Castleblaney — 1832
Clones — 1856
Clontribet — 1825
Corlea — 1835
Crieve — 1819
Derryvalley — 1816
Drumakeen — 1856
Loughmorne — 1847
Middletown — 1829
Newbliss — 1856
Scotstown — 1855
Stonebridge — 1821

CO. SLIGO
Sligo — 1824

CO. TYRONE
Albany — 1838
Agheritain — 1836
Aughnacloy — 1843
Ballygawley — 1843
Ballygoney — 1834
Ballyreagh — 1843

Brigh	1836	Sandholes	1844
Castlecaulfield	1834	Seskinore	1826
Castlederg (First)	1823	Stewartstown	1814
Clenaness (Lower)	1840	Strabane	1828
Cookstown (First)	1836	Urney & Sion	1837
Donagheady	1838		
Douglas	1831	**CO. WATERFORD**	
Drumellin	1845	Waterford	1770
Dungannon (First)	1790		
Glenderry	1945	**CO. WEXFORD**	
Eglish	1837	Wexford	1849
Glenhoy	1850		
Gortin	1843	**CO. WICKLOW**	
Killeter	1839	Bray	1836
Moy	1852		
Newmills	1846		
Orritor	1827		
Pomeroy	1841		

5

CATHOLIC CHURCH RECORDS

James G. Ryan

5.1 Introduction

The vast majority of the people of Ireland belong to the Catholic Church and this has been the case for many centuries. Unfortunately, the records of the Catholic church are sparse until the beginning of the 19th century. Nevertheless the records which do exist are a major source for the history of those Irish families whose activities and position have not resulted in any other forms of record. Catholic Church records are often the only evidence of the existence of a large proportion of the population of late eighteenth and early 19th century Ireland, and particularly of those people who did not own or formally lease land; nor make wills or deeds; nor join armies or societies; nor sign petitions; nor live in areas for which census information survives. A huge proportion of small farmers, labourers, servants, beggars and many others have left no record of their existence except that of their church. Because of their importance for the history of these, and other, families it is useful to understand the background to the compilation of these records. To do so requires some insight into the history of the Catholic Church, and into the political and social significance of its membership at various periods of Irish history.

5.2 History

In 1534 Henry VIII of England enacted the Act of Supremacy by which he, and his successors, became head of the Church of England. In 1536 the Irish Parliament declared him also head of the Church of Ireland. From that time onward religious affiliation assumed a political significance in Ireland. In the eyes of the English administration it was no longer possible to be loyal both to the crown and to the Catholic Church. However, in practice, the new religion had little immediate influence in Ireland for several reasons. One was the general lack of commitment on the part of the English administration to its introduction. The result of this lack of commitment was that no serious effort was made to find Church of Ireland ministers and preachers who could spread its doctrines among the Irish people. Even if the commitment to provide ministers had existed, it would have been (and later proved to be) difficult to find ministers who spoke the Irish language; which was the sole language of the vast majority of the Irish people.

A second factor in the slow penetration of Protestantism in Ireland was a general unwillingness on the part of the English authorities to impose those penalties which were laid down for non-observance. The final factor was that large parts of Ireland were not in any practical sense under English control. Thus the north, the west and the bulk of the southern parts of Ireland were at this time predominantly Gaelic in outlook and therefore culturally either opposed or unaffected by English influence. There was, in short, general disaffection with the English monarch among the great bulk of the Irish people, and a consequent unwillingness to yield to his authority in any matter, particularly religion.

The adherents to the new Church in Ireland were mainly those who did so out of loyalty to the Crown. These included the members of the English administration in Ireland and those families which had, or hoped to gain, royal favour. The Protestant church was effectively confined to the Pale i.e. the area around Dublin in which English administration was dominant. Even within the Pale the majority of the Anglo-Norman families remained Catholic. Indeed Catholicism was to prove a major bond between Anglo-Normans, or "Old English", and the Gaelic people of Ireland in the following centuries. In practice therefore, the vast bulk of people remained Catholic although all of their church buildings were now officially Church of Ireland and, in some places at least, overt practice of the Catholic religion was unwise.

From the point of view of the family historian, the Irish Catholic church up to the late 17th century has provided virtually no records. All the evidence suggests that in this period the Catholic Church in Ireland was in administrative disarray. Particularly in the period after the establishment of the Church of Ireland, it would appear that the laity were poorly instructed, if at all, the sacraments poorly administered, and the clergy both uneducated and unresponsive to their bishops. It can be imagined that the keeping of records was a low priority in a church which was internally disorganised, and externally under legal, if not practical, threat of extinction.

In the seventeenth century the difficulties of the Catholic Church became even greater. At the beginning of this century the ancient Gaelic clan system was finally broken. This was symbolized by the departure from Ireland in 1609 of Hugh O'Neill and his allied Chieftains in the so-called "Flight of the Earls". Their departure, and the subsequent plantation of their Ulster lands with settlers, who were predominantly Presbyterian Scottish (See Chapter 4) was a major blow to the Irish Catholic Church. The Catholic Church in the northern counties, which had previously been under the protection of the Gaelic Chieftains, now became very restricted by local planter administrations who equated Catholic with rebel.

Conditions in the 17th century were, legally, not as difficult for Catholic priests as they would become in the 18th century. Nevertheless, it is clear that priests in many parts of the country experienced practical difficulties in administering their duties. One of the results of this situation was the apparent failure of priests to keep records. Although Synods in 1614 and after had ordered the keeping of registers of births and marriages, there is no evidence that these recommendations were acted upon. If they were, then none of the registers from the early 17th century have survived.

During the mid 17th century the struggle for control of the English crown had the effect of gradually reducing the rights and influence of Catholics. At this stage, it should be remembered, not only were the vast majority of the population Catholic, but also the majority of the landowners and 'gentry'. In the face of this erosion of their rights the Gaelic and Norman Catholics united and rebelled against English rule. In 1641 they formed the Catholic Confederacy and established an independent parliament in Kilkenny City which governed the country for the following seven years. This rebellion was finally and brutally suppressed by Oliver Cromwell in 1649, and resulted in the confiscation of the lands of those Catholics who had been involved, and a further very significant reduction in Catholic influence.

In 1660, after the Restoration; to the English Crown of Charles II there was a temporary easing of conditions for Catholics in both England and Ireland. A Synod of Irish Catholic Bishops in 1670 again ordered priests to keep parish registers of baptisms and marriages.

Some of these records do survive (eg Wexford Town) and it appears that others were kept, although few survive.

The Irish Catholics were still very discontent with the way in which they were being treated by the English establishment, and in 1690 a further opportunity arose for them to advance their cause. In this year the Catholic King James II fought the Protestant William of Orange for the British crown. Although neither was Irish, the existence of a large body of Catholic support in Ireland caused James II to fight his war in Ireland. This war led to James' defeat at the famous Battle of the Boyne, and effectively precipitated the enactment, in 1703, of the "Act to prevent the further growth of Popery". This, and a series of succeeding laws which together are known as the "Penal Laws", severely and formally restricted the political rights of Catholics and the practice of the Catholic religion.

The Penal Laws effectively removed the rights of Catholics to public office, succession of land ownership, and the professions. It was designed to keep Catholics politically impotent or, as one historian put it, "to make them poor and to keep them poor". In regard to the church administration the authorities had earlier (1697) passed an Act banishing Catholic priests (described as "papists exercising any ecclesiastical jurisdiction and all regulars of the popish clergy") from Ireland and England as of 1 May 1698. However, it would appear that this effort was a failure as few priests actually left the country. The authorities, realizing that they could not effectively ban all Catholic priests from Ireland, instead decided to register them. An act to this effect was passed in 1704 and a total of 1089 priests was registered. Only these registered priests were permitted to perform ecclesiastical duties and it was clearly intended that no further registrations would be permitted.

Other priests did exercise their function in Ireland and, for them conditions remained hazardous, although the degree of hazard varied from one place and time to another. In some parts of the country and at some specific periods they were persecuted, whereas in other places and times they were ignored. The attitude of the local Protestant population, and particularly the landlord, was a major factor in this. A further factor was the ability of the people to support a priest. Where there was a surviving Catholic gentry class, as in parts of Galway and Clare, the church administration had patrons who allowed them to operate more freely. Elsewhere, however, they were dependent on a populace who were themselves in economic distress and without power.

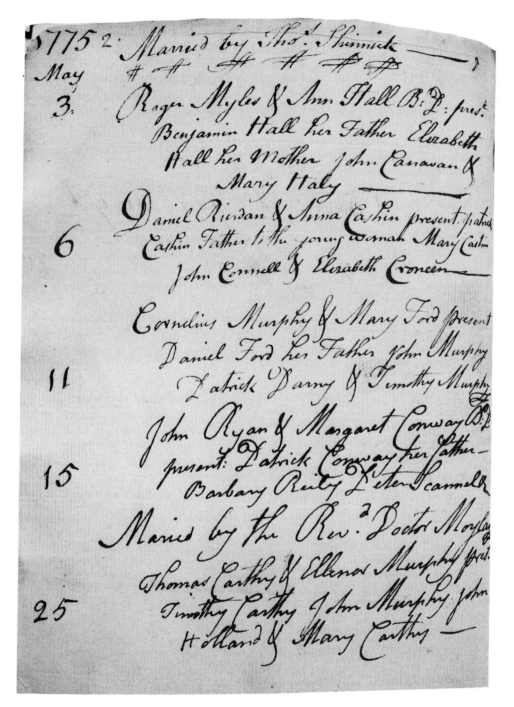

Fig. 5.1   *Marriage Register of the South Parish (St. Finbar's), Cork City of 1775.*

It is certain however, that very few priests dared to produce the damning evidence of their ecclesiastical duties which church records would have constituted. This would have been both foolhardy and also virtually impossible in practice given the fugitive, and generally impoverished, status of the majority of these priests.

From about 1740 onward the grip of the Penal Laws began to be relaxed. The exercise of priestly duties became easier and the Catholic church administration began to be quietly rebuilt. Although it was still prudent to keep a low profile, the everyday practice of the Catholic religion could be resumed. The re-emergence of the Catholic church was strongest in the cities and large towns. This was because the Penal Laws were mainly based on control of property and influence. Catholics were therefore not prevented from trading and many Catholic merchants became very wealthy, and actively funded the rebuilding of the church infrastructure. This mainly occurred in the cities since this is where the merchants tended to live. In the cities it was also easier to "hide" mass houses. There are many descriptions of stables and other buildings which were in regular use for mass. Church records began to be compiled in city parishes in larger numbers from about the 1730's.

In the rural areas the picture was very different since the influence of landowners on the behaviour of their Catholic tenants, and of local officials on the administration of the law in regard to priests, was more significant. In addition there was the very significant fact that the majority of Catholics of these areas were extremely poor. Consequently in only a few areas could these communities afford to build churches and maintain clergy until much later in the century or even well into the 19th century.

The status of Catholics generally improved throughout the late 18th century and early 19th century. This was partly due to the improving economic circumstances of Ireland, and the consequent increasing resources of the Catholic people. This resulted in increasing donations and fees to the Catholic church, which were used for church building and for education of priests. Towards the end of the 18th century, the pressure for equal rights for Catholics grew and was assisted by the spirit of liberty, equality and fraternity which was then growing in Europe. The French Revolution greatly alarmed the Protestant ascendancy. The threat of a populist revolt by the Catholic and Presbyterian people of Ireland was recognised by the ruling classes. The fear of the guillotine caused an effective split between the Protestant supremacists who would meet the threat by increased repression, and the liberals, who believed that the solution was to be found in the granting of more concessions to the Catholic majority. In the General Election of 1790 the liberal party was defeated, much to the despair of the Catholics, who continued their political pressures for civil liberty. This did have some results, in particular the passage of a new Catholic Relief Act in 1793 which gave some concessions but fell far short of demands. A significant development in the organisation of the church was the establishment of a seminary at Maynooth in 1795. This was the first seminary to operate in Ireland in some 150 years and provided an increased supply of priests for the growing number of Catholic parishes. Before this, Catholic priests had been educated abroad in Spain or, more commonly, in France.

Among the rights granted in the 1793 Catholic Relief Act was a limited right of Catholics to vote. However, as this right was based on property ownership, and Catholics were still poor in proportion to their fellow-citizens, their effective representation was low. In addition, Catholics could not themselves be parliamentary representatives. In 1823 Daniel O'Connell and others formed the Catholic Association, a movement to win political representation by Catholics and to allow them to hold government posts. This Association enrolled huge numbers of members and acted through the electoral process to elect candidates who were in favour of Catholic Emancipation. This finally resulted in the election of Daniel O'Connell as MP for Clare. Although he was a Catholic and therefore legally ineligible, the authorities realised that refusal to admit him to Westminster would have been inviting Civil War and he was allowed to take his place. In 1829 a bill repealing many of the remaining penal laws was passed and although some legislation remained, and some new legislation was enacted, this year is seen as the effective victory-date for Catholic emancipation.

While the political barriers to development of the Catholic church were thereby removed, the poverty of the bulk of the Catholic population and the devastation later caused by the Great Famine of 1845-47 and the subsequent emigration, had obvious effects on the ability of many poor parishes to provide themselves with churches until much later in the century. From the 1830's the period of churchbuilding began in earnest and a massive reconstruction of the church infrastructure commenced.

5.3 The Maintenance of Church Records

Thus, from the history of the Catholic clergy and people we can develop a picture of the position in regard to the maintenance of Catholic church records. Briefly there are none before the late 17th century.

TABLE 5.1

The date of the earliest baptismal records in each province, and the number of Parishes which commenced recording baptisms in the 18th century and in each decade from 1800.

	Earliest	1700's	1800	1810	1820	1830	1840	1850	1860-90	Total
Ulster	1752	8	3	6	23	48	56	35	51	**230**
Connaught	1723	5	10	6	18	36	35	34	40	**184**
Leinster	1671	91	24	41	52	36	21	23	15	**303**
Munster	1706	37	41	61	62	51	38	22	13	**325**
Total		**141**	**78**	**114**	**155**	**171**	**150**	**114**	**119**	**1042**

After 1670 it would appear that some records were kept but few survive. Again in the 1690's the period of major persecution of Catholic priests begins and few records were kept. In the 1730's, due to relaxation of the Penal Laws and growing toleration, formal religious observation was possible again in some areas, but mainly in the urban areas.

The number of churches keeping records increases in the later 18th century and early 19th century. However, there is very clear regional variation in the progress of church building and record keeping. For instance if we examine the dates on which Irish parishes began keeping records, we find that 30% of those in the province of Leinster, and 11% of those in Munster, began baptismal record-keeping before 1800 *(Table 5.1)*. The comparable figure is only 3% in Connaught and Ulster. Taking another measure, we find that well over half of the Ulster and Connaught parishes began keeping baptismal records after 1840 whereas in Leinster over half had begun by 1810 and in Munster by 1820. However, despite these regional generalizations, there are some churches with early records in all parts of the country.

The regional variations in the impact of Catholicism have been reviewed by Whelan *(1)*. Among the factors identified which would have had a strong impact on the keeping of records was the training of priests. Priests in the early 18th century were either trained in Ireland or on the European continent, usually in France. Due to the conditions in Ireland, and the urgent demand for priests, those ordained in Ireland

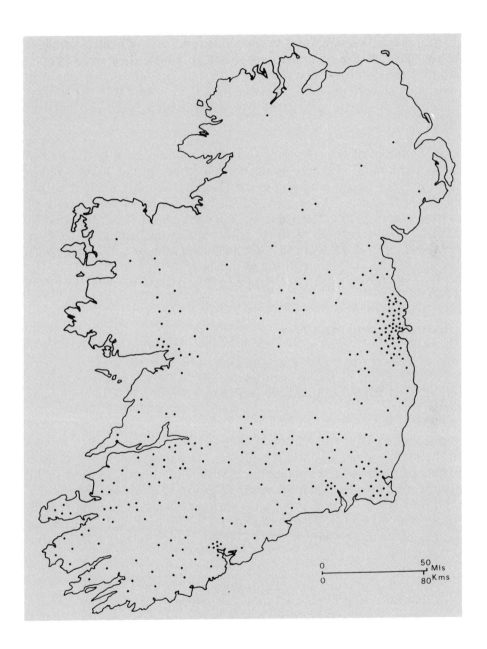

Fig. 5.2 *The Distribution of Continental trained priests in 1704 - from Whelan (1).*

were often inadequately trained either intellectually or in church teaching. Those who graduated from the well-organised continental seminaries were fully trained both in the requirements of the church (including record-keeping) and in the skills required. Whelan's analysis (1) of the distribution of priests according to where they were trained shows that the continental-trained priests were predominantly based in the parishes of Leinster and Munster (*Fig. 5.2*). As Table 5.1 shows, the parishes in these provinces are those which have the earliest records.

Another factor of direct relevance to record maintenance is the wealth of the parishioners. If there is no church, there is not likely to be a register, and the better endowed is the church, the more likely it is that a register will exist. The income of Catholic parishes was purely by voluntary subscription. The values of the parishes in 1800, reported by Whelan (1) shows that all of those with an annual income of £200 or more are situated in Leinster or Munster, while almost all of those with an income of £50 or less are situated in Ulster or Connaught. Thus the wealth of parishes again reflects the likelihood of their keeping registers.

5.4 Record-Keeping Practices

Having examined the reasons for the lack of records we must now turn to a consideration of those records which do exist and the factors which affected their compilation and their current value to the family historian.

At various times over the centuries instructions were issued to priests as to the maintenance of church registers. Occasional early Synods of the Irish Church issued instructions which in theory applied to all priests in all dioceses. Each Diocese, or group of Dioceses, could also issue instructions to their priests on various issues, including record-keeping. The Synod of Drogheda of 1614 for instance issued the "Statutes of Armagh" which among other things covered baptismal record-keeping.

> "Parish priests are recommended to have, when possible, one baptismal font, well secured in a proper place, where all children are to be baptised, except in danger of death,   excessive cold or other more urgent reason. They are also recommended to bring with their ritual a blank book, for the insertion of names of children, parents, sponsors etc. No priest

on account of friendship or other motive, can admit
more than two sponsors - one of each sex"

The statutes also dealt with Matrimonial records;
"Parish priests are recommended to keep a book for
inserting the names of the married couple, their
parents, the time, place and witnesses of the contract,
dispensations etc, which book they are to preserve
carefully ..."

Interestingly, no instructions were issued in regard to burial records.
However, if the instructions on baptismal and marriage records were
obeyed, then little evidence of them has survived.

On balance, it would appear that records were not kept by the majority
of priests. One of the central problems seems to have been the general
disorganisation of the church and the failure of Catholic bishops to
exercise control over their parish priests. Because of the lack of central
control, it is also likely that records which were kept by individual
priests were removed by the families of those priest after their deaths,
on the basis that they were personal belongings.   The issue of diocesan
administration is more fully dealt with by Corish (2). Another factor,
already mentioned, is the basic training of those priests who had been
hurriedly ordained, without adequate education, during the period of
urgent demand for priests.

There are a few first-hand accounts of the failure of priests to keep
records. For instance, when Patrick Plunkett, the newly appointed
Bishop of Meath, made his first visitation of parishes in June 1780, he
admonished almost all of his clergy for their failure to keep records and
instructed them to be "made out immediately". In the case of the parish
of Churchtown and Rathcondra, for instance, he seemed to be
dissatisfied with the form in which the records were kept and
instructed that

"The register of birth, marriage and death should be a
book, or three distinct books, bound and written
clearly and legibly and kept with care" (3).

Following the very stern instructions issued by Plunkett to the priests
of his diocese, most of them seemed to have begun to keep records.
Certainly this is one of the few dioceses to have kept death records.

Thus one of the significant reasons for the differences in record-keeping

Notetur Numeris.	Anno Domini 18 79		Natus		Ex parentibus legitimo Matrimonio junctis
	Baptizandi Nomen.	Cognomen.	Die.	Mense.	Nomina Parentum.
854	Mary	Magrath	17	Januarii	Michael McGrath et Ellen Egan
855	Elizabeth	Buckley	18	"	John Buckley et Anne Regan
856	Elizabeth	Regan	18	"	William Regan et Julia Ahorne
857	Alice	O'Sullivan	8	"	David O'Sullivan et Eliza Keating
858	John	Russell	18	"	Edward Russell et Ellen Murfaley
859	Henry George	Harper	13	"	William M. Harper et Dorah Emilia Cox
860	Thomas	Potter	21	"	Simon Potter et Brigid Callaghan
861	Michael	Horgan	20	"	Daniel Horgan et Mary Cremerty

Fig. 5.3 Baptismal Register of South Parish, Cork of 1879 showing a pro-forma register with columns for various items of relevant information. Only part of the register is shown - other information provided includes residence, name of priest etc.

practices between different dioceses can be shown to be the directions issued by the Irish Bishops. For instance, in 1808 the Bishops of Munster issued regulations for their clergy which stated:

> "It being of extreme importance that ostensible registers of baptism and marriage be regularly kept, by every parish priest, in legible handwriting and due form, our parish priests are hereby required *sub poena suspensionis* to keep the same in their respective parishes and to insert, or to have inserted the baptism and marriage of their parishioners   as the Council of Trent requires. They must for this purpose provide, at least one large well-bound, blank book, of folio or quarto size capable of containing the baptisms and marriages of many years. No other records are to be kept in that book".

These instructions were not fulfilled by a large proportion of the Munster clergy. It is noteworthy that no reference is made by the Munster Bishops to the keeping of death records, whereas Plunkett in Meath was insisting on death records 30 years before.

The practicalities of record-keeping are best illustrated by the books which do survive and the type of detail they contain.   Until the latter half of the 19th century, the books in which the records are entered generally have neither lines nor columns (i.e they are the 'blank books' referred to above).   In the 1860's pro-forma registers, ie customised books with detailed printed columns and headings seem to have become more commonly used.

The records are written in either English or Latin in handwriting which varies from copperplate clarity to illegibility. The ink has faded in some records, damage to the edges of the volumes has affected the peripheral records in some cases and more serious damage has mutilated other records.

Apart from the date, the minimum details usually provided are;

Baptism:	Child, parents and godparents names
Marriage:	Names of couple and witnesses.
Burial:	Name of person interred

In some cases the residence (usually the townland or street name) is given, and rarely an occupation may be stated. There are also a variety of other annotations used to describe the person or their condition e.g "vagrant", "stranger" etc can occasionally be found. Not so uncommon is the annotation "illegitimate" or even "Bastard" on baptismal records.

Some of the abbreviations commonly used in the records are given in Table 5.2.

In some parishes it is clear from the handwriting that the records have been compiled by several priests. This often creates a confusion of dates and record types within the one record-book. It would appear from this that these records were periodically transcribed from the priests' notes into the main register. The practicalities of performing their duties (see next section) would suggest that this must have been a usual practise in many rural parishes.

Having considered the record books, it is useful to look at the way in which the records of the different events were compiled. Since all of the rites of passage are major family occasions, the compilation of church records is affected by the customs surrounding these events, as well as the church's efforts to record the relevant details.

The factors affecting each of the "rites of passage" are discussed below.

In deciphering Latin records a rudimentary knowledge of Latin is an obvious advantage. Although many of the Latin name forms are easily decipherable (Johannis or Joannis for John; Petrus for Peter; Henricius for Henry; Michaelis for Michael; Anna for Ann; Brigida for Bridget; Honora for Honor etc), others are less obvious (Jacobus for James; Guillielmus for William etc). A useful rule of thumb is that the ending -am indicates a female and "-um" or "-em" a male. Difficulty often arises in distinguishing names in the accusative case (e.g. Johannem for John, or Johannam for Johanna) or the genitive case (e.g. Johannis for John and Johannae or Johanne for Johanna).).

If events which are thought to have occurred are not recorded in the church registers, there are several possibilities which may explain the situation. Firstly, remoteness of the family's residence may have caused the event not to be recorded. Another possibility is the failing of the priest who, it must be remembered, worked in very bad conditions in many parishes. There is also the possibility that the priests may have demanded a fee for the sacrament which the family could not afford. There is substantial evidence to show that many priests insisted on payment of a fee for baptism and, more particularly, marriage. This question of clerical avarice has been well documented and was obviously of concern to the church *(4)*. The existence of the problem is clear from the following newspaper notice *(5)*.

> "...We earnestly desire you to be as little burdensome to the people under your care as you possibly can...... and we strictly enjoin that no clergyman under our care be so meanly mercenary as to demand anything for the administering of sacraments, but having performed the sacred functions of their ministry then gratefully accept the dues conformable to the regulations of the prelates."

That such admonitions were being placed in the public press is an indication that the problem existed and that it was necessary to show the public that it was being addressed.

One major problem facing the family historian is to determine whether the starting date of the records is also the date on which the church was built. If it is found that the records do not start early enough for research purposes, the two possibilities which exist are (a) that the church existed but no records were kept, or (b) that the church did not exist and the family of interest either attended a neighbouring church, or were ministered to by a priest operating without a church. Unfortunately there is no comprehensive list of the dates of construction of churches. Useful references in this regard are local parish histories. Another useful general reference is Samuel Lewis' "Topographical Dictionary of Ireland" *(6)*. This describes each civil parish in the country and for most it gives an indication of the Catholic parish which served the area, and the location of chapels. It therefore provides a general guide as to whether a church existed at that time, and also of the location of the chapels. The latter is important in many parishes since, even when the funds for construction of a church were available, in many cases it was not possible to obtain a site which was central to the parish. Thus some parishioners must have been at considerable distances from their churches.

A further problem is to establish which Catholic parish might have been attended by a resident of a particular townland, parish or street. There are several guides which correlate RC parishes and civil parishes. These include Ryan *(7)* and Mitchell *(8)*.

5.5 Baptismal Records

Baptism is the most recorded event in church records since most dioceses did not maintain death records and not everyone married (at all, or before emigrating). For doctrinal reasons children were baptised as soon as possible after birth. However, in many rural parishes access to a church, or even a priest, was often not possible immediately after birth. A description of rural parishes of the early 19th century is provided in the "visitation" or inspection reports of various bishops.

TABLE 5.2

Abbreviations and Terms Commonly Used in Catholic Church Records

Bapt.	Baptised
conj.	"conjunxi": ie joined in marriage
coram	in the presence of
cum dispens-atione in bannis	With dispensation by Banns. (see p.126)
Derelictus	Abandoned i.e abandoned child
de.	"of" usually denoting a person as being "of" a particular place or a child as being "of" a parent
Dau.	daughter
et	and
Filia	daughter of (parent's name)
Filius	son of (parent's name)
fil.leg.	"Filius;/Filia legitimus/a"Legitimate son/daughter
ignotes parentibus	parents unknown
Gemini	Twins
Illeg	Illegitimate
in tertio/ quattuor etc consanguineo	Where the bride or groom were closely related, dispensation was needed to allow them to marry. The degree of relationship was stated in the dispensation, eg "tertio consanguineo" means that the couple were first cousins; "quattor consanguineo" that they were second cousins etc.
Patrini	A term occasionally used for Sponsors
Peregrini	Travellers
Sp.	"Sponsoribus" ie the Sponsors or Godparents
Ss. or Sps.	Sponsors i.e Godparents
Sub Conditione	A child considered to be in danger of death, or apparently dead, could be baptised by the mother or other person. This child was subsequently also baptised by the priest "sub conditione" or "on condition" that the earlier emergency administration of the baptism had not been performed correctly. This annotation suggests that the child was in poor health at birth but had survived.
Test.	"Testibus;" or Testator ie Witness
Ws.	Witness(es) (in the case of a marriage)

These show that most rural priests had horses and that a good deal of their work required them to visit their parishioners and administer the sacraments. Access to a priest for many parishioners must, of neccessity, have been only occasional and the keeping of records by the priests serving such parishioners must have been difficult. Baptism by the mother (ie *sub conditione see Table 5.2)* was allowable where the child was in danger of death and no priest was available.

It is not entirely clear where baptisms were usually performed. Until the mid-nineteenth century the use of baptismal fonts was not general and descriptions of churches of this period rarely mention baptismal fonts. There was thus no practical reason to attend the church even if one were available and accessible. In areas where churches did not exist it must have been in the home or in the priest's house. However, as with virtually all other church activities, the practices varied widely between dioceses and regions. For instance a newspaper notice from the Bishop of Cloyne and Ross in 1786 *(5)* states that "Christenings are generally performed at the chapel or the priest's house".

The register of the Parish of St. Nicholas Without, Dublin, contains statistics of the numbers of baptisms performed in homes and the church in every year from 1828 to 1851. This shows a gradual move towards church baptisms. In 1828 there were 999 baptisms of which 431 were at home and the remainder in the church. By 1851, when there were 1151 baptisms, only 139 were performed in the home. In general it would seem that as the availability of churches increased, the ceremony moved to the church. It was not until 1850 that the Synod of Thurles recommended that baptisms be performed in church. When this recommendation was communicated to Rome for verification, it was made mandatory. From then on it became the normal practice and undoubtedly this change assisted in the orderly maintenance of records.

Godparents are invariably recorded for baptisms. The godparents of Catholic children were generally chosen so as to strengthen family ties and are frequently aunts, uncles or older cousins. Prior to the mid-17th century each child would have had many godparents, many of whom were only children themselves. In the early 17th century several decrees were issued to limit the number of godparents (to one or at most two which could be either male or female, or two males). It is not uncommon to find two males or two females recorded as "godparents". The practice of children becoming god-parents; was stopped by a decree that they must be well-instructed in the religion and should also be of an older generation.

Children were almost always baptised with only one personal name, and this was the practice until well into the twentieth century. Ancestor-hunters outside Ireland will often quote a second name for a child. There are several possibilities for the origin of this name, but they are outside the scope of this article. The usual pattern of naming was that the first son was named after the paternal grandfather, the second after the father and the third after the maternal grandfather. Successive daughters were named after the maternal grandmother, the mother and the paternal grandmother respectively. There are obviously variations to this pattern, for instance if a child, or a close relative, died it was not uncommon for the next-born child of the same sex to be given the same name. In many cases it is clear from the record that a child has been named after a god-parent. Nevertheless, the above naming pattern is a very useful rule of thumb.

5.6 *Marriage Records*

The preferred times of the year for Catholic marriages were the autumn and spring months. Marriage during Advent (the four weeks before Christmas) and Lent (the forty days before Easter) was not allowed without a special dispensation from the church. A popular time was therefore just before Lent, ie during February and early March. The other period in which many marriages occurred was September to October.

A much-noted feature of Irish marriage was the practice of marrying within social class. Thus, by and large, labourers sons tended to marry labourers daughters, large farmers daughters to marry large farmers and so on. This was ensured by the dowry system, whereby the family of the groom would expect the bride to bring with her a dowry suited to her groom's status. Many, if not most, marriages among more prosperous families were arranged through matchmakers who ensured that the couple were socially suited. Another feature of Irish marriage was that among the poorer classes marriage tended to occur at an early age, while the more prosperous usually married later. A full account of the social history of Irish marriage is given by Cosgrove *(10)*.

Like baptism, marriage was generally celebrated in the home, for all the reasons previously stated. As for baptisms, the ceremony gradually moved to the priest's house, and then to the church as these facilities became available. In 1850 the Synod of Thurles made it mandatory for marriage to be performed in church unless there was some grave reason to do otherwise. Priests are invariably in attendance at these marriages and there is considerable evidence that a large part of the

Married in the South Parish
1810.

June 21. Eugene McCarthy to Judith Reilly = Lr. Barry's = B.D.   Eugene McCarthy
    Witnesses, Thomas Reilly & Margaret Callanan ... Thos Barry, Vicar   Judith Reilly

    21. Cornelius Sweeny to Margaret Riordan . B.D.   Cornelius Sweeny
    Witnesses, William Riordan & John Donovan ... T. Barry   Margaret Riordan

    21. Denis McCarthy to Joanna Kane . B.D.   Denis McCarthy
    Witnesses, Patrick Casey & Timothy Callaghan ... T. Barry   Joanna Kane

    24. Denis Tuomey to Catherine Forrest = Penrolies Cross = B.D.   Denis Tuomey
    Witnesses, Jane Tuomey & Mary Forrest ... Patk Cremen, Vicar   Catherine Forrest

    30. Jeremiah Hayes to Mary McCarthy = Quaker Road = B.D.   Jeremiah Hayes
    Witnesses, Denis Connell & Margaret McCarthy ... T. Barry   Mary McCarthy

    30. John Pollard to Mary Magrath = Gallows Green = B.D.   John Pollard
    Witnesses, Timothy Moriarty & Joanna Magrath ... T. Barry   Mary Magrath

July 1. Daniel Murphy to Catherine Wagner = Mayole Road = B.D.   Daniel Murphy
    Witnesses, Patrick Driscoll & Henry Henright ... T. Barry   Catherine Wagner

    4. Denis Mehegan to Ellen Desmond = Quarry = B.D.   Denis Mehegan
    Witnesses, Timothy Horagan & Joanna Desmond ... T. Barry   Ellen Desmond

    4. John Burke to Honora Heaphy = Rutland Street = B.D.   John Burke
    Witnesses, John Cullinane & Charles Donovan ... T. Barry   Honora Heaphy

    8. Timothy Mullins to Ellen Callaghan = Barrack Street = B.D.   Timothy Mullins
    Witnesses, John Callaghan & Jeremiah Murphy ... T. Barry   Ellen Callaghan

    8. Eugene Sullivan to Mary Ring = Nicholas Church Lane = B.D.   Eugene Sullivan
    Witnesses, Bartholomew Ahern & Eugene Sullivan ... T. Barry   Mary Ring

    10. Thomas Horagan to Ellen Callaghan . B.D.   Thomas Horagan
    Witnesses, George James Drinan & Catherine Callanan ... T. Barry   Ellen Callaghan

    12. Daniel Sullivan to Ellen Brien . B.D.   Daniel Sullivan
    Witnesses, Daniel Brien & Anne Sullivan ... T. Barry   Ellen Brien

    14. Thomas Hurly to Joanna Murphy = Glasheen = B.D.   Thomas Hurly
    Witnesses, Daniel Leary & Denis Murphy ... T. Barry   Joanna Murphy

    15. John Clifford to Elizabeth Connor . B.D.   John Clifford
    Witnesses, William Clifford & Michael Connor ... T. Barry   Elizabeth Connor

    16. Maurice Walsh to Margaret Duggan . B.D.   Maurice Walsh
    Witnesses, William Donovan & Mary Sullivan ... P. Cremen   Margaret Duggan

    17. John Baker to Anne Baker. Dispensed in 2° & 2° Consang. grad   John Baker
    Witnesses, Philip Reilly & Honora O'Leary ... T. Barry   Anne Baker

    17. James Higgins to Ellen Harrington . B.D.   James Higgins
    Witnesses, John Higgins & John Harrington ... P. Cremen   Ellen Harrington

    21. Maurice Dinneen to Judith Kieffe . B.D.   Maurice Dinneen
    Witnesses, Maurice Dinneen & Elizabeth Kieffe ... P. Cremen   Judith Kieffe

Fig. 5.4   *Records of Marriages conducted at the St. Finbar's South Parish, Cork in 1810*

priest's income came from the fee received at weddings. This was particularly so in the southern counties. Indeed, the major reason for the Synod's ban on marriages in private houses was because of the abuses that had developed in connection with the practice. In particular, it had become customary for a collection to be made for the priest at these occasions and these collections often yielded considerable sums. In consequence some priests came to regard such collections as a right and would not officiate unless the marriage took place at an occasion where a collection was possible, or where an equivalent sum was paid *(9)*.

In 1786 the marriage fee recommended by the bishops was 7 shillings and sixpence. In 1808 an increase to one guinea (21 shillings) was agreed by the Munster bishops who noted "...how justly a laborious and zealous clergy are entitled to a proper support from those to whom they increasingly minister in all spiritual things." In notifying the clergy of the increase in marriage fee, the bishops felt the need to impose a penalty of suspension on any priest demanding more than this and also to direct that the clergy should accept from the poor a "half guinea or less, when offered." Significantly, they continue...."there is surely every reason to hope that on those occasions no Roman Catholic clergyman will refuse his ministry"

In addition to the priest's fee, a fee was legally due also to the minister of the Church of Ireland. Before marriage it was legally required that the Banns be read, i.e that the intention of the couple to marry was read out or otherwise published so that any obstruction to the marriage could be notified. The fee to the minister was technically to obtain a dispensation from the banns. This was because their publication, in some areas at least, had come to be regarded as an indication of the poverty of the couple or simply as a unwonted invasion of their privacy. Most couples in such areas therefore strove to pay this dispensation fee. An indication of the dislike of the banns can be judged from an article in the Dublin Morning Post of 8 Jan 1824 which stated " The first marriage by Banns in this neighbourhood for many years took place at Blessington on the First of January.....Many people who cannot procure a licence preferring to be married by unauthorised clergymen rather than submit to have banns published". The question of these unauthorised clergymen, or couple-beggars, is further discussed below.

Although dispensation was usually readily given, priests were absolutely required by their bishops to read the Banns in certain cases where there was legitimate doubt about the marital status of one of the parties. These included marriages which involved strangers to the

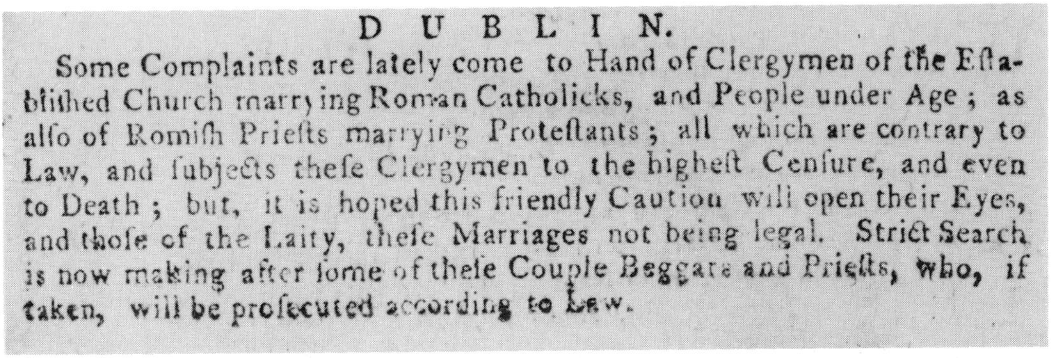

D U B L I N.

Some Complaints are lately come to Hand of Clergymen of the Eftablifhed Church marrying Roman Catholicks, and People under Age ; as alfo of Romifh Priefts marrying Proteftants ; all which are contrary to Law, and fubjects thefe Clergymen to the higheft Cenfure, and even to Death ; but, it is hoped this friendly Caution will open their Eyes, and thofe of the Laity, thefe Marriages not being legal. Strict Search is now making after fome of thefe Couple Beggars and Priefts, who, if taken, will be profecuted according to Law.

Fig 5.5. *A "friendly caution" against the activities of couple-beggars from Faulkner's Dublin Journal of 17 Jan 1764.*

parish, and marriages of other persons who had no certain place of abode and also of Catholic military. In the latter case it was also required that a certificate of the freedom of the soldier or officer to marry should be obtained from the commanding officer.

The fee to the Church of Ireland minister was considerable, given the incomes of the time. The Marriage Register of Mullingar from 1738 onward contains references to the amount paid to the Church of Ireland minister. This varied from 2s 8d to 4s 6d at a period when a day-labourers wages were 6d per day. This was in addition to the priest's marriage fee.

Unlike England, there was no legislation which required that marriages should take place in the Established Church. The Catholic authorities seem to have been careful not to provoke the establishment of such legislation by objecting too strongly to the payment of the fee to the Church of Ireland minister.

The significance of these fees to the family historian is that they may have contributed to the apparently high level of runaway marriages and elopements which seem to have occurred in Ireland. Although runaway marriages would also have occurred for the usual romantic reasons, for poor people the high fees exacted by some priests and ministers may have been a factor.

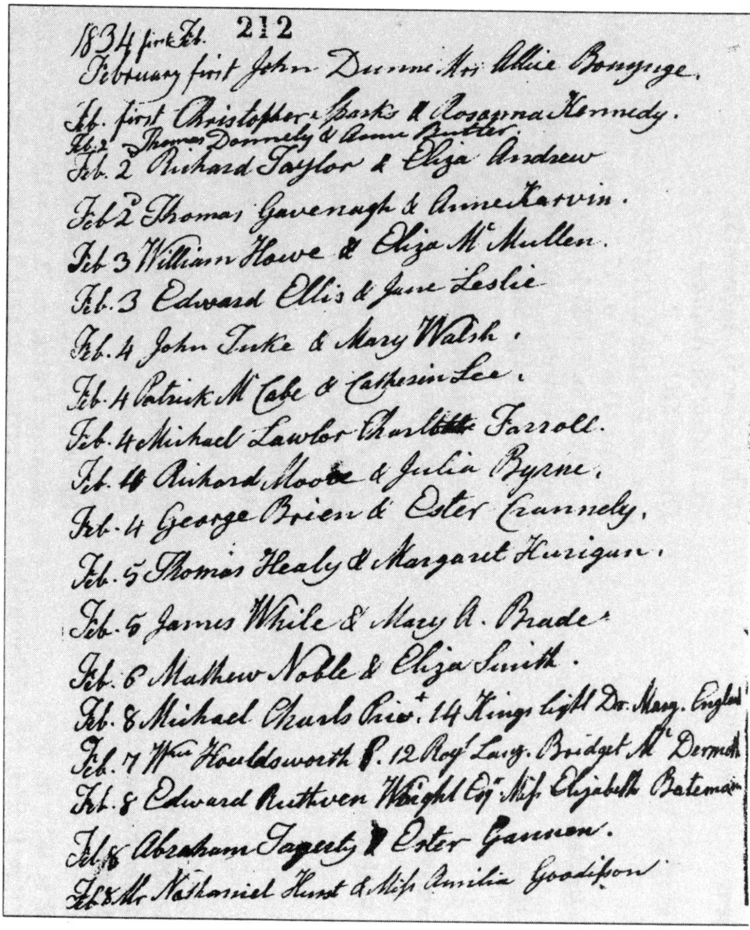
1834 first Feb. 212
February first John Dunne & Mrs Allice Bonynge.
Feb. first Christopher Sparks & Rosanna Kennedy.
Feb. 2 Thomas Donnelly & Anne Butler
Feb. 2 Richard Taylor & Eliza Andrew
Feb 2 Thomas Gavenagh & Anne Karvin.
Feb 3 William Howe & Eliza McMullen.
Feb. 3 Edward Ellis & Jane Leslie
Feb. 4 John Tuke & Mary Walsh.
Feb. 4 Patrick McCabe & Catherine Lee.
Feb. 4 Michael Lawlor Charlotte Farrell.
Feb. 4 Richard Moore & Julia Byrne.
Feb. 4 George Brien & Ester Crannely.
Feb. 5 Thomas Healy & Margaret Hurigan.
Feb. 5 James White & Mary A. Brade.
Feb. 6 Mathew Noble & Eliza Smith.
Feb. 8 Michael Charls Price, 14 Kings light Dr. Mary England
Feb. 7 Wm Houldsworth P. 12 Roy Lang. Bridget McDermott
Feb. 8 Edward Ruthven Wright Esq. Miss Elizabeth Bateman
Feb. 8 Abraham Fagerty & Ester Gannon.
Feb. 8 Mr Nathaniel Hunt & Miss Amilia Goodison

Fig. 5.6 *An extract from the records of Feb. 1834 of the Dublin Lutheran Church showing marriages performed by Rev. J.G. Schulze*

As noted earlier, in the late 18th and early 19th century it is clear that many priests charged fees which must have been difficult for the people to pay, and militant action was taken by Catholic parishioners in some areas to limit the fees imposed. Finally the bishops were forced to impose restraint on the clergy in regard to fees and other payments-in-kind. Marriage fees were a particular source of agitation. In 1786, it is reported that the maximum fee for marriage in Munster was 7s 6d, at a time when the labourer's daily wage (when work was to be had) was only 6 pence (i.e the fee was more than two weeks of a subsistence wage). In addition the fee for dispensation from the Banns was a further 5 shillings. There are indications that at least some priests did not perform these sacraments for those who could not pay.

A further reason for runaway marriages is the universal one of family or clerical disapproval. Those who, for this reason, chose to elope were possibly married in other parishes, or by Couple-beggars or Tack-'ems. These were usually defrocked clerics, or persons posing as clerics, who performed marriages for a small fee. Many of these couple-beggars are reported to have conducted hundreds and even thousands of marriages and some even advertised their services in the newspapers. One of the notorious couple-beggars Samuel D'Assigny is reported to " have joined many thousands pairs in wedlock, although he was never in Holy Orders, yet wore a band and gown etc and so imposed on the credulous and hasty lovers" *(11)*. The attractions of the Couple-beggar were, the secrecy such a ceremony afforded to eloping couples etc the low cost; and the speed which resulted from the fact that no notice was required. Some eloped couples returned home after their marriage, their union safe by the very fact of their elopement. The usual practice of the church in these situations was a forced period of separation of the couple, followed by their "official" marriage in the church.

Despite the stern disapproval of the church, couple beggars were very widely used, particularly in urban areas. Their Catholic trade ended in 1827 when the church decided that Catholic marriages were invalid unless celebrated by a Catholic priest. Few records of any of their marriages survive, although some were kept, and some were even accepted in court as proof of legal marriage. A series of 28 registers from one group of couple-beggars were among the documents destroyed in the PRO fire of 1921*(11)*. This series alone was reported to have contained the records of " an estimated 30,000 marriages, of which, in most cases, no other record exists and all ranks and creeds seem to have taken advantage of this expeditious and generally inexpensive method of celebrating marriages" *(12)*.

One set of marriage records, of which a significant proportion seem to have involved runaway couples, is that of the Dublin Lutheran church of Minister Rev. J. G. Schulze. Records of the 4,000 unwitnessed marriages which he conducted are held at the Registrar General's Office. A significant proportion of these marriages are of Catholics.

> ## A Clergyman of the established Church, unprovided for,
>
> WHO never has been diſqualified by any eccleſiaſtical Cenſure from performing all prieſtly Functions, lives quite private and retired, where he is always to be ſeen, and will occaſionally attend at any Diſtance, by applying at his Houſe, No. 10, Paradiſe-Row.
>
> ## A Clergyman, and a Son of the Church.
>
> A CLERGYMAN, of the eſtabliſhed Church, out of Place, "*and not diſqualified to exerciſe any Eccleſiaſtical Function*;" no ſelf-intereſted Proſelyte emerged out of Obſcurity, and ſilenced for ————, but a Native of the Church (if the Expreſſion may be uſed) and, not long ago in Eminence, driven by a ſingular and cruel Misfortune, to take this Method of informing the Public, that if he be wanted, on a PARTICULAR OCCASION, may be found at No. 4, Tighe-ſtreet, formerly Gravel-walk.
>
> *Alas! That great Things ſhould be compared with ſmall.*

Fig. 5.7   *Advertisment from the Hibernian Journal of 6 Nov. 1780 for the services of clergymen or couple-beggars in Dublin.*

A particular mention should be made of the position in regard to marriages of Catholics with non-Catholics. The couple attempting such a union found themselves at the centre of a major conflict between church and state. From a legal viewpoint there was never an impediment to a marriage between two Catholics. Such a marriage was governed only by common law, and therefore required only consent of both parties before an approved witness. It could therefore be conducted by a Catholic priest. Marriages between Catholics and other denominations were also governed by common law until 1745, although there were severe penalties, including death, for any Catholic priest who officiated at such a marriage. The common law status of these mixed marriages was ended by a statute of 1871.

Catholic church law, however required the Catholic partner to marry in a Catholic church and also that there should be an undertaking that the children be brought up as Catholics. The Catholic church recognized mixed marriages up to 1827 when the Tridentine decree, that such marriages were generally void, came into force. This Decree was not observed in Ireland, or in several other countries. The Synod of Thurles in 1850 re-emphasised the church ruling and insisted that the children of the union must be raised as Catholics, and that the marriage must occur without sacred rites. No such ruling was made in England, however, and it would appear that after 1850 wealthier Catholics who wished to marry non-Catholics were marrying in England so as to avoid these conditions *(9)*. Accordingly the practise in England was altered to prevent this practice.

The significance of this for the family historian is that the marriage of a practicing Catholic partner may be recorded in Church of Ireland records, or in an English Catholic church for wealthier couples in the early 1850's. In many cases a couple who were married in the Church of Ireland subsequently went to the Catholic priest where a modified ceremony also took place. How, and if, such ceremonies were recorded by the Catholic priest is uncertain. Also relevant to the family historian is the fact that it was common in practice for the boy children of such a marriage to be brought up in their father's religion and the girls in their mothers.

5.7 Burial Records

The existence of burial records (or equivalent records of death e.g anointing etc) is very variable. A general survey of the burial records now available shows that only 29 parishes have burial records from the 18th century, mainly in Meath (9 parishes) and Westmeath (7 parishes). This was due to the actions of Bishop Plunkett described earlier. Only 214 Irish parishes have kept burial records at any stage up to 1880, as compared to 1042 parishes which maintained baptismal registers.

It is also noticeable that burial records were not consistently maintained by those parishes which began them. In many parishes burial records stop and restart (or stop and never restart) for periods which are independent of breaks in the other records. Some of the factors which affect these records are discussed later. However, it would appear that maintenance of burial records was mainly due to the conscientiousness of individual priests rather than to any parish or diocesan policy.

To fully understand the background to the compilation of burial

TABLE 5.3

Earliest date of burial records* in each province, and numbers of parishes which began burial records in the 18th century and in each decade from 1800-1870.

	Earliest Record	1700's	1800	1810	1820	1830	1840	1850	1860	1870	**Total**
Ulster	1805	-	3	2	6	13	16	16	8	2	**66**
Connaught	1770	1	-	2	-	-	2	-	-	1	6
Leinster	1741	25	8	12	22	12	6	6	6	1	98
Munster	1786	3	6	3	11	7	8	3	2	1	44
Total		**29**	**17**	**19**	**39**	**32**	**32**	**25**	**16**	**5**	**214**

*   *Note that many of these records have not been maintained consistently from their start date.*

records, it is useful to review the customs and legalities surrounding the burial of Irish Catholics and the internal and external church conflicts which affected these practices. It was the custom throughout Ireland that the dead were 'waked' i.e that the corpse was 'laid out' in their home and that the friends and neighbours would spend the night in the house mourning their loss and comforting the relatives. The long hours of the wake were occupied by an elaborate set of wake amusements, many of which were of ancient origin. These were mainly elaborate party-games involving role-playing by the participants and included eg mock-marriages and various kissing games (13).

Another feature of the wake was keening i.e a lamentation over the corpse in the form of a melodious wailing performed by women, who were often hired for the purpose. Several features of these wakes were the subject of continued censure by the church. The first was the keening, which was severely criticized by the church on the basis that such immoderate grief suggested that the souls of those persons would not rise again. The church also censured the wake amusements because of the lewd content of some of them, and also because of the mockery which was made of the priests and of church rites in some of the games. Synods of priests and bishops from the seventeenth to the present century censured against attendance at wakes, and against keening. The fact that these practices continued until this century is an indication of how deep-rooted these practices were in popular custom.

Among the penalties prescribed by these synods against keening and wakes was with-holding of the mass, and of attendance of the priest on the deceased. It is difficult at this remove to know how often this penalty was actually applied and how significantly it might have affected the records in those parishes which maintained them.

Another factor which is of relevance to the family historian, is the question of control and choice of graveyards. During the early 17th century, when the parish system was being established and priests were in short supply, the monastic orders took an active role in administering to the people in their locality. In consequence, monastic graveyards came to be used for local burials and there is much evidence to suggest that they were a preferred burial location of the local people. When the diocesan clergy began to establish parish graveyards, the local people were often presented with a choice of burial sites, and the monastic and diocesan clergy were involved in some unseemly wrangles over the rights to the funeral fee when the burial was at the monastic site.

The second area of conflict was that graveyards were, in civil law, the property of the established church and the local Church of Ireland minister was therefore entitled to a fee from burials. The burial was permitted but no Catholic service was technically allowed, although in practice it did occur. In the 1820's the Catholic church finally began to purchase its own graveyards and from that time specific Catholic graveyards existed.

Although the burial records may not exist, gravestone inscriptions are available from some graveyards. Ryan *(7)* lists the sources then available of graveyard inscriptions from each county. Family burial plots in such graveyards are an excellent source of genealogical information since families would often keep using them for generations after they had moved away from the area.

5.8 Other Records

Apart from birth, marriage and death records, there are occasionally other forms of record which are useful to the family historian. Parish registers will occasionally include records of individuals making payment of parish dues; receipt of contributions for certain causes (particularly building of churches); the entry of converts (ie baptism of adults) and other items. There is also diocesan archival material, much of which can be useful to family history and even more of it to local history. Useful items include petitions from parishioners to the dioceses for various favours, eg to retain, or remove, a priest; reports from priests or bishops on the conditions of parishes, etc. These archives are maintained by each Diocese but most are not indexed.

In some cases it can be useful to establish information about Catholic clergy. Many middle-class families had a son in the priesthood, and family folklore will often recall the existence of a brother or uncle as a priest. The existence of a nun in the family seems not to be recalled as frequently. Information on the lives of priests or nuns is sometimes available in Diocesan and Parish magazines, and on gravestones. Consequently, it may be more productive to seek information about the family by researching the priest's life than by looking for records on his secular kinfolk. The Irish Catholic Directory, published annually from 1836, lists all of the Diocesan priests in the country, as well as the parishes in which they served.

Another useful source is "Maynooth Students & Ordinations Index" *(14)*. This lists all of the students who entered this seminary during the first 100 years of its existence, together with their date of entry, the diocese from which they came, and their date of ordination (if any). This, together with the Catholic Directory, can reveal the entire career of a priest, and identify the parishes in which further research may reveal specific family information about the priest and his family.

A further useful source of information about Catholics is newspapers. The unrest of the 18th and early 19th century resulted in many groups of Catholics publishing petitions, pledges of loyalty etc in their local newspapers. In addition there are newspaper listings of persons contributing to various Catholic causes or charities. A useful index of these notices is given in "Catholics & Catholicism in the 18th Century Press" *(15)*. These notices are of limited usefulness for family research since they will generally do little more than place a person in a specific area at a particular time. Relationships to others is rarely given.

However, as in all family history, a careful use of all such local sources can build up a picture of local conditions and lead to the discovery of other sources of more direct relevance to the history of a family.

5.9 *Availability of Catholic Church Records*

Parish records are the property of the church, and more particularly of the diocese within which they were compiled. Access to the records within each diocese is controlled by the Bishop or parish priest. The general attitude of the Catholic Bishops to the use of parish registers is that the records are not public documents but private records to which the local bishop holds copyright. However, they are willing to make them available to "bona-fide researchers" *(16)*. Even access to records which have been microfilmed and are retained in public archives are subject to the continuing permission of the Bishop. This permission has, in several cases, been withdrawn when the Bishop considers that the conditions imposed have not been complied with.

The Catholic Bishops fully cooperated with the National Library in the microfilming of the records during the 1950's. They have also agreed to, and cooperated with, the current project to index these records of Ireland. This is being coordinated by the Irish Genealogical Project, and carried out by Heritage Centres in participating counties. During the early 1980's the Genealogical Library of the Church of Jesus Christ of Latter-Day Saints (the LDS Library) offered to microfilm all of the records again and had started to do so but a decision was made by the Irish church not to allow this to continue *(16)*. Many of the archive records of the church are not available for access due to their confidential nature. However parish records have been made available.
The birth, death and marriage records of the Catholic church are available in several formats and locations. Briefly there are the original records, microfilms of these records, and (for some counties and years) indices of the records.

The Original registers are almost all held in the parish in which they originated and can be examined there by permission of the local priest. However, since the church has made these records available for microfilming and, in many cases, for indexing, some priests will take the understandable view that researchers should consult these copies rather than seek access to the originals. For this reason, written requests to a parish priest for a search of their records will often remain unanswered. Many priests are, of course, very helpful to researchers, but in general it is perhaps more considerate, and effective, if the records in Heritage Centres (see below) or other archives are accessed rather than the originals.

Microfilm copies of the Catholic church records were made by the National Library in the 1950's to ensure the preservation of the records as a valuable social record. However not all of the records were microfilmed and many of those which were filmed are in poor condition. The records were microfilmed up to the date 1880. This cut-off date was chosen "partly to avoid problems over confidential information and partly because government records from that time are very adequate" *(17).* The National Library's policy is to make all of the records available to researchers, but it must also respect the wishes of individual parish priests and bishops, who retain copyright. Some bishops have already placed restrictions on access to the National Library microfilms and there is continuing uncertainty as to what might happen when the Heritage Centres, which are currently indexing the records, begin to offer a complete service. At this stage, it is felt, there may be pressure on the bishops to restrict access to the microfilmed records in other archives. The Irish Catholic church has no apparent intention of establishing any general policy in regard to access to records. Individual bishops will continue to exercise their individual copyright to the records of their respective dioceses.

The Genealogical Library of the Church of Jesus Christ of Latter-Day Saints (the LDS Library), based in Salt Lake City, Utah, USA has a large collection of genealogical materials acquired " to assist individuals and their designated representatives in furthering personal family history research" *(18).* The LDS Library have copies of some of the microfilms made by the National Library of Ireland. All of the microfilmed Irish Catholic church records are available for research at the LDS Library except those of the Diocese of Limerick which are not available by directive of the Bishop of Limerick. The Limerick Diocese records are however accessible at the National Library and also at the Regional Archive Office, The Granary, Limerick where they are under the care of the Regional Archivist, Dr Chris O'Mahoney.

Indices to Parish Records are the most significant recent development in regard to use of the Catholic church records by family researchers. The process of indexing is being coordinated by the Irish Genealogical Project with the aid of funding from the State and from the International Fund for Ireland. The object of this project is to index the church and other records of each county and to offer a genealogical research service based on the resulting database. In practice this involves developing a cooperative network of the centres which had already begun indexing in certain counties, and encouraging their establishment in other counties. As might be expected the progress in the different counties varies considerably. Some counties, eg Armagh, Sligo and Clare, have completed the indexing of church records (although not necessarily on computer) while others have not even begun. For further information on this project and the services offered contact the Irish Genealogical Project, 1 Clarinda Park North, Dun Laoghaire, Dublin.

In conclusion, the records of the Catholic church are a major resource for Irish genealogical and social research.   However, like the families whose lives they record, they have been subjected to the forces of Irish history.   Consequently they are not as plentiful as researchers might hope, nor are the surviving records as detailed and accurate as might be desirable. Nevertheless, for certain periods of Irish history they are the only documents to record the existence of millions of Irish people. Understanding their history and the background to their compilation may therefore be useful in making best use of this incomparable resource.

REFERENCES

(1) *Kevin Whelan.*   **The Regional Impact of Irish Catholicism 1700-1850. in   Common Ground; Essays on the Historical Geography of Ireland.** pp253-277. Cork 1988.

(2) *Corish, Patrick J.*   **The Irish Catholic Experience - A Historical Survey.** Dublin 1985.

(3) *Cogan, Anthony.* **Ecclesiastical History of the Diocese of Meath;**, 3 Vols. Dublin 1862-1870.

(4) *Larkin, Emmet.* **The Problem of Irish Clerical Avarice in the Nineteenth Century.** Eire-Ireland, Fall 1989, pp 33-41

(5) **Dublin Evening Post** of 28 Sept. 1786 - newspaper notice inserted by the Rev. Matt McKenna, the Bishop of Cloyne and Ross.

(6) *Samuel Lewis.* **Topographical Dictionary of Ireland**, 2 Vols. London, 1839.

(7) *Ryan, James G.*   **Irish Records - Sources for Family and Local History.** Salt Lake City, 1988

(8) *Mitchell, B.* **A Guide to Irish Parish Registers,** Baltimore 1988.

(9) *Barry, P.C.* **The Legislation of the Synod of Thurles, 1850.** Ir. Theol. Quart. XXVI (1959).

(10) *Cosgrove*, Art (Ed.). **Marriage in Ireland.** Dublin 1985.

(11) **Report of the Deputy Keeper of Public Records of Ireland,** No.33, p. 7.

(12) **Report by Mr Herbert Wood on certain registers of irregular marriages celebrated by unlicensed clergymen, known as couple-beggars. Report of the Deputy Keeper of Public Records of Ireland;,** No.34 Appendix II.

(13) *Connolly*, S.J. **Priests and People in Pre-Famine Ireland 1780-1845.** Dublin 1982.

(14) *Hamell, Patrick J.* **Maynooth Students & Ordinations Index 1795-1982.** Maynooth, no date.

(15) *Brady, J.* (Ed.), **Catholics & Catholicism in the 18th Century Press.** Maynooth 1982.

(16) **Personal Communication from Bishop Michael Smith ,** Secretary of The Irish Episcopal Conference, June 1991.

(17) **Personal Communication from B. McKenna,** Keeper of Manuscripts, National Library of Ireland, August 1991.

(18) **Personal Communication from Paul F. Smart,** Supervisor of the British Reference Section, Genealogical Library, Salt Lake City.

6

METHODIST RECORDS IN IRELAND

Marion G. Kelly

6.1 Introduction

The investigation of church records relating to Irish Methodists requires some understanding of the complex interrelationships between the various groups which formed the Methodist Church in Ireland and also of the relationship between Methodism and the Church of Ireland or, occasionally, the Presbyterian church.

As a result of the spiritual awakening that ocurred under the leadership of Rev. John Wesley and Rev. Charles Wesley in eighteenth-century England, churches have emerged in the Methodist tradition over the past two centuries in ninety countries of the world. At the Sixteenth World Methodist Conference held in Singapore in 1992, 4000 delegates represented just under twenty five million baptised members, with more than fifty four million community members. Seven participants from Ireland represented around 60,000 Methodists, including full members and adherent or community members.

The beginning of Methodism in Ireland may be linked with the evangelical George Whitefield in 1738, but the clearest reference to the gathering of a Methodist Society, numbering 300 members, is to the work of Thomas Williams in Dublin in 1746. John Wesley, the co-founder of Methodism with his brother, Charles the hymn-writer, came to Ireland in 1747. John subsequently visited Ireland on twenty other occasions, establishing new Societies throughout the country. The original conception of John Wesley was that those who followed him should be a Society inside the Established Anglican church. As a clergyman he was strongly opposed to any separation from Anglicanism, hence the itinerant preachers were not recognised as clergymen. Methodists went to the parish church for the administration of Baptism and Holy Communiion. This position was maintained until after John Wesley's death in 1791.

The early Irish Methodists wished to continue as full members of the Established church, but there was little support in the Established Church for Methodist evangelistic 'enthusiasts' whose zeal made the clergy uncomfortable or outraged. For many who were enrolled in Methodist Societies there had been no previous connection with the Church of Ireland. Consequently, Methodists desired their own preachers to exercise the full functions of clergymen, especially in the Administration of the Sacraments. Conference received many petitions asking permission for the Administration by all Methodist preachers, to ease the work of those few Methodist preachers who were ordained within the Anglican community. In 1816 Conference granted this permission to some Circuits in the north of Ireland, thus loosening the connection with the Established church. The traditional loyalty of Irish Protestants to the Church of Ireland as 'the principal permanent support which the doctrines of the Reformation had in the island' led to a split between those who wished to retain the old idea of being a Society within the church, and those wishing to adopt the characteristics and functions of an independent church with its own ministry in charge.

From 1818, two separately constituted Methodist bodies, the Primitive Wesleyan Methodist, and the Wesleyan Methodist, Connexions existed side by side. By 1870 the Disestablishement of the Church of Ireland, and the continued emphasis on original Methodism as taught by John Wesley led eventually to the Union of 1878 which formed the Methodist Church in Ireland.

6.2 Four Methodisms, or more

Since 1878 the Methodist Church in Ireland can be considered as representing the main body of Methodists in the country. However, there have been periods when four clear Methodist groups were identified. These were:

1. The Wesleyan Methodist Connexion
2. The Primitive Wesleyan Methodist Connexion
3. Methodist New Connexion
4. Primitive Methodist Connexion

The Wesleyan Methodist Connexion effectively represents the original Methodist establishment in Ireland. In 1818, the Primitive Wesleyan Methodists had separated from them after a period of disagreement about the Administration of the Sacraments by preachers who were not ordained in the Church of Ireland. In 1878 these two groups re-united to form the Methodist Church in Ireland. . This union was eased by the disestablishment of the Church of Ireland. At that time the Wesleyan Methodists had 19,950 members, and the Primitive Wesleyan Methodists had 6,650 members, making a total for the Methodist church in Ireland of 26,600. The Terms of Union required " that in all official documents of the Uniting Conference the terms 'Wesleyan' and 'Primitive Wesleyan' be dropped and the term 'Methodist' alone be used". Since 1878 the Methodist Church in Ireland can be considered as being the main body of Methodists in the country.

The extent of the overlap in administrative structures between the two groups is evident from the sale of excess chapels which followed the union, and also from the extensive Revision of Circuits which was authorised in the minutes of the first conference of the united church in 1879. The records of many members who were previously Primitive Wesleyan Methodist are likely to be found in the Church of Ireland registers, as there was often dual membership of the Methodist Society and the Church of Ireland. There are also a few noted cases of dual membership with a Presbyterian Meeting House.

After the decision to come together, earlier problems regarding Rights of Burial required a legal statement on clarification of rights in churchyards or graveyards attached, or belonging, to the Church of Ireland.

The smaller groups of Methodists, ie the Methodist New Connexion and the Primitive Methodist Connexion were historically administered from England. Their records were therefore prepared as the records of the Mission Stations of various British circuits. In 1905 the administration of the Irish property and congregations of the Methodist New Connexion was transferred to Ireland. The main congregations of this connexion were at Salem, York Street in Belfast; Zion in Newtownards; Queens Parade, Bangor, Broomhedge and Priesthill, Co Down; and Ballyclare, Co. Antrim. In 1910 the administration of the Primitive Methodist church was also transferred from the British Conference to Ireland. The records of the New Connexion (pre-1905) and of Primitives (pre-1910) can be researched at the archives of their English parent bodies, which were eventually united in 1932. Their archives are located at The John Rylands University of Manchester, Manchester,

England M13 9PP. Further information is provided by Leary *(1)*.

Some fine remnants of local circuit records of these groups have also been traced eg those of Broomhedge and Priesthill published by Law *(2)*.

6.3 Structure of the Methodist Church in Ireland

In the Methodist church the members are enrolled in Classes, each class being under the pastoral care of a Leader.

The church is composed of courts, as follows:
The Classes in each locality are grouped into a Society, the administration of which is entrusted to a Leader's Meeting. One or more Societies in an area may form a Circuit, the administrative body of which is the Quarterly Meeting. The Circuits are grouped in accordance with the rules of conference into Districts, and the business of each district is administered by a District Synod. The governing body of the Methodist Church in Ireland (since 1878) is the Conference, which meets annually in June. The Vice-President of Conference is the President of the Methodist Church in Ireland, whose term of office commences on 1 July each year.

6.4 Duties of the Superintendent Minister

The care of records is specifically included among the duties of Superintendent Ministers, who are the senior leaders of each Circuit. The Manual of Laws of the Methodist church (for which see Jeffery *(3)*) specify duties of relevance to the compilation, and maintenance, of records. These include;

> Para 152 *(2)* To admit into, and exclude from, church membership, in conjunction with the Leader's meeting; to arrange for the quarterly visitation of the classes by himself or his colleagues; to keep lists of members received from or removed to other circuits; to forward the membership schedule to the Secretary of the Membership Bureau; to enter all necessary particulars in the Circuit Schedule book; to forward in due time to the proper officers of the district all such statistical information relating to his Circuit as may be required by rule.

> Para 152 *(11)*. To see that the Baptismal Register, the Circuit Schedule Book, the Furniture Book, the Circuit Register of Members and Classes, lists of families belonging to the

congregation with their names and addresses, lists of orphans on the circuit who are receiving grants from the Child Care Society, with all other books, lists or forms required to be kept, are duly and accurately filled, kept and presented to the appropriate authorities, or left for his successor, or otherwise dealt with as the regulations of the conference may require. The names of members of Society shall be entered in the membership register and Quarterly Class roll. The Membership Register and Quarterly Class Roll shall be submitted to the September and Spring Synods for examination and report.

From all of these records, those of most relevance to the family historian are:

Register of Members and classes: which provides the names and addresses of members, listed by "Class" and date of birth (if under 18). A separate listing is made of junior members. Some Societies maintain a Cradle Roll which records the name, date of birth and date of infant baptism.

Baptismal Register: *(see 6.6)*

Fig. 6.1 *A class ticket or Quarterly ticket issued to each member of a Methodist Class*

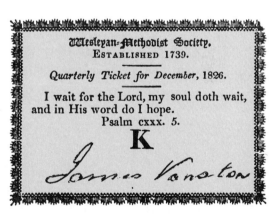

Wesleyan-Methodist Society.
ESTABLISHED 1739.

Quarterly Ticket for December, 1826.

I wait for the Lord, my soul doth wait, and in His word do I hope.
Psalm cxxx. 5.

K

James Vanston

Members leaving or joining the Circuit: Statistics on members leaving or joining a Circuit were maintained but only numbers, rather than names are listed.

Lists of families: These are listed by name and address.

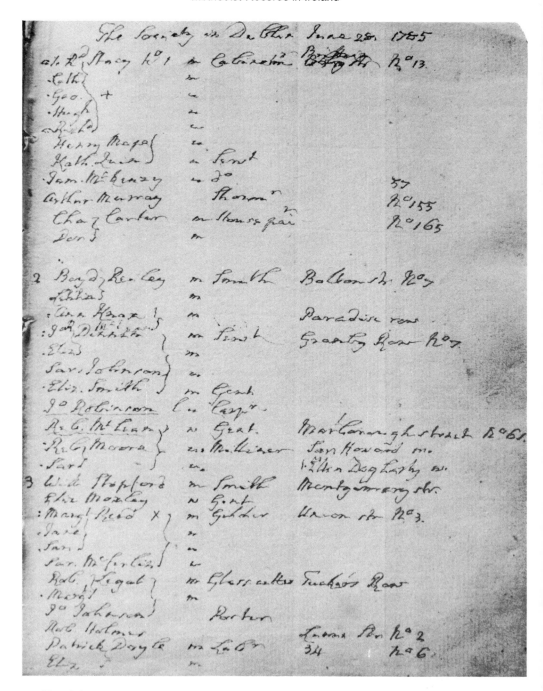

Fig. 6.2   *A page from the Dublin Class List of 1785 which was drawn up by John Wesley.*

6.5   Class Lists

As we have seen, local Methodist Societies are sub-divided into Classes for pastoral care. Since the Eighteenth century Class lists have formed an important part of Wesleyan information about members. They often showed the Leader's name, the place of meeting , and a record of class money contributions.   The Class money, which was initially one penny per week, was contributed towards the welfare of needy Society members.   Members also contributed quarterage money, which was contributed for the maintenance of the central Methodist administration.

Figure 6.1 shows an example of a class-ticket, and Fig. 6.2 of the Dublin class list of 1785. This was drawn up by the co-founder of Methodism, John Wesley, at the age of 82 years, and records the number of the class, the members' names, addresses and occupations. John Wesley's journal for 28 June 1785, which began for him at four in the morning, reads:

Tuesday 28
4 Prayed, Psa cxvi;   12 writ society

There are similar entries for the days following. Among the occupations noted are cabinet maker, smith, carpenter, glass cutter, printer, labourer, coachman, taylor, gentleman, hatter, stone cutter, milliner, gunsmith, goldsmith, victualler, cutler and hairdresser.   Another example of a class list, of Bluestone, Co. Armagh can be found in the recently published booklet by Caroline M. Jones *(4)*.

6.6 Baptismal Registers

Infant baptism has been generally observed throughout Methodist Societies.   Baptismal registers generally give details of the child's name, parents names and residence and (sometimes) occupation of the father, together with the dates of birth and baptism, and the signature of the preacher (see Fig. 6.3).   Some registers give only minimum details, eg dates of birth and baptism and officiating preacher's name. The registers are retained at Society or Circuit premises in accordance with the duties of Circuit Superintendent Ministers.   Present regulations require the safe keeping of a standard register, and no return to a central register is now required.

Baptism of adults occurred in the cases of converts to Methodism.   On John Wesley's journeys, he recorded in his Journal the occasions when

			13			

BAPTISMS solemnized in the Wesleyan-Methodist Chapels & Congregations Manorhamilton Circuit in the County of Leitrim, Cavan & Fermanagh _____ in the Year 1842 / 1843

When Baptized.	Child's Name, Son or Daughter.	Parents' Name.		Abode.	Child's Age when Baptized.	The Minister by whom the Ceremony was performed.
		Christian.	Surname.			
1842. Nov 23 No. 33.	Isabella, daughter of	Jas. & Mary	Crawford,	Moneygashel Co. Leitrim,	5 days,	Robt Bamford
Nov 26. No. 34.	Margret, daughter of	Simon & Mary	Elliott,	Moniculum Co. Leitrim,	5 weeks,	Robt Bamford
6th Jan 1843 No. 35.	Mary A. daughter of	Geo & Sarah	Gordon,	Killataslan Co. Fermanagh	7 weeks,	Robt Bamford
6th Jan. No. 36.	Mary, daughter of	Wm & Mary	Burch,	Cultin, Co. Fermanagh	2 months,	Robt Bamford

Fig. 6.3   A page from the Baptismal Register of the Wesleyan-Methodist chapel of Manorhamilton Circuit, Co. Leitrim, of 1842/3.

he was called on to baptise adults, for instance former Quakers or, in one instance, a former Jew. Some Irish Methodists like to claim an ancestor who was baptised by John Wesley.

The earliest baptismal registers have been preserved in stoutly bound volumes. A fine example is the Carrickfergus Circuit register which has been in continuous use since the early 19th century.

There is evidence to suggest that Wesleyan ministers were required to forward details of baptisms to a central register. A composite volume of entries at many Circuits throughout Ireland has been deposited at the PRONI and is available on microfilm (Ref. MIC 1E). This volume contains baptismal entries from 1817 to 1850. This manuscript has deceptively clear penmanship, but the details transcribed do not always correspond with the originals held at circuit level either in accuracy or completeness. This volume covers the whole of Ireland with the notable exception of Dublin and district. This would suggest that a sister volume was recorded but has not yet been traced. A transcription of the Baptismal registers of Dundalk (1837-1865) and Drogheda (1829-65) is given in an article by Turner *(5)*, which also includes a fine introduction to the baptismal practices of Methodist Societies.

6.7 Marriage Registers

Since state registration of marriages began in 1845, the standard registers of marriage have usually been retained on Circuit premises. Before this, there is no clear evidence for a standard procedure of recording marriages among Methodists. R.Lee Cole *(6)* states that 'it was in 1863 that Methodists were first given power to perform marriages in their churches". Marriages may also be found in other records. For instance in the Louth Baptismal registers *(5)* there are also four marriages recorded, and marriages (and burials) may also be recorded in class lists.

Finding the register may be difficult due to the closure of preaching houses and other changes. When a preaching house closed, the register was passed to the next circuit, and was sometimes renamed. It is therefore essential to know the composition of circuits in order to trace registers. The Minutes of Conference are a useful source of information for this purpose, since they list the stations of each methodist preacher by the name and number of their Circuit appointment. Unfortunately the official name of a circuit may not reveal all of the divisions, especially in areas where Methodists are

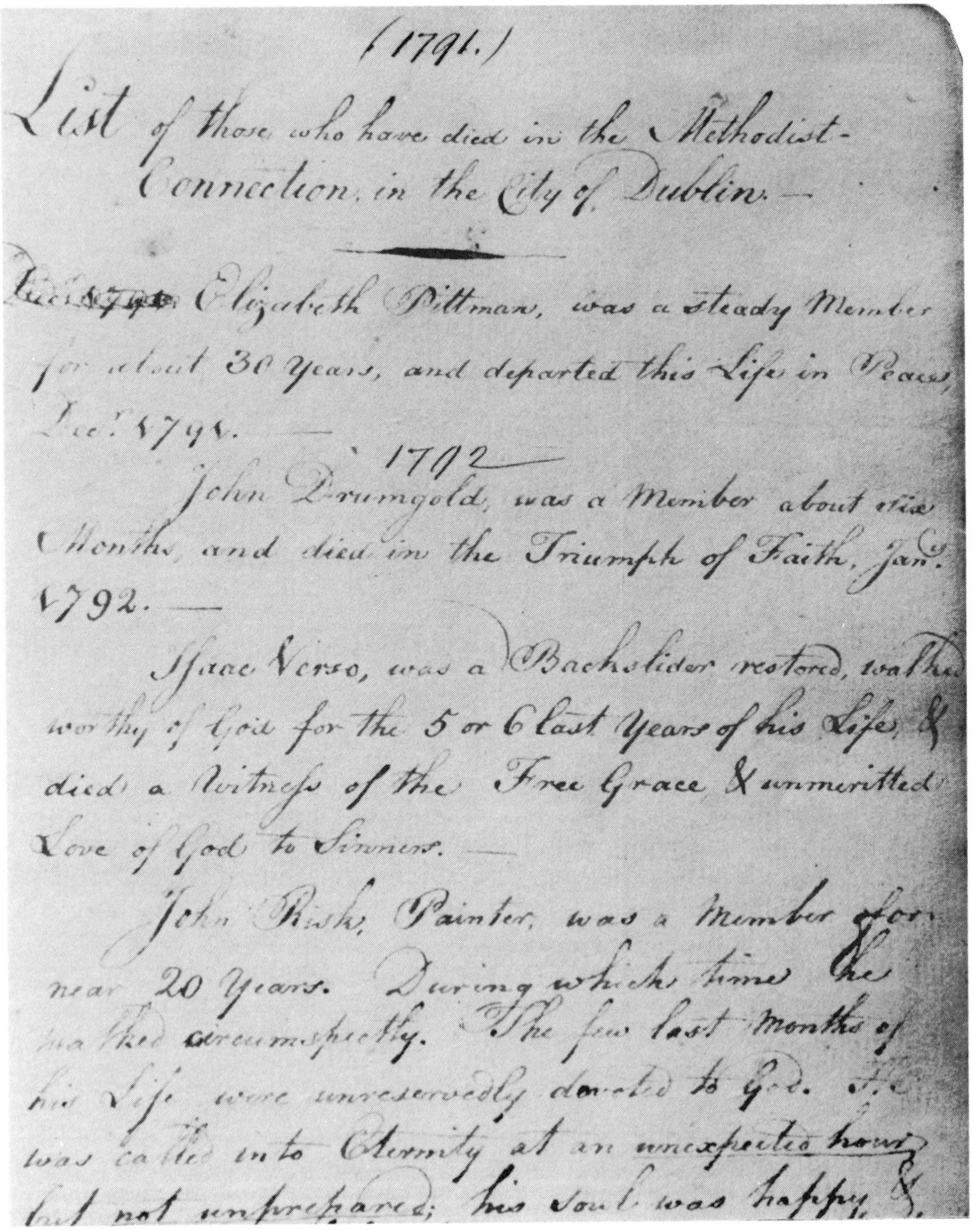

(1791.)

List of those who have died in the Methodist-Connection, in the City of Dublin. —

Elizabeth Pittman, was a steady Member for about 30 Years, and departed this Life in Peace, Dec.' 1791. —

1792

John Drumgold, was a Member about six Months, and died in the Triumph of Faith, Jan.' 1792. —

Isaac Verso, was a Backslider restored, walked worthy of God for the 5 or 6 last Years of his Life, & died a Witness of the Free Grace & unmeritted Love of God to Sinners. —

John Rush, Painter, was a Member for near 20 Years. During which time he walked circumspectly. The few last Months of his Life were unreservedly devoted to God. He was called into Eternity at an unexpected hour, but not unprepared; his Soul was happy &

Fig. 6.4   A "List of those who have died in the Methodist Connection in the City of Dublin" in 1791, - Bound in with the Dublin Class List of 1785 - see Fig. 6.2.

scattered over a wide area in small societies. More recent Minutes of Conference list each Society alphabetically, and by district number and Circuit number. A listing of Societies by District and Circuit number is given in Appendix 6.1. Minutes of Conference from 1752 have been printed and are available in Methodist archives. A limited number of the current Minutes of Conference can be purchased from the Methodist Bookroom, Aldersgate House, University Road, Belfast, Northern Ireland.

6.8 Burials, Deaths and Obituaries

There is no standard form of recording deaths or burials in Irish Methodism. Only a few early Methodist preaching houses had graveyards as part of their property. Members of Wesleyan families therefore used the local Church of Ireland parish graveyard, or less commonly the Presbyterian graveyard. Disputes arose between the Methodist and Church of Ireland Clergy about rights of Burial and these led to the 1868 Act on Burials in Ireland (31 and 32 of Victoria, cap 103). This legislation gave to Non-Conformists the right of burial in Parish graveyards, with such religious ceremonies as were customary among the parties concerned. However, after the Irish Church Act of 1869, misunderstandings arose which appeared to assume that the 1869 Act had repealed certain of the provisions of the 1868 Burials Act. In one case a Rector had declared that he could 'keep methodists and dissenters of all kinds, out of the graveyard, as the Church Act gave him power". A request was made in 1879 by the Methodist "Committee of Exigency" to the Representative Church Body of the Church of Ireland for a clarification of the authority of Church of Ireland clergy. The reply stated that "wherever a person, not a member of the Church of Ireland, has a right of burial in a churchyard, the Minister of the Church to which he belonged, has the right to perform the burial service.." .

In spite of this clarification, from time to time individual clergymen refused to allow the Methodist clergy to conduct graveside services, even ordering the gates to be locked, and refusing permission for graves to be opened. In 1893, the Lord Bishop of Ossory found it necessary to confirm in writing " the full and perfect legal right of the Methodist Minister to perform the service in Johnstown graveyard over a member of his congregation".

As many incumbents continued to be unaware of the law relating to the rights of Methodist clergy, calls were made for the provision of burial grounds where new places of worship were erected.   Methodist church buildings were therefore provided with small burial grounds whenever it was felt necessary. This is particularly evident in Co. Fermanagh and Co. Armagh. In Belfast the Ballymacarett Wesleyan burying ground was widely used from 1826 for almost a century. Regrettably, no register of burials can be traced and all of the gravestones were removed when the site was developed for commercial purposes. In County Fermanagh, the Sydare Methodist Cemetery has been extended several times and is the graveyard for the local community. Contrary to popular belief, there are many Methodist graveyards throughout the country, A comprehensive listing is not yet available.

Obituaries and Death Notices in Methodist publications are very variable in terms of the detail provided, apart from the spiritual attributes of the deceased. Obituaries of Methodist Ministers only are found in the Minutes of Conference, but notices of the laity are to be found in the general Methodist periodicals listed in Section 6.10. These notices are generally provided by the local Circuit Minister and vary widely in tone and content. Some list extensively the positions held within the church with short references to the immediate family, while others concentrate on the deceased's Methodist antecedants and the connections with other family groupings *(see Fig. 6.4)*.

6.9 Other Family History Sources

There are also other items which may prove of interest to those who wish to know more about their Methodist, or Methodist-associated, ancestors.

Conference Minutes and Journals: Conference minutes contain notes about items affecting the members of the society, including departures, arrivals, censures etc. The Journals will usually add further detail to items mentioned in the minutes. Subscription lists, such as the Jubilee Missionary Appeal provide some surprising details of families, and can be useful when the specific circuit, to which a family member belonged, is known. Local Building fund appeals depended for success on published lists of benefactors to 'encourage the others', even though such publicity is not in the mode of John Wesley who, in his lifetime gave away all his earnings. The report of the Chapel Fund Committee (1852) published the names of subscribers giving more than two shillings and sixpence. This practice was continued for several years but few lists can be traced.

Local Celebratory Histories: invariably include a chronological list of preachers who, as itinerants, may have been stationed for one year

788 *Obituary.*

daughter, who had been in a declining state for some time, would be established. But how unsearchable are the ways of Providence! In six months, from our removal, I was deprived of both: first witnessing the peaceful and happy death of my child, on the 10th of October, and that of my wife on the 8th of the succeeding month. A little while before her departure, she said, " I am going to launch into eternity, and I go without a doubt or fear. Unbelief is not permitted to assail me; I rest my entire confidence in Jesus, who died for sinners; there is no other ground for confidence." Thus in sure and certain hope of eternal life, she entered into the joy of her Lord, aged fifty-four years, leaving four daughters and a husband to deplore their loss.

DANIEL PEDLOW.

4. Died at New-Ross, Ireland, Nov. 12th, Michael M'Cormick, esq., aged seventy-eight years. Early piety, in all cases advantageous, was to Mr. M'Cormick a peculiar blessing. In him was united a temper naturally fierce and fearless, with a body of unusual stature and strength. Hence a controlling power, more efficient than mere education can supply, became necessary. This he met with in an early conversion. Being favoured with the ministry of the Rev. John Wesley and his fellow-labourers in Ireland, he was turned from darkness to light, and from the power of Satan unto God; and approving heartily of the discipline which he found amongst the Methodists, he became a member of their Society. Many were the changes of place and circumstance which marked his subsequent years; but never did he wholly lose the influence of that change in his character which took place on his conversion to God. Zeal for the cause of the Redeemer, unawed by shame or fear, was a disposition which never forsook him. Often has he risked his life in the protection of the early Preachers from popular insult, while those men of God were delivering their message, " in the streets and lanes of the city." Thus he rendered essential services to the cause he loved; for which indeed he was eminently qualified by an appearance the most commanding, (not a little heightened when attired in mili-

introducing the Preachers into new places, and extending to others the blessings of that Gospel, which he had found to be " the power of God unto Salvation." Upon retiring from the army, he commenced business in New-Ross, and was present in the memorable engagement of June 5th, 1798. On that day a host of twenty thousand rebels attacked the town; but after a desperate conflict they were repulsed by the King's troops under the command of General Johnson. In this action, Mr. M'Cormick displayed such heroic bravery as called forth the thanks of the General, to whom he acted as Aide-de-camp during the day, and procured for his name a conspicuous place in all the histories of that dreadful time. Indeed many are of opinion that to him, under Divine Providence, was greatly owing the victory of that day. Prior to his leaving the army, he had married, nor had he ever reason to regret his choice. Though Mrs. M'Cormick has been dead many years, the memorial of her piety has bidden defiance to the lapse of time: still her name lives in the hearts of many, as a woman in whom were displayed all the virtues of conjugal, parental, and social life, enriched by the beauties of Christian holiness. The loss of such a wife was a severe trial; and as Mr. M'Cormick was now extensively engaged in trade, and had the charge of a large family, the weight of his relative duties was much increased. In this sphere he moved with diligence and integrity. But it was in the close of life, that God, who is rich in mercy, was pleased most remarkably to bless his servant. During his latter years, he suffered much from injuries received in the service of his country; yet the language of complaint he rarely used. When I came into this Circuit in August, 1825, his health was visibly declining; but his soul appeared to be maturing in grace; for there was in his spirit a meekness, quite the reverse of his natural temper. When he perceived the rapid approach of death, he frequently charged his family to observe the strictest economy in his interment; ordering that the funeral should be perfectly plain: the money saved thereby, he directed to be given to the poor. I had the privilege of witnessing

Fig. 6.5 *Sample Obituary from Wesleyan-Methodist Magazine of December 1826 (see 6.10)*

only. Society and Circuit stewards, Sunday School teachers, organists, trustees and Class leaders are also commonly listed, as are Rolls of Honour, which name former members who served in various wars.

Stewards books: provide a back-up to membership rolls, and often give the names and addresses of pew-holders, the rents from which were an important source of revenue in preaching houses.

Some early Sunday School Registers have also survived.

Lists of Subscribers: Society expenditure is now met by weekly Freewill offerings. When this system was introduced in 1875 many societies listed the names of subscribers, and amounts subscribed, in their annual reports. These can be useful in researching the economic history of specific families.

Students & Staff of Methodist College: A rich source of information about the past students and staff of the Methodist College, Belfast was compiled by Paul Fry (7). This complements the work of Henderson (8).

6.10 Methodist Publications

Family records can also be found in many specifically Methodist publications, such as the 'Armenian Magazine' (1778 - 1797) and, more recently, the 'Methodist Recorder', journals which served Methodists in both Britain and Ireland.

An annual index to the death notices and biographical items appearing in the Armenian Magazine can usually be found bound with each year's issue. There is also a composite index for the years 1778 to 1839 which may be consulted at Wesley Historical Society (WHS) Irish Branch (see 11.4). However this does not cover the short run of the Dublin Edition of the magazine. The index is entitled:

"An Index to the Memoirs, Obituary Notices and Deaths together with the references to the local histories of Methodism as contained in the Armenian Magazine (1778- 1797), The Methodist Magazine (1798-1821) and the Wesleyan Methodist Magazine (1822-1839)"

An Irish Periodical - The Irish Evangelist - was published to communicate the Progress of the 1859 Evangelical revival, and was continued until 1883. This publication carried short notices of births, deaths and marriages. A card index of these was compiled by the Wesley Historical Society (WHS) - Irish Branch in 1984 and is available at their Library *(see 11.4).*

The 'Irish Christian Advocate' appeared as a weekly newspaper for Methodist families from 1883 until 1971. The items of important biographical interest and local history which received more than half a column print space have been indexed at the WHS Irish Branch. A monthly Methodist Newsletter began publication in 1974 and remains as a channel for similar material.

Among the interesting family research uses of the Irish Christian Advocate index has been the origins of the Physicist and Nobel Laureate Professor E.T.S. Walton. When the town of Dungarvan wished to honour Prof. Walton, who was the son of the local Methodist Minister, they were unsure of his specific birthplace. His birth notice in the Irish Christian Advocate revealed that he had been born in Epworth Cottage. The local committee was thereby able to identify and mark the site.

Magazines similar to the Armenian Magazine were also published by other Methodist Conferences in Britain. Irish Methodists associated with the Primitive Wesleyan Conference were served by a monthly magazine which was indexed yearly. This is the main source of information on this body and contains reports of the Annual conferences and the stations of the preachers, as well as obituaries and local society history. For details of British publications see Methodist Study Guide No IA *(9).*

6.11 Irish Archives containing Methodist Material

Methodist Archival Policy: Unlike the British Methodist Conference, the Irish Conference has not found it necessary to appoint a separate custodian and registrar responsible for the preservation and safe custody of Connexional documents. The system of Methodist Archives in Britain has been reviewed by the current British Connexional Archivist, William Leary *(1).*

The smaller scale of Irish Methodism does not, perhaps, warrant an equivalent system of Archivist and District Archivist. In practice, the Conference Safe, Dublin has been the designated repository for documents from circuits not provided with a suitable safe. The Statutory Trustees of the Methodist Church in Ireland, 1 Fountainville Avenue, Belfast BT9 6AN have accepted the responsibility for the custody of deeds and documents. The policy of the British conference is that all minute books and account books, when no longer needed for reference or the protection of confidence, should be deposited on a

AN ALPHABETICAL ARRANGEMENT

OF

THE WESLEYAN-METHODIST MINISTERS AND PREACHERS ON TRIAL

IN IRELAND.

ALLEY, GEORGE.

1852	Boyle	1
1853	Kilkenny	2
1855	Carlow	2
1857	Enniskillen	1
1858	Carrickfergus	3
1861	Dublin, South	1

APPELBE, W. P., LL.D.

1834	Londonderry	2
1836	Roscrea	1
1837	Dublin	3
1840	Limerick	3
1843	Drogheda	1
1844	Coleraine	3
1847	Dublin, South	3
1850	Dublin, North	3
1853	Cork	3
1856	Belfast, North	2
1858	Dublin, South	3
1861	Dungannon	1

ARMSTRONG, ANDR.

1855	Brookborough	1
1856	Rathdrum	1
1857	Portadown	1
1858	Killala	1
1859	Donegal	1
1860	Clifden	2

ARMSTRONG, JOHN.

1816	Ballymena	2
1818	Killesandra	2
1820	Armagh	2

1822	Enniskillen	1
1823	Monaghan	1
1824	Lurgan	2
1826	Downpatrick	1
1827	Cavan	3
1830	Donegal	3
1833	Newtownlimavady	3
1836	Portrush	2
1838	Dungannon	2
1840	Lurgan	2
1842	Omagh	2
1844	Lowtherstown	2
1846	Brookborough	3
1849	Donaghadee	2
1851	Aughnacloy	1
1852	Dungannon	3
1855	Moira	3
1858	Lurgan	2
1860	Belfast, S., *Sup.*	2

ATKINS, JAMES B.

1856	Sligo	3
1859	Belfast, South	1
1860	Wexford	1
1861	Roscrea	1

ATKINS, JOHN H.

1838	Institution	1
1839	Skibbereen	1
1840	Belfast	3
1843	Limerick	3
1846	Castlebar	3
1849	Ballina	3
1852	Bandon	3
1855	Kinsale	1
1856	Skibbereen, *Sup.*	6

BAKER, THOMAS W.

1847	Tipperary	1
1848	Skibbereen	1
1849	Cavan	1
1850	Magherafelt	1
1851	Belmullet & Erris	3
1854	Killala	2
1856	Manorhamilton	2
1858	Magherafelt	2
1860	Ballyclare	2

BALLARD, JOHN W.

1851	Wexford	2
1853	Armagh	2
1855	Roscrea	2
1857	Dublin, South	2
1859	Ballymena	2
1861	Coleraine	1

BALLARD, THOMAS.

1818	Tullamoore	1
1819	Tandragee	1
1820	Enniskillen	2
1822	Castleblaney	1
1823	Mallow	2
1825	Monaghan	2
1827	Dungannon	1
1828	Donaghadee	3
1831	Downpatrick	1
1832	Skibbereen	3
1835	Youghal	3
1838	Donaghadee	3
1841	Downpatrick	2
1843	Lisburn	2
1845	Waterford	3
1848	Donaghadee	1

Fig. 6.6   A page from "Hill's Arrangments" or "An Alphabetical Arrangement of all the Wesleyan Methodist Ministers, and Preachers on Trial, in Ireland" by Rev. William Hill, London, 1885.

permanent loan basis with an appropriate record office. This is not a general policy of the Irish Methodist Church, although some Irish circuits, such as University Road Circuit in Belfast, have, on their own initiative, deposited such papers with the Public Record Office of Northern Ireland. In other cases, for example the non-current Cloughjordan (Co. Tipperary) items, some Circuit and District papers have been forwarded to the Wesley Historical Society, Irish Branch

Public Record Office of Northern Ireland (PRONI): Considerable progress has been made, with the permission of Conference officials and the cooperation of local circuits, in the copying of registers held by Circuits in Northern Ireland. These are catalogued by name of Circuit, content and date, and distinction is made between Wesleyan and Primitive Wesleyan where appropriate. These copies are in the PRONI (Ref MIC CR3 MIC 1E).

In the interest of safe-keeping, permission was also given for the transfer to the PRONI of important volumes of documents relating to the Primitive Wesleyan, and Wesleyan Methodist Conferences. These include Conference Minutes, Journals (which contain the more specific detail of items referred to in the Conference Minutes and are often of genealogical relevance), District Synod Minutes and Registers of Property.

Local History Societies: Some local history Societies have also received permission to copy registers held locally outside Northern Ireland. A full list of these transcriptions is not available.

Wesley Historical Society (Irish Branch). The Wesley Historical Society was founded in 1893 and the Irish branch was established in 1926. The Irish Branch, whose library and collection are located at Aldersgate House, 9-11 University Road, Belfast has the following items in its collection.

    (i)   An important library of Printed Books about Irish Methodism; sets of Minutes of Conference; Methodist Magazines; Newspapers of Methodist origin; the Proceedings of the Wesley Historical Society (Published since 1897 -); The Bulletin of the Irish Branch (Published twice-yearly since 1986); a large collection of Irish Methodist local histories; Biographies; early Methodist pamphlets and reference books such as 'Hills Arrangements' *(11)(Fig. 6.6)* and 'Hall's Circuits and Ministers' (1765 - 1912).

(ii) A wide collection of Manuscript material, such as letters and diaries of itinerant preachers, preaching plans and class tickets, minute and account books. A select list of this material has been provided to Mr Homer Calkin of the World Methodist Historical Society, Lake Junalaska, North Carolina, for inclusion in his Catalog of Methodist Archival and Manuscript Collections.

(iii) A set of Microfilm copies of Registers made by the PRONI.

<u>Edgehill Theological College, Belfast:</u>   Similar material as at (i) and (ii) above is held in the library of Edgehill Theological College, Lennoxvale, Malone Road, Belfast, Northern Ireland.

REFERENCES

(1)   *Leary, W.* (1983) The Methodist Archives. **Archives** Vol. XVI (69)

(2)   *Law, Isobel* **A Tale of two Churches: Two centuries of Methodism at Priesthill 1786-1986**. Privately Published 1986.

(3)   *Jeffery, F.* **Irish Methodism; An Historical Account of its Traditions, Theology and Influence**. Epworth House, Belfast 1964.

(4)   *Jones, Caroline.* **Bluestone: Gem of Irish Methodism 1789 - 1989.** Privately Printed 1989.

(5)   *Turner, B.S.* (1974) Methodist Baptismal Registers of County Louth 1829-1865. **J. Co. Louth Arch. & Hist. Soc.** XVIII (2).

(6)   *Lee Cole, R.* **History of Methodism in Ireland.** Vol IV. Belfast: Irish Methodist Publishing Co. 1960.

(7)   *Fry, Paul.* **Register of Methodist College.** Belfast 1868-1984. 880pp. Privately Published.

(8)   *Henderson, J.W.*   **Methodist College Belfast 1868-1938;   A survey and retrospect in 2 Volumes.**   Published by and for the Governors of the Methodist College,   Belfast 1939.

(9)   *E. Alan Rose.*   **Checklist of British Methodist Periodicals: Methodist Study Guide No 1A**.   WHMS Publications 1981: ISBN 0 9505559.3.2

(10)   *Leary, W.* **Local Methodist Records: Methodist Study Guide** No. 2.   WHMS Publications. (1981) ISBN 0 9505559.4.0

(11)   *Hill, Rev. William.*   **An Alphabetical Arrangement of all the Wesleyan Methodist Ministers, and Preachers on Trial, in connection with the British Conferences.** Wesleyan Methodist Book Room. London, 1885.

FURTHER READING

Crookshank, C.H. **History of Methodism in Ireland;** Vol 1. Wesley and his Times; Vol II. The Middle Age;   Vol. III. Modern Development. 1885- 1886.

Smith, W., **A Consecutive History of the Rise, Progress and Present State of Wesleyan Methodism in Ireland.** Dublin 1830.

APPENDIX 6.I

METHODIST SOCIETIES AND THEIR CURRENT DISTRICT AND CIRCUIT REFERENCE NUMBERS

The districts to which each of the societies belong are indexed by the following numbers: I Dublin; II Midlands and Southern; III Enniskillen and Sligo; IV Londonderry; V NorthEast; VI Belfast; VII Down; VIII Portadown. The abbreviations used are:

Jt. C. of I.	=	Joint Church of Ireland Ministry
Alt. P.	=	Alternating Ministry with Presbyterian Church
Jt. P.	=	Joint Presbyterian Ministry

Abbey Street (Dublin)	I/2	Ballyclare	V/35
Adare	II/18	Ballyconnell	III/26
Aghyaran	IV/30	Ballydehob	II/16
Antrim	V/38	Ballyholme	VII/59
Ardara	IV/33	Ballyhupahaun	II/11
Arklow	I/7	Ballymena	V/39
Armagh	VIII/72	Ballymoney	IV/29
Athlone	II/14	Ballynafeigh	VI/49
Athy	II/11	Ballynahinch	VII/64
Augher	VIII/73	Ballynanny	VIII/73
Aughnacloy	VIII/73	Ballynure	V/35
Avoca	I/7	Banbridge	VIII/79
		Bandon	II/16
Bailieborough	III/26	Bannfoot	VIII/74
Ballina	III/27	Battlehill	VIII/67
Ballinacorr	VIII/74	Belvoir	VI/49
Ballinamallard	III/25	Bessbrook	VIII/68
Ballinary	VIII/67	Birr	II/14
Ballinasloe (P)	II/13	Blacklion	III/19
Ballineen	II/16	Blackrock	I/6
Ballingrane	II/18	Blackscull	VIII/76
Ballintra	III/32	Blackwatertown	VIII/69
Ballybay	III/26	Bloomfield	VI/50

Bluestone	VIII/74	Donaghmore	VIII/79
Borrisokane	II/12	Donegal	IV/32
Boyle	III/27	Donegall Road	VI/47
Braniel (Jt.P)	VI/54	Donegall Square	VI/42
Bray	I/6	Downpatrick	VII/65
Broomhedge	VII/66	Drimnagh	I/4
Brookeborough	III/22	Drimoleague	II/16
Brownlow	VIII/74	Dromore	VII/66
		Drumady	III/22
Carlisle Road (L'Derry)	IV/28	Drumquin	IV/31
Carlow	II/9	Drumshanbo	III/27
Carnalea	VII/60	Dun Laoghaire	I/6
Carnlough	V/37	Dundonald	VI/54
Carrickfergus	V/36	Dundrum (Co. Down)	VII/65
Carryduff	VI/42	Dundrum (Dublin)	I/4
Castlecaulfield	VIII/70	Dungannon	VIII/70
Castlederg	IV/30	Dunkineely	IV/33
Cavandoragh	IV/30	Dumanway	II/16
Cavehill	VI/43		
Centenary (Leeson Park)	I/1	Edenderry	VIII/67
Churchill	III/20	Enniscorthy (p)	I/8
Clabby	II/23	Enniskillen	III/19
Clonakilty	II/16	Epworth	VIII/67
Clontarf	I/3		
Clooney Hall (L'Derry)	IV/28	Finaghy	VI/55
Cloughjordan	II/12	Fintona	IV/31
Coleraine	IV/29	Fivemiltown	III/23
Collooney	III/27	Florencecourt	III/29
Comber	VII/62		
Cookstown	VIII/71	Galway (Alt.P)	II/13
Cork	II/15	Glacknadrummond	IV/28
Corlespratten	III/26	Glastry	VII/63
Craigmore	VIII/77	Glenavy	VIII/77
Craigyhill	V/37	Glenburn	VI/51
Cregagh	VI/51	Glencairn (Jt. C. of I.)	VI/48
Crumlin Road	VI/45	Glengormley	V/34
Cullybackey	V/40	Gorey (Alt.P)	I/8
		Greencastle	V/34
Derryanville	VIII/67	Greenisland	V/36
Derrygonnelly	III/20	Grogey	III/23
Derrylee	VIII/69	Grosvenor Hall	VI/56
Doagh	V/35		
Donacloney	VIII/76	Hamilton Road, Bangor	VII/58
Donaghadee	VII/61	Holywood	VII/57

Hydepark	V/34	Manorhamilton	III/27
		Markethill	VIII/78
Innishmore	III/21	Mayne	IV/31
Inver	IV/32	Moira	VIII/76
Irvinestown	III/24	Monaghan	VIII/73
Islandmagee	V/36	Monkstown (Jt.C of I)	V/34
		Mossley	V/34
Jennymount	VI/44	Mountmellick	II/11
Joanmount	VI/45	Mountpottinger	VI/50
		Movilla Abbey (Jt.C of I)	VII/62
Kells	III/23	Movilla	IV/28
Kilcoo	III/20	Moy	VIII/69
Kilkenny	II/9	Mullaghy	III/19
Killarney	II/15		
Killylea	VIII/72	Newbuildings	IV/28
Killymaddy	VIII/72	Newcastle	VII/65
Kinsale	III/16	Newry	VIII/68
Knock	VI/54	Newtownards (Regent St.)	VII/62
Knockbreda	VI/49	Newtownards Road	VI/52
Knockloughrim	V/41	Newtownbutler	III/22
Knockninny	III/19	Newtownkelly	VIII/70
		Newtownstewart	IV/31
Laghey	VIII/70		
Larne	V/37	Omagh	IV/31
Letterbreen	III/19		
Limavaddy	IV/28	Pettigo	III/24
Limerick (Alt.P)	II/17	Port Laoise	II/11
Lisbellaw	III/21	Portadown (Thomas St.)	VIII/67
Lisburn (Seymour St.)	VII/66	Portaferry	VII/63
Lisburn Road	VI/46	Portrush	IV/29
Lisleen	IV/30	Portstewart	IV/29
Lisnaskea	III/22	Priesthill	VII/66
Lissacaha	II/16	Primacy (Jt.C of I)	VII/60
Longford	III/26		
Lucan	I/2	Queen's Parade (Bangor)	VII/60
Lurgan (High Street)	VIII/74		
Lurgan (Queen Street)	VIII/75	Rathcoole	V/34
		Rathgar (Brighton Rd.)	I/4
Maghaberry	VIII/76	Richhill	VIII/78
Magherafelt	V/41	Roscrea	II/12
Magheragall	VII/66	Rostrevor	VIII/68
Maguiresbridge	III/21		
Mahon	VIII/67	Saint Columba's (Lisburn)	

(Jt.P)	VII/66	Togherdoo	IV/31
Sandy Row	VI/56	Toneyloman	III/19
Sandymount (Alt.P)	I/5	Tramore (Alt.P)	II/10
Seymour Hill	VI/55	Trillick	III/26
Shankill	VI/48	Tullamore	II/14
Shannon (Jt. P.&C. of I)	II/17	Tullyboy	III/26
Shinrone	II/12	Tullycherry	III/24
Skerries	I/3	Tullyroan	VIII/69
Skibbereen	II/16		
Sligo	III/27	University Road	VI/46
Springfield	III/20	Upper Falls	VI/55
Springfield Road	VI/56		
Stewartstown	VIII/70	Warrenpoint	VIII/68
Strabane	IV/28	Waterford (Alt.P)	II/10
Strathfoyle (Jt.C of I)	IV/28	Wexford (Alt.P)	I/8
Sutton	I/3	Whiteabbey	V/34
Swanlinbar	III/19	Whitecastle	IV/28
Sydenham	VI/53	Whitehead	V/36
		Wicklow	I/7
Tandragee	VIII/78	Woodvale	VI/48
Tempo	III/21		
Tierwinney	III/24	Youghal	II/15

IRISH JEWISH RECORDS AS A
GENEALOGICAL SOURCE

Raphael V. Siev

"Jews, whom Christians tax with avarice, are of all races the most given to intermarriage." as James Joyce says in Ulysses (1). This is a strange remark but at the same time a very true assessment of Jewry, not only at the present time but also in earlier generations.

Within this century the Nazis went to extreme lengths to ascertain whether a person was truly Aryan and would discriminate even against anyone who had a single grandparent who might have been Jewish. From what has been written of that period, it would appear that intermarriage in Germany must have been very widespread from the period of the Enlightenment, namely the middle of the 18th Century, and that by the 1930's a considerable number of persons in Germany had Jewish genes.

From a cultural and ethnic point of view, a gene may be defined as an hereditary factor and thus genealogy is an account of descent from ancestors or an account of pedigree.

It is not generally appreciated that the study of descent from one's forebears was a recognised and inbuilt feature of the Bible and, in particular, the Old Testament. In most of the Biblical examples, the Bible provides lists of names indicating the ancestors or descendants of a particular leading character or of someone involved in a particular situation. The main listings of genealogies are found in the first five books of the Bible, the five books of Moses, and secondly towards the end of the Old Testament in the books of Ezra, Nehemiah and Chronicles. In many of the listings there is an insertion of some additional information concerning the individual referred to, e.g. his age, when his son was born, or how old he was when he died. Very often the sequence of names is used to trace the ancestry of an individual back to some eminent personage of a much earlier period.

It is more than probable that this usage was also necessary for legal purposes, for example, to establish title to lands, properties and possessions, and also rights to position in society and to tribal, family and dynastic rights and privileges - an example of this can be found in the book of Ruth. What is significant is that none of the lists trace their origins back to a god, as was the custom among so many nations.

It is not the purpose of this chapter to set out the reasons why people leave or change their religion. Jews do not encourage non-Jews to convert to Judaism, although conversions do take place. On the other hand, in every generation Jews have left their faith and have converted and/or have married non-Jews. Ireland has been no exception to this practice and in addition there has been a long standing tradition among non-Jewish groups to seek out Jews and to encourage them to convert. Intermarriage between a Jewish person and a non-Jewish person invariably led to the conversion of the Jewish spouse, most often to christianity. Another factor which led to intermarriage was that Jewish people settled in parts of the country where there were few opportunities to mix and meet other Jewish people. In such

TABLE 7.1

JEWISH POPULATION IN IRELAND 1881-1981

Year	No.	Year	No.
1881	472	1937	5221
1891	1779	1946	5381
1901	3769	1961	4446
1911	5148	1971	3592
1926	5315	1981	2644

circumstances, it was only natural that their Irish born children should integrate and marry into their local non-Jewish communities. Thus many non-Jewish people in this island have Jewish ancestors. Indeed some family names clearly indicate their Jewish origin e.g. Coen, Levy, while others, e.g. Bannon, Briscoe and Dunleavy can be of either Irish or Jewish origin.

Parents' Name	Residence	Sex	When Born
David Davis	Baggot St	Girl	December 27th 1858
Henry Yack	Parliament St	Girl	December 31st 1858
Morris Cohen	Fownes St	Girl	January 15th 1859
Meyer Erlich	Anglesea St	Girl	January 20th 1859
...... Woman, called Rachel	Stevens St	Boy	January 30th 1859
Abraham Cohen	New Row	Girl	February 10th 1859
David Jacobs	Dame St	Boy	April 16th 1859
Hyman Davis	Stephens Green	Girl	July 30th 1859
Morris Salaman	Gloucester St	Boy	August 1st 1859
Samuel Dutch	Sandymount	Girl	August 7th 1859
E. Samuelson	Dawson St	Girl	August 20th 1859

Fig. 7.1 Page from the Registry Book of the Hebrew Congregation in Dublin of 1858-1859.

A further factor stimulating intermarriage was the small size of the Jewish population of Ireland, certainly less than a hundred Jewish persons lived in Ireland in the eighteenth century. The rise and decline in numbers over the last century is shown in Table 7.1.

In 1992 it is estimated that the total number of Jews in the whole island of Ireland is less than 2000 persons.

It would appear that the few dozen Jews who were in Ireland in the 18th century were mostly descendants of Jews expelled from Spain and, in particular, Portugal. They formed organised communities in Dublin and Cork and established two cemeteries, one at Ballybough in Dublin and the other between Kemp Street and Douglas Street in Cork. The Dublin cemetery still exists while the one in Cork is now a car park!

In the nineteenth century, and particularly after the Napoleonic wars, a new influx of a hundred or more Jews arrived in Ireland from Central Europe. The vast majority settled close to the existing synagogue in Mary's Abbey, off Capel Street in Dublin of which they became members. From this time, purely Irish Jewish records exist. The final and most recent influx of Jews came from the Baltic States, mainly from Lithuania, in the late 1800's and early 1900's. These Jews settled in the towns of Limerick, Cork, Waterford, Dublin, Drogheda, Belfast and Derry.

The Irish Jewish Museum was opened by Dr. Chaim Herzog, the Irish born and Irish educated President of Israel, on 20 June 1985. It is located in a former synagogue in the once densely Jewish populated district of Portobello in Dublin. It is a voluntary institution having no paid permanent staff. It relies for its existence on the goodwill of friends and wellwishers. Fortunately, these have been generous, and continue to be generous, in supplying artifacts and memorabilia. In this way, the museum possesses four important ledgers of prime interest for genealogical information and research.

The oldest register which the Museum possesses is entitled the Registry Book of the Hebrew Congregation in Dublin, namely, the aforementioned Mary's Abbey Synagogue. It commences with the record of the birth of a baby girl on 20 February 1820, and concludes with the birth of a baby boy on 7 May 1879. The total number of entries for these 59 years is 336. This register has an additional value as it contains a register of deaths commencing on 5 January 1842 and concludes after recording 40 deaths on 8 February 1879 *(see Fig. 7.1)*.

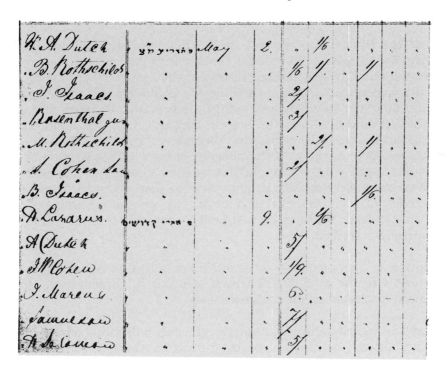

Fig. 7.2   *Extract from the Membership register of the Dublin Hebrew Congregation of 1846.*

In addition to the above, the Museum also has the Membership Register of the Dublin Hebrew Congregation. This begins on 16 September 1841 and has entries down to 7 April 1883 (*see Fig. 7.2*). In the margin of this book notes of births and deaths are also recorded, not just from Dublin but also from other places in Ireland.

A third source book containing valuable material is the maternity attendance book of Mrs. Ada Shillman who might be described as the midwife of the Dublin Jewish Community. It is a 64 page record of all the deliveries she attended from 9 April 1896, when a Ms. Beigel was born, up to 29 April 1908 with the birth of another girl, a Ms. Wachman. It is significant that her charge for the delivery in 1896 was 12 shillings (or 60p in current currency) while her charge in 1908 had gone up to one pound. Each of the first 25 pages contain some 36 entries and thus approximately 900 births are recorded. The remainder of the book contains details concerning each family, (1) their address, (2) the full name of the father, (3) the full name and maiden name of the mother, (4) the first name of the new child and occasionally (5) the occupation of the father. Mrs. Shillman's work did not extend beyond the few streets around the Portobello district of the South Circular Road, Dublin. Its value is nevertheless immense as the largest concentration of Jewish settlement was in that area. When one recalls that the vast majority of the Irish Jewish population of child bearing age had only arrived in Ireland within the previous 10 years and that most of them did not know the English language, or of the requirement that all births had to be registered, the value of this record takes on a new dimension. Because of the absence of the civil registration of the births of a number of Jewish children at the beginning of this century, the Museum has been called upon over the last few years to confirm the validity of a family belief of a birth. On several occasions it has been able to do so and has even supplied additional information of the type already described.

The museum also possesses a record book of deaths occurring in the mid-1930's to the mid-1940's which sets out in considerable detail relevant information about each deceased.

Whilst the overwhelming majority of Jews born in Ireland have remained Jewish by religion, belief or practice, there is yet a sizeable number of persons who were born Jewish but have converted out of the faith or by marrying non-Jews. The number of intermarriages over the last 50 years is estimated as being in the region of 250. Thus the records of the museum will be of benefit to a considerable number of Irish families.

This article begins with a quotation from James Joyce's Ulysses on intermarriage as it is a most relevant quotation in regard to the contents of this paper. Over the past six years, the museum has been approached on numerous occasions by various Christian and non-Jewish people with requests for information about their forebears. The museum has been able to confirm on all occasions except one that their grandparent or great-grandparent was Jewish and that their family information was correct. Many other Irish people, or people of Irish ancestry could also benefit from the material held and the facilities of the museum are available to all genuine enquirers. The Irish Jewish Museum is located at Walworth Road (off Victoria Street), Portobello, Dublin 8.

REFERENCES

(1)   Ulysses, James Joyce, Bodley Head, London 1960. P.264.

FURTHER READING

Hyman, Louis. **A History of the Jews of Ireland.** London/Jerusalem. 1972.

Shillman, Bernard, **Short History of the Jews of Ireland.** Dublin 1945.

Siev, Raphael, **The Irish Jewish Museum,** Bulletin of the Department of Foreign Affairs, Dublin, August 1987, Issue No. 1039.

HUGUENOT CHURCH REGISTERS IN IRELAND

Vivien Costello

8.1 Introduction

As specifically Huguenot sources in Ireland are at best scarce and for some regions of the country non-existent, one can expect research into Huguenot ancestors to involve much effort, time and patience. The still extant primary sources are scattered in various repositories necessitating also much legwork. In order to undertake successful research it is initially necessary to have a basic knowledge of the pattern of Huguenot emigration to Ireland and the principal locations of the settlements. Information gleaned from documents relating to Huguenots will inevitably have to be augmented by searches of general Irish genealogical source material.

8.2 The Origins of the Huguenots

The Wars of Religion in Europe spanned over two centuries. From the early 16th to the middle of the 18th Century much persecution was engendered and many refugees left their native lands. The French Protestants fled abroad in successive waves, seeking refuge principally in Switzerland, Prussia, Denmark, Sweden, Poland, Russia, Staten Island, Virginia, South Carolina, S. Africa, Holland, England and Ireland.

It is important to note that scarcely any Huguenot refugees arrived in Ireland directly from France. They usually came via England, often having initially fled to a neighbouring continental country such as Switzerland, Germany or Holland. The problems of piecing together a pedigree of the first generation of a refugee family are thus often almost insurmountable. A couple might for example have been married in Germany, and had children baptised in Switzerland, Holland and England before finally settling in Ireland. If a family had older children before leaving France, some of these may well have opted to settle in a different country to their parents. In the case of families with property, the eldest son often became a Catholic to inherit the property, whilst the rest of the family fled abroad. Surprisingly, the family relationships between the Catholics and Protestants usually remained good. There are many collections of correspondence which demonstrate this.

The flight of the Huguenots to England and Ireland occurred in four waves:

1.   During the 2nd half of the 16th Century when French and Flemish fled together from the persecutions under Catherine de Medici in France and the Duke of Alva in the Netherlands.

2.   During the beginning of the 17th Century when Richelieu's policies brought about the siege of La Rochelle.

3.   After the revocation of the Edict of Nantes in 1685. The penal laws enacted against Huguenots were enforced for a period of some 60 years.

4.   After the Peace of Aix-La-Chapelle which ended the war of Austrian Succession in 1748. French soldiers released from eh war were sent, in conjunction with Jesuits, to hunt down the remaining Huguenot communities in France which still existed in isolated pockets.

8.3 The Huguenots in Ireland

Ireland was not an ideal place of settlement for Protestant refugees. It had religious wars of its own and in some periods it was a case of "from the frying pan into the fire". The first refugees recorded in Ireland came in the reigns of Henry VII and Edward VI. A group of mainly Walloons employed in silver and lead mines in Co. Wexford in 1551 were attacked by the locals. The fate of a group of mainly Flemish weavers who were settled in Swords, Co. Dublin under Viceroy Sir Henry Sidney in the reign of Elizabeth I is not known, but it is likely that the project did not last long.

During the 1620's a number of Dutch, Walloon and Huguenot merchants began to settle in the main Irish ports such as Dublin, Cork,

Waterford, Limerick and Galway. These were often very successful and are frequently mentioned in the Corporation records of these towns. The 1641 Rebellion of Irish Catholics dispersed these settlers and forced many to flee to England.

In 1649, it was again the turn of the Catholics to suffer. Cromwell's campaign denuded large parts of Ireland of almost all Roman Catholics, driving them "to Hell or to Connaught". The countryside was ravaged and many towns and cities became semi-derelict, depleted of tradesmen, artisans and shopkeepers. There were incidentally some Huguenot names amongst the Cromwellian soldiers, some of whom settled in Ireland.

In 1660 after the Restoration of Charles II to the English throne, the Duke of Ormonde was appointed Viceroy of Ireland. A member of the very prestigous Butler family who owned large estates, principally in Cos. Kilkenny and Tipperary, the Duke of Ormonde had himself been forced into exile on the Continent during the Cromwellian era. He had himself witnessed the persecution of the Huguenots in France. Ormond, who was a Protestant, was nevertheless not personally hostile to Catholics, indeed most of his own Butler family were Catholics. Politically however, he could not risk restoring to Catholics what they had lost under Cromwell. He was determined to rebuild Ireland, industrialise it and return it to prosperity. He decided that one means to this end would be to settle Huguenots, with their many trades and skills, into urban areas. In 1662 he introduced into the Irish Parliament "An Act for Encouraging Protestant Strangers and others to Inhabit Ireland". Under the act Huguenots became citizens and freemen of the corporate towns and the Freemen lists of many towns and cities are a rich source for tracing Huguenots. Ormonde was also responsible for organising groups of Huguenots to come to Ireland, by giving them grants of land. Linen weavers were established at Chapelizod, on the outskirts of Dublin, woollen manufacturers in Clonmel and Carrick-on-Suir and ore smelters were settled in Enniscorthy.

After the Revocation of the Edict of Nantes in 1685 even larger numbers of Huguenot refugees flooded into Ireland, especially the larger urban areas. These were quickly augmented still further by the members of the five Huguenot Regiments recruited in Holland by William of Orange and brought to Ireland to fight against James II's troops (1689 - 91). There were three regiments of Foot under La Meloniere, Du Cambon (succeeded by Comte de Marton, later Earl of Lifford), La Caillemotte Ruvigny (killed at the Battle of the Boyne and succeeded by Pierre

Belcastel), one of Horse under Marshal Schomberg (also killed at the Boyne and succeeded by the Marquis de Ruvigny, later Earl of Galway) and one of Dragoons commanded by Miremont. After William III's victory these regiments were sent to live in Flanders and were disbanded after the Peace of Ryswick. Many of these officers and men served in new Huguenot regiments under different colonels for the further campaigns on the continent in the reign of Anne. William III granted pensions to Huguenot officers when they became old, wounded, sick or disbanded on condition that they settled in Ireland. The Huguenot communities in England had become very overcrowded and he wished to force them to settle in Ireland.

New places of settlement for Huguenots were established during the reign of William III. Louis Crommelin, a refugee who had settled in the Low Countries was invited to establish a linen manufacture in the ruined town of Lisnagarvey (now Lisburn) with 75 Huguenot families. Similar projects were set up in Waterford and Kilkenny, silk and poplin weaving was introduced in Dublin, sailcloth manufacture in Cork and the making of cambric in Lurgan and Dundalk.

In 1692 William III granted the Lands of Portarlington to Henri de Massue, Marquis de Ruvigny, later Earl of Galway, his General who had served him well in his campaign against James II. Ruvigny became the most important spokesman for the Huguenot communities in Ireland and he set up a settlement of initially mostly military pensioners in the town of Portarlington.

By 1710 the Huguenot population in Ireland was at its height. An accurate estimate of the number at that period is not yet possible, but we know there were at least several thousand. From then on the number began to decline, because of unfavourable economic circumstances, not least the many trade laws enacted against Ireland by the Westminster Parliament. These were supposed to suppress the Catholics but equally affected Protestant tradesmen and artisans such as the Huguenots. Many Huguenots began to emigrate from Ireland to England, the Continent and America in search of prosperity. Some wearied by hardship and suffering went back to France and became Catholics.

The very last Huguenot settlement established in Ireland was that of Inishannon, Co. Cork. In 1765 Thomas Adderley, M. P. for Bandon brought 65 Huguenot families to the area to manufacture silk. Houses were built for them and mulberry trees were planted. However the silk worms died in the damp climate and so the project was abandoned after about 20 years.

8.4 Irish Huguenot Communities with a Church & Minister

Dublin - had one church from 1665, 4 churches - 2 conformist and 2 non-conformist by the early 18th Century.

The two conformist churches were: The Lady Chapel in St. Patrick's Cathedral begun in 1665 and the Chapel of St. Mary begun in 1701 in Meetinghouse Lane off Capel Street. The originals of both sets of

The French Refugees were so numerous on their first introduction as to form, in the year 1695, three congregations. A meeting-house in Lucas-lane, and another in Peter-street, were erected for those of the Calvinist persuasion, and a chapel under the roof of St. Patrick's Cathedral was assigned to those who were of the established Church; but as they were not supplied by any accession from abroad, the members gradually amalgamated with the population of the Metropolis. Many families became extinct in the, male line, and those who retained their name, lost, with their vernacular language, the distinctive character of their sect. The two first places of worship are closed, and the congregation of the latter is nearly extinct. It consists of about twenty individuals, for whom the liturgy is still read, and the sermon preached in the French language. Government allows the minister a stipend of £150. per annum. Their present pastor is the Rev. Mr. Letablere.

In 1723, a school was established in Myler's-alley, Patrick's-close, for the maintainance and education of those whose parents were in distress. At first it included boys and girls. It now supports only eight girls, who are lodged, maintained, educated, and apprenticed at a proper age. They are all the children of Refugees. The income of the school arises from the interest of debentures, occasionally a charity sermon, and a few subscribers.

Fig. 8.1   *A contemporary account of the Huguenot Churches of Dublin from the "History of the City of Dublin", J. Warburton, Rev. J. Whitelaw, & Rev. R. Walsh, London 1818*

registers were destroyed in the PRO fire but had fortunately been published by the Huguenot Society of London.

The conformist cemetery was "The Cabbage Garden" beside St. Patrick's Cathedral. It is now a public park and very few headstones survive.

The Registers of the Dublin Conformist Churches are contained in Volume 7 of the Publications of the Huguenot Society of London, edited and indexed by J.J. Digges La Touche. This volume is available in the National Library of Ireland. Contained therein are the following:

	Baptisms	*Marriages*	*Burials*
St. Patrick's	1668-1687	1680-1716	1680-1716
St. Mary's	1705-1716	1705-1715	1705-1715
United Churches	1716-1818	1716-1788	1716-1830

The two non-conformist churches were The Chapel of St. Brigide's which was a rented private house in Wood Street off Bride Street. It was begun in c.1690 but when difficulties arose with the lease of the house at Wood Street a new church was built in Peter Street in 1711. The Chapel of Lucy Lane was completed in 1693 (Lucy Lane is now Chancery Place). It was sold to the Presbyterian congregation of Skinner's Row in 1773. The original registers of the non-conformist churches were likewise destroyed but had also been previously published by the Huguenot Society.

The non-conformist cemeteries included one at Newmarket used by the Wood Street congregation until a burial ground at Peter Street was opened in 1711. This cemetery was the subject of a High Court case in the 1960s and the site was taken over by Jacob's Biscuit Factory. The headstones were removed to Mount Jerome Cemetery, Harold's Cross.

A further cemetery is at Merrion Row, St. Stephen's Green. The history of this cemetery is more fortunate. It is still maintained by the French Huguenot Fund, a Dublin Huguenot Charity with its roots in the early 18th Century. The cemetery was restored in 1989 through a joint project of the French Government and Fás as part of the Dublin Millenium celebrations. Hundreds of burials are recorded in the non-conformist registers, but very few headstones are visible. All particulars are recorded in Danny Parkinson's booklet "The Huguenot Cemetery, Merrion Row, Dublin" (including the burial register extracts).

The non-conformist Dublin Huguenot Registers were published in Volume 14 of the Publications of the Huguenot Society of London,

L'ÉGLISE FRANÇOISE DE PORTARLINGTON 91

Bapteme. Du Dimanche 15 Janvier, 1726.

Judith Joly.—Le Lundy 9ᵉ Janvier, 1726, est né une fille à David Joly et à Ester Joly, sa femme, laquelle a eté batisee cejourdhuy par Monsʳ de Bonneval, Ministre de cette Eglise, presentée au Sᵗ Bapteme par Monsʳ le Colonel de Boiron, parrain, et par Madame de Lalande, marraine, et on la nommée Judith.

Bapteme. Du Dimanche 26ᵉ Fevrier, 1726-7.

Charlotte Gautier.—Le Vendredy 17 Fevrier sur les cinq heures du matin est né une fille à Pierre Gautier et à Marie Guerié, sa femme, laquelle a eté batisée cejourdhuy par Monsʳ de Bonneval, Ministre de cette Eglise, et a esté presentée au Sᵗ Baptême par Monsʳ le Colonel de Boiron, parrain, et par Madame de Mezerac, marraine, et on lui a imposé nom Charlotte.

Bapteme. Du Dimanche 17ᵉ Septembre, 1727.

Pierre Debreuil.—Le Lundy 4ᵉ Septembre sur le midy est né un fils à Jean Debreuil et à Susanne Le Conte, sa femme, lequel a été baptisé cejourdhuy par Monsʳ de Bonneval, Ministre de cette Eglise, et a presenté au Sᵗ Bapteme par Pierre Debreuil, parrain, et par Marguerite Conte, marraine, et on luy impose nom Pierre.

Jean Debreuil.

Baptême. Du Vendredy 29ᵉ Septembre, 1727.

Jeanne Dufay Dexoudun.—Le Sammedy 21ᵉ Septembre, 1727, est née une fille au Capᵐᵉ Josué Dufay Dexoudun et à Dame Marie de Vignoles Dexoudun, sa femme, laquelle a été baptisée cejourdhuy par Monsieur de Bonneval, Ministre de cette Eglise, et a été

Fig. 8.2   An extract from the Baptismal records of 1727, from the printed **Registers of the French Church of Portarlington, Co. Laois**, Huguenot Society Publications: Vol 19, published in 1908

edited and indexed by Thomas Philip Le Fanu. This volume is also available in the National Library of Ireland.

Registers	Baptisms	Marriages	Burials
Combined	1701-1731	1702-1728	1702-1731
Non-conformist			1771-1831

Also included in the non-conformist registers are Reconnaissances 1716-1730. A reconnaissance was the readmission into the Protestant church of a member who, because of persecution in France, for a time attended Roman Catholic services.

It will be noticed that a substantial portion of the non-conformist registers has been lost. In 1771 thieves broke into the vestry of St. Peter's and finding no valuables, set the registers alight in annoyance. In addition the baptism and marriage registers post 1771 were lost in the early 19th Century.

Portarlington - one church from 1692.
Portarlington grew rapidly in the period 1692-1703. By 1703 many houses had been built, there were 2 churches, 1 French and 1 English, 2 schools, 1 French and 1 English and 1 cemetery. The French church is now the Church of Ireland and both it and the cemetery are in excellent repair. The original Huguenot registers are still extant in the parish but have also been published in the Hug. Soc. Pubs. Vol. 19.

Waterford - one church was established in part of the ruins of the Franciscan Friary c.1700.
Waterford had a substantial Huguenot population in the early 18th Century. On 27th March 1693 the Corporation of Waterford resolved to provide houses for 50 Huguenot families to establish a linen industry in the city. The Huguenot registers are lost, but many Huguenot names occur in the Church of Ireland registers and the Corporation records.

Cork - one Huguenot church was built in 1712, but services had previously been held in a court house. As the second city of Ireland and an important commercial port, Cork attracted Huguenot settlers from the 16th Century onwards and had a huge influx after 1685. Its registers are lost.

Lisburn (Lisnagarvey) - one church from c.1717, but had had a minister since 1704.
This was the most important Ulster Huguenot settlement. William III's bill to foster the linen trade in 1697 caused 75 French families organised by Louis Crommelin to establish the industry in Lisburn, using 1,000 looms. This was the one such project to have a long-lasting success. Some refugees who arrived in Lisburn before 1704 attended the Church of Ireland in Lambeg or Lisburn Cathedral. Both registers contain many Huguenot names. The actual Huguenot registers were lost in the mid-nineteenth Century and all subsequent efforts to trace them have failed. Many Huguenot names appear in the local Church of Ireland registers.

Carlow (Caterlow/Caterlough) - one church, established c.1693.
Because very little information is now available on the Carlow Huguenot community it is often omitted from articles on the Huguenots in Ireland. Nevertheless it was a major Huguenot settlement in the early 18th Century. At least 50 families must have settled there for it to have been granted a church and minister. The registers were lost

Enterrement de Jean Massy.—Le trentième de Decembre, dixhuit cent douze, est mort et le troisième de Janvier, dixhuit cent treize, a été enterré Jean Massy, agé de neuf ans.

1813.

Enterrement de Jane Johnson.—Est morte au Park Jane fille de Jane Johnson, le 3ᵉ de Janvier, 1813; enterrée le 4ᵉ du dit mois, agée de dix mois.   J. REBILLET.

Enterrement d'Anne Melton.—Le second de Janvier est morte et le quatre du dit mois a été enterrée Anne Melton, agée d'environ vingt-cinq ans, l'an dixhuit cent treize.
J. REBILLET.

Enterrement de Marianne Walsh.—Le Jeudi vingtième Mai, dixhuit cent treize, a été enterrée Marianne Walsh, agee d'environ dixhuit mois.

Enterrement de Buckingham Sexton.—Le Jeudi vingtième Mai, dixhuit cent douze, a été enterré Buckingham Sexton, agé de quelques mois.

Enterrement de Thomas Stannus.—Le Lundi dixseptième de Mai, dixhuit cent treize, est mort au Seigneur, et le Vendredi vingt et unieme du dit mois a été enseveli, Thomas Stannus, Ecuier, par moi.
Agé d'environ quatrevingt ans.   J. REBILLET.

Enterremt de Sidney La Combe.—Le 3ᵉ de Juin est morte, et le vingt-cinquième a été enterrée, Sidney La Combe, agée d'environ un an.

Fig. 8.3   *An extract from the Burial records of 1813, from the printed **Registers of the French Church of Portarlington, Co. Laois,** Huguenot Society Publications: Vol 19, published in 1908*

and the Church of Ireland registers pre 1744 are also gone. Nevertheless even post 1744 the Church of Ireland registers contain many Huguenot names as do the registers of neighbouring parishes such as Tullow.

8.5 Huguenot Communities with a Minister but no Church

Wexford - The Huguenots worshipped in St. Mary's Church of Ireland and had their own minister from 1684.
In the 1680s some 42 Huguenot families are recorded as having lived in Wexford. Ms. 1619 in the National Library contains an extract from the Registry Book of the Diocese of Ferns & Leighlin dated 21.4.1684 in which Huguenots in the town of Wexford petition for the setting up of a French church. It is signed by 10 heads of families.

Kilkenny - had a Huguenot minister from 1694.
The Duke of Ormonde had established a Huguenot community in

Kilkenny from the 1660s and it is known to have had a Huguenot minister from 1694, but no records now remain. It is even reputed to have had a French University for some years during the 1690s, but it has not been possible to find documentation of a possible church, university or congregation. On of the few original documents on Kilkenny Huguenots is a petition by 10 heads of families for a church c.1712 - (Microfilm NLI P.521). There are enough references to Huguenots in Kilkenny for us to be sure that a substantial community was settled here and many varied sources yield the names of several dozen settlers, but we lack data about the majority.

Clonmel (Co. Tipperary) - had a Huguenot minister from 1699.
The Duke of Ormonde endeavoured to establish woollen manufacture both in Clonmel and Carrick on Suir in the 1660s. A Captain Grant was appointed as his agent in Clonmel. Some 500 families were reputed to have been invited from the overcrowded Huguenot community of Canterbury to the towns. No records now exist on these communities, except for a few fragments in the Calendar of Ormonde manuscripts.

Dundalk (Co. Louth) - had a Huguenot minister from 1737.
A colony of weavers for the manufacture of cambric was established in Dundalk under the de Joncourt brothers in 1736 under the auspices of the Linen Board. They were granted a minister, but the colony did not last long and left no lasting impression on Dundalk.

Inishannon (Co. Cork) - had a Huguenot minister from 1760.
As stated previously, this was the last formal project to settle Huguenots in Ireland. The silk manufacture was not a success and the community had dwindled within 20 years. There is no trace of any register entries for this community.

Additional small settlements without either a church or minister are on record for:
Belfast, Lambeg, Lurgan, Dromore, Castleblaney, Chapelizod, Collon, Edenderry, Killeshandra, Enniscorthy, Wicklow, Bandon, Kinsale, Youghal, Limerick, Tallow, Killaloe, Galway, Killala and Sligo. Perusal of miscellaneous Church of Ireland registers of towns throughout Ireland would suggest that nearly all of them had a least one or two Huguenot families if not more, with the possible exception of some parts of Connaught. The best documented of these smaller communities is Youghal, with extant Church of Ireland registers.

The foregoing will have already indicated to you that trying to trace

Huguenots in Ireland who did not settle in either Dublin or Portarlington, whose registers are still available, is not easy. It should not however prove impossible to those with time and tenacity. Many general sources exist which are likely to yield results.

9

IRISH BAPTIST CHURCH RECORDS

H.D.Gribbon

9.1 Historical Background

So far as is known with any certainty, the earliest Baptist churches in Ireland were established by Cromwellian and Commonwealth soldiers and settlers around the middle of the seventeenth century. Cork had its first Baptist Church in 1651; Dublin possibly in 1647, certainly by 1653; Waterford in 1650. Others established at around the same time included Athlone, Bandon, Carrickfergus, Clonmel, Cloughkeating (or Cloughjordan), Galway (1652), Kilkenny (1652), Limerick (1654), Rahugh, Wexford and Youghal.

With the restoration of the monarchy in 1660 and the imposition of disabilities on Catholics and dissenters, many of the original churches disappeared. Decline rather than growth marked most of the eighteenth century and it was not until the nineteenth, again under the influence of the Baptists from Great Britain, that renewed vigour and church planting heralded a fresh advance. By 1847 Thom's Irish Almanac and Official Directory was able to list thirty-nine Baptist churches in Ireland, and there may have been a few omissions from their list.

Emigration following the famine of 1845-49 halted the expansion, and indeed in the southern and western parts of the country reversed it. The closing decades of the century however saw a slow advance which continued, particularly in the North into the twentieth century. Following the second world war the advance continued, in terms of new churches established. This growth was most marked in the growing urban and suburban centres of Ulster, but there have also been fresh developments in the south (e.g. in Dublin, Carrigaline, Sligo & Dundalk) as well as in the north and west in Donegal, Tyrone and Fermanagh.

Numerically, Baptists have never been more than a very small fraction of the total population of Ireland. Although statistical evidence is lacking, even in their seventeenth century hey-day they must have

Leinster		Connaught	
Carlow County	2	Galway Town	2
Dublin City	185	Galway County	16
Dublin Suburbs	74	Leitrim County	15
Dulin County	28	Mayo County	13
Kildare County	9	Roscommon County	8
Kilkenny City	1	Sligo County	65
Kilkenny County	15		—
King's County	46		119
Longford County	-		—
Louth County	2		
Meath County	1		
Queen's County	-		
Westmeath	73		
Wexford	8		
Wicklow	11		
	—		
	455	Ulster	
	—	Antrim County	859
Munster		Armagh County	35
Clare County	-	Belfast Town	227
Cork City	66	Cavan County	2
Cork County	62	Donegal County	136
Kerry County	5	Down County	319
Limerick City	13	Fermanagh County	9
Limerick County	1	Londonderry County	1534
Tipperary County	17	Monaghan County	6
Waterford City	52	Tyrone County	311
Waterford County	9		—
	—		3438
	225		—
	—	Ireland : TOTAL 4237	

Fig. 9.1   *Number of Baptists in Ireland by counties and cities 1861. Extract from H.D. Gribbon "Irish Baptists in the Nineteenth Century" Ir. Baptist. Hist. Soc. J. XVI (1983/84) pp4-18.*

been numbered in hundreds rather than thousands. By 1800, membership of the surviving five churches was probably around 500 which, post-famine in 1863, had become 800. By 1900, churches affiliated to the Baptist Union of Ireland i.e. the great majority, had about 2,600 members, in 1950 4,700, and by 1990 8,500.

The number of people claiming to be Baptists in Government censuses would be approximately double the above figures. In 1901 for instance there were 7,000 Baptists enumerated. To understand the difference between numbers of recorded church members, and those listed as 'Baptists' for census purposes, and incidentally to explain some of the peculiar features of Baptist church records, it is necessary to say something about Irish Baptist belief and practice.

9.2 Baptist Beliefs & Practices

Baptists maintain that the scriptural injunction 'believe and be baptised' was, and is, of continuing validity. Thus the sprinkling, christening or baptising of infants can have no spiritual significance: faith must precede baptism (Acts 8, v 36-39). And the mode of baptism practised in apostolic times. i.e. total immersion, also continues valid. Most Baptists at the present time, and it is probable in the past, have been baptised on profession of faith, in their late teens or early twenties, although baptism in early teens is not unknown and in riper years relatively common. Faith, rather than age, is the criterion.

Men or women who have been baptised may apply to join a local Baptist church, consisting of a body of baptised believers. If accepted they are placed on the roll as members, and are expected to play a full part in the life of the church. They also become eligible to take part in church business meetings as distinct from public worship services. At church business meetings the day-to-day running of affairs - finance, discipline, reception of new members, the calling of a pastor, arrangements for special meetings etc., are discussed. These discussions are conducted under the guidance of elders and deacons, the former having responsibility in spiritual, and the latter in secular, matters. In a small church the pastor or minister may be the only elder but with large congregations it is usual to have more than one.

Each church is independent, but there has always been a degree of co-operation and mutual assistance amongst them, the nature and extent of which has varied over time. In the seventeenth and eighteenth centuries the churches sent their ministers and 'messengers' to annual association meetings, reporting their state and needs. At these meetings matters of common interest or concern were discussed, ministers were ordained, a circular letter was drafted for transmission to all the churches and there was occasional correspondence with similar associations in Great Britain. If a church was without a minister it was arranged that the vacancy be covered on an ad hoc basis (since baptism and the Lord's Supper could be administered only by an ordained minister). The association had no authority over the churches and there was no permanent secretariat. At each meeting the time and place of the next were agreed. It became the practice to meet alternatively in Dublin and one of the other Centres.

9.3 Baptist Records

Because of the above system of church administration, there was no central repository for the records of the Baptist church. Each church kept its own minute book which incorporated a roll, a record of business meetings, obituaries, copies of association correspondence and accounts of day-to-day affairs like upkeep of property, that is, the church building and graveyard where there was one. The same book could be used to record marriages of church members.

Opposite each name on the roll was recorded the date of coming into membership, whether by baptism or by transfer from another Baptist church, and in the final column 'deceased', 'emigrated to', 'removed', 'transferred to' etc. These last entries should have been dated but generally were not, or only by the year on periodic revision of the roll. The Cork church book is extant and covers the period from 1653 to 1875 with certain gaps (1680-1700, 1798-1823, 1820-1840). Some Dublin records exist from 1748, dealing with the Education Fund used to train men for the ministry, but there are trust deeds with references back to 1735 and a church minute book from at least 1835. Both Dublin and Cork churches owned land and there are title deeds recording changes of tenure etc. Nothing is known of the original records of Cloughjordan and Rahugh or of those churches which existed in the seventeenth and eighteenth centuries but which subsequently disappeared. Certain contemporary items of correspondence either with individual churches or with the association have however been recorded by White (1), Rogers (2) Anon (3) & Whitley (4).

While not reproducing contemporary records the publications of Apslund (5), Rippon (6) and Backus (7) are also of relevance to the situation of Baptist churches in Ireland in the eighteenth century.

The Irish Baptist Association of Churches continued in existence into the nineteenth century, but after 1821 became moribund until it was re-organised in 1862. Meantime, the work of evangelism in Ireland was

CONSTITUTION AND RULES OF THE SOCIETY.

ADOPTED IN 1814.

1. That a Society be now formed, and designated " THE BAPTIST SOCIETY FOR PROMOTING THE GOSPEL IN IRELAND, INSTITUTED IN THE YEAR 1814."

2. That the principal objects of this Society be, to employ Itinerants in Ireland, to establish Schools, and to distribute Bibles and Tracts, either gratuitously, or at reduced prices.

3. That a Subscriber of ten guineas at one time, be a Governor of the Society for life, and eligible to be on the Committee.

4. That any person subscribing one guinea annually be a Governor, and eligible to be on the Committee ; and any person subscribing half a guinea annually, or five guineas at one time, shall have the privilege of voting at all its public meetings.

5. That the concerns of the Society be managed by a Treasurer, Secretary, and a Committee of twenty-seven Governors.

6. That a general meeting of the Subscribers and Governors be held annually in London, in the third week in June,* when the Treasurer, Secretary, and two-thirds of the Committee, who have most frequently attended, be eligible for re-election.

7. That the Treasurer present to the Committee, half-yearly, an account of the state of the funds; and not pay any bills on behalf of the Society, without an order signed by two members of the Committee ; and that Auditors be annually appointed by the general meeting to examine the accounts.

8. That a general meeting of the Society may be called, by any seven members of the Committee, on giving one month's notice to the Secretary.

9. That all Ministers, who are members of the Society, be at liberty to attend and vote at all meetings of the Committee.

* Now changed to the end of April, or beginning of May.

Fig. 9.2   *Extract from The Rules of the Baptist Irish Society extracted from "The Baptist Irish Society, its Origin History & Prospects..." London 1845.*

taken up by the London-based Baptist Missionary Society, which was responsible for establishing in 1814 the Baptist Irish Society (see Fig. 9.2). Agents of this Society organised in 1841 a short-lived Association of Churches in Southern Ireland. Thereafter, accounts of churches founded or aided appear in the 'Irish Chronicle' appended to the monthly 'Baptist Magazine' published in Great Britain. Individual churches continued of course to keep their own records which for some included, after 1845, a marriage register. Besides founding and aiding churches, the Baptist Irish Society embarked on an extensive education programme, establishing schools in mainly rural areas. In 1832 they had reached a peak of 91 schools having about 10,000 pupils. Details appear in the Society's Annual Reports. Most of the Baptist Irish Society's schools closed in the years following the great famine of 1845-49, the last one in 1865. But there were a few others lasting into the present century and attached to individual churches - Brannockstown, Co. Kildare; Lisnagleer, Co. Tyrone; Antrim Road, Belfast; and Banbridge, Co. Down.

Some of the school registers among the manuscript records deposited in the Public Record Office of Northern Ireland are listed by McMullan *(8)*. Other Baptist records of the first half of the nineteenth century include three letters of 1822-23 from the Cloughjordan church, which are reproduced by Thompson *(9)*. Also, for several northern parishes there are the '"Ordnance Survey memoirs 1834-37" discussed by Gribbon *(10)*. These Memoirs are not in any sense Irish Baptist records but they do contain contemporary descriptions of several Baptist Churches supplied to the writers by local Baptists.

The churches forming the Irish Baptist Association derived fresh vigour from the 1859 Evangelical Revival *(11 & 12)*. In 1877 the Association began publishing its own periodical, "The Irish Baptist Magazine", which naturally included news about local churches and personalities. This magazine was by no means parochial and its interests and contributors ranged fairly widely. Meantime, the Baptist Irish Society had become the British and Irish Home Mission Society with an increased Irish input but still controlled and largely financed from Great Britain and reported on in the Baptist Magazine. However, it was increasingly felt that Baptists in Ireland had become strong enough to stand on their own feet (Disestablishment and Home Rule were both currently in the air).

Accordingly, in 1888, control was transferred to Ireland with the formation there of the Irish Baptist Home Mission. Finally, in 1895, the Irish Baptist Association of Churches was wound up and replaced by the Baptist Union of Ireland. Thereafter this Union became responsible not only for the Home Mission, but also for the Irish Baptist College, established in 1892 to train men for the ministry; the Annuity Fund, and the Loan and Building Fund (1902); the Orphan Society (1916); and the Foreign Mission (1924). Property was held, and centralised financial services were provided by the Baptist Union of Ireland Corporation Ltd. The Union had, and has, a permanent secretariat and headquarters in Belfast. The practice was continued of holding annual Assembly meetings at various centres in Ireland but of recent years most usually in Belfast.

Reports from the Assembly, and particularly the Assembly Handbook provided for ministers and delegates, contain a wealth of detail about the current state of Irish Baptist affairs. The Irish Baptist Historical Society was formed in 1968 and its annual Journal makes reference to most of the known records dealing with the denomination's history. There is always a hope that fresh material will turn up and if it does it will be noted in the journal.

The Baptist Union of Ireland, whose present headquarters is at 117 Lisburn Road, Belfast, serves and is supported by the churches but does not control them. They have a common basis of doctrine and a common form of church government but each is responsible for its own internal affairs including the keeping of records. Certain records, particularly legal or financial may be lodged with the Union for safe keeping but remain the property of the churches. Anyone wanting to consult the records of a particular church must first approach the church through its secretary (whose name and address are listed in the Handbook) and, if the records are in the Historical Society's collection or are in the Union's legal/financial custody, approach should then be made to the secretary of the Society or of the Union.

Churches will generally be most reluctant to open their records to researchers looking for genealogical material. However, very old records like the Cork or Waterford church books may be made available subject to the hundred years rule. However, for general purposes, many churches have published handbooks on the occasion of the opening of new buildings or to celebrate a centenary. These usually give some detail on early local events. Some further articles of interest to general Irish Baptist history, or to the history of specific communities, are listed below *(13 - 18)*.

REFERENCES AND FURTHER READING

1. *B.R. White*, **'The Irish correspondence of 1653'**, Association records of the Particular Baptists of England, Wales and Ireland to 1600. Part 2 (London, 1973), pp. 110-124.

2. *John Rogers*, **Ohel or Beth-shemish** (London, 1653) pp.302-8

3. 'The Messengers of several churches .. assembled at Bridgewater to the Churches of Christ assembling in Dublin, Wexford or elsewhere in Ireland ... 1655' Tract T 323 16. Library of the Society of Friends, Friends House, London.

4. *W.J. Whitley* (ed) **Minutes of the general assembly of the General Baptists**, 2 vols. 1654-1728, 1731-1811, I, p.138.

5. *John Apslund*, **Register of Baptist Churches in Britain and Ireland** (1710)

6. *John Rippon*, **The Baptist Annual Register** (1791-93)

7. *Isaac Backus*, History of the Baptist Warren Association from the year 1767 to the year 1792 (unpublished Ms. in Angus Library, Oxford).

8. *R.C.McMullan*, **'Baptist Education in Ireland** (1844-1970) Ir. Baptist Hist. Soc. Jn, III (1970-71) pp. 21-54.

9. *J. Thompson* in **Ir. Baptist Hist. Soc. Jn.**, XVI (1983/83), pp.28-37.

10. *H.D. Gribbon* in 'Some lesser known sources of Irish Baptist History' **Ir. Baptist Hist. Soc. Jn.**, VI (1973-74), pp. 66-68.

11. *J. Thompson*, "The Irish Baptist Association in the eighteenth century" **Ir. Baptist Hist. Soc. Jn.**, XVII (1984/85) pp. 18-31

12. *J. Thompson*, 'Irish Baptists and the 1859 Revival' **Ir. Baptist Hist. Soc. Jn.** XVII (1984/85), pp 4-10

13. **The Baptist Irish Society: its origin history and prospects** (London, 1845).

14. *Ernest V. Liddle*, "An Apology for Irish Baptists" **The Chronicle**, xx, no. 4 (Pennsylvania, 1957).

15. *David P. Kingdon*, **Baptist Evangelism in 19th Century Ireland** (Belfast, 1965)

16. *Louis E. Deens*, **Man of stature: Hugh D. Brown 1884-1914.** (Belfast, 1968)

17. *Robert A. Boggs*, **Alexander Carson of Tobermore** (Belfast 1969)

18. *Robert Dunlop*, **Plantation of Renown: the story of the La Touche Family of Harristown and the Baptist church at Brannockstown in Co. Kildare** (1970)

INDEX